RELIGION, ALLEGORY, AND LITERACY
IN EARLY MODERN ENGLAND,
1560–1640

For Pam

Religion, Allegory, and Literacy in Early Modern England, 1560–1640

The Control of the Word

JOHN S. PENDERGAST
Southern Illinois University, Edwardsville, USA

ASHGATE

© John S. Pendergast, 2006

All rights reserved. No part of this publication may be reproduced, stored in a retrieval system, or transmitted in any form or by any means, electronic, mechanical, photocopying, recording or otherwise without the prior permission of the publisher.

John S. Pendergast has asserted his moral right under the Copyright, Designs and Patents Act, 1988, to be identified as author of this work.

Published by
Ashgate Publishing Limited
Gower House
Croft Road
Aldershot
Hants GU11 3HR
England

Ashgate Publishing Company
Suite 420
101 Cherry Street
Burlington
VT 05401-4405
USA

Ashgate website: http://www.ashgate.com

British Library Cataloguing in Publication Data
Pendergast, John S., 1963–
  Religion, allegory, and literacy in early modern England, 1560–1640 : the control of the word
  1. English literature – Early modern, 1500–1700 – History and criticism 2. Christianity and literature – England – History – 16th century 3. Christianity and literature – England – History – 17th century 4. Books and reading – England – History – 16th century 5. Books and reading – England – History – 17th century 6. Christian literature, English – History and criticism 7. Social control – England – History – 16th century 8. Social control – England – History – 17th century 9. Literacy – England – History – 16th century 10. Literacy – England – History – 17th century
  I. Title
  820.9'003

Library of Congress Cataloging-in-Publication Data
Pendergast, John S., 1963–
  Religion, allegory, and literacy in early modern England, 1560–1640 : the control of the word / John Pendergast.
      p. cm.
  Includes bibliographical references (p.   ) and index.
  ISBN 0-7546-5147-9 (alk. paper)
 1. English literature – Early modern, 1500–1700 – History and criticism. 2. Christianity and literature – England – History – 16th century. 3. Christianity and literature – England –History – 17th century. 4. Books and reading – England – History – 16th century. 5. Books and reading – England – History – 17th century. 6. Christian literature, English – History and criticism. 7. Social control – England – History – 16th century. 8. Social control –England – History – 17th century. 9. Literacy – England – History – 16th century. 10. Literacy – England – History – 17th century. 11. Allegory. I. Title.

PR428.C48P46 2005
820.9'003–dc22

2004019640

ISBN 0 7546 5147 9

Printed and bound in Great Britain by TJ International Ltd, Padstow, Cornwall.

Contents

List of Figures		*vii*
Acknowledgments		*ix*
1.	Introduction: Reading Salvation	1
2.	Augustine and Early Modern Literacy	17
3.	The Control of the Word: Renaissance Exegesis and the Education of the Reader	37
4.	The "Real" Word of God	67
5.	The Grammar of Embodiment and Biblical Interpretation	101
6.	John Donne's Metaphoric God	119
7.	Educating Gentlemen: Allegory, Literacy and Spenser's *Faerie Queene*	133
8.	Lily, Latin Literacy and "Enfranchisement" in Shakespeare's *Love's Labour's Lost* and *Two Gentlemen of Verona*	153
Bibliography		*177*
Index		*183*

List of Figures

1	John Marbeck, *Concordance*	53
2	Henoch Clapham, *A Briefe of the Bible's Historie*	55
3	Simon Wastell, *Microbiblion*	59
4	Christopher Syms, *An Introduction to* ...	84
5	Henry Edmundson, *Lingua Linguarum*	87
6	Joseph Webbe, *Pueriles Confabulatiunculae*	91

Acknowledgments

Parts of chapter 6 originally appeared in *Studies in Philology* (Summer) 1996; reproduced by permission of the University of North Carolina Press. Parts of chapter 4 originally appeared in *ELH* (65), 1988; reproduced by permission of Johns Hopkins University Press.

Chapter 1

Introduction: Reading Salvation

Who also hath made us able ministers of the new Testament, not of the letter, but of the Spirit: for the letter killeth, but the Spirit giveth life.

(II Corinthians. 3:6)

John Guillory notes in *Cultural Capital* that "literacy is not a simple matter of knowing how to read or write, but refers to the entire system by which reading and writing are regulated as social practices in a given society." [1] A system is multifaceted, and any attempt to define a system by only one of its parts leads to distortion. Earlier in his book Guillory defines literacy as "the systematic regulation of reading and writing." Such regulation raises serious questions: Who reads? What do they read? How do they read? In what social and institutional circumstances? Who writes? In what social and institutional contexts? For whom? Although I will not be able to answer or explore all these questions, the Protestant emphasis on literacy as a relation between parties, as a rhetorical construction as opposed to a static one, will be my overarching focus. The one thing all these questions have in common is that the practices of reading and writing are regulated or "normalized" by some extrinsic force or standard, and by examining this regulation or normalizing, we can learn more about the interpretive practices of early modern readers.

But no matter how one eventually interprets, one always reads through the body, and therefore understanding begins in sensation. Further, since the body is in the world, for Christian apologists such as St Augustine who were influential in developing modern concepts of literacy this suggests that these sensations must be "realigned" or brought into line with good moral behavior. Likewise, the sensations produced on and by the body are merely the starting point for understanding. For St Augustine, in the words of Meyrick H. Carre, "sensations are necessary for a knowledge of things." On the other hand, sensory perception implies, as we have seen, general notions "inferred or assumed."[2] Even at the sensory level, the movement is toward contextualization, which could be defined here, as throughout Christian exegesis, as a form of "norming." In the words of Augustine, "we contemplate indestructible truth, by means of which we define precisely, as far as we can, not the nature of one particular man's mind, but the nature it ought to be according to the eternal reasons." This distinction is key: no interpretation is really private and "correct." All understanding is arrived at via prior Truths, i.e. what should be believed or is generally believed. As we shall see in the pages which follow, beginning in the sixteenth century, arriving at those prior Truths became a dominant and persistent goal of pedagogues and theologians alike; a "particular man's mind" was free to arrive at theological and exegetical conclusions only to the extent that those conclusions were in alignment with "the nature [of what] ought to be."

Those who were charged with teaching what "ought to be" were helped by one central ontological and epistemological truth: perception itself is reliant upon "higher" faculties: "But that capacity of ours which is concerned with the treatment of corporeal and temporal things is, indeed, rational in that it is not common to us and the beasts, but is drawn, as it were, out of that rational substance of immutable truth, and which is deputed to handle and direct the inferior things."[3] This is illustrated in the illusion of the bent oar in the water—our senses are corrected, usually instantaneously, by our rational faculties which have access to "True" universals. These "True" universals are the standard by which individual perceptions (that which is "in the world") are judged.

This privileging of the general over the specific leads Myrick Carre to an important conclusion regarding Augustine's exegetical methods: "The existence of material bodies in the physical guise in which they appear to us, or, more strictly, in the manner in which the mind reproduces them, remains a point not of knowledge but of belief."[4] The exegetical theories of Augustine of Hippo are a starting point for this study since throughout his work he emphasized that true understanding is based not on the direct perception of the sensual (i.e. material) world but rather must be seen in the clear light of the spiritual world. All concepts of interpretation and literacy (which after Augustine cannot be separated) must take into account correctness and contextualization as fundamental aspects of reading comprehension. The fact that ultimately standards cannot be defined (but are nonetheless assumed to exist), could be seen as a residual element of Christian ontology. In the chapters which follow I will examine the manner in which meaning is manifested in language in accordance with the following suppositions:

1) The most fundamental separation between "illiterates" and literates comes in the form of *correctness*. Whether we are considering literacy in spoken or written forms, the first criteria are that language be used in a socially conforming manner and that the words spoken or written are used according to prescribed rules. The role of education is to assure that this correctness is understood. In other words, at its most basic level, literacy is equated with *norming*, with the dissemination of set standards. This norming is not restricted simply to sentence- level correctness; right reading and right understanding are just as important as correct writing.

2) It is textual. "One can be literate without the overt use of texts, and one can use texts extensively without evidencing genuine literacy."[5] However true Brian Stock's observation may be for literacy in theory, the assumption in almost all definitions or uses of the word "literate" involves the privileging of language in a "textual" manner, i.e. treating it as something repeatable and contextual, as opposed to the momentary and situational nature of oral discourse.

In the paradigm shift treated in the following pages, literacy gradually becomes defined almost exclusively as textual. The Lutheran Reformation, for example, was primarily textual. In the years prior to the focus of this study there was a huge increase in the number of vernacular texts available for public consumption. Martin Luther alone was responsible for approximately 20 percent of the 10,000 pamphlet editions (first editions and reprints) which were published in Germany between 1500 and

1530.[6] Although there are no corresponding figures for the English Reformation, as we shall see in the pages which follow, the debates began by Luther were propagated via the printed word in England. Further, Luther's translation of the Bible into the vernacular further emphasized the material/printed nature of spiritual truths.

3) The term "literacy" is a value laden term, used to describe a culturally defined ideal. Brian Stock writes that literacy is a difficult term to define because "the term's connotative field in English has no precise equivalent in other languages." Worse, Stock writes, is the fact that the term has no value-free meaning, even in English.[7] A value-free, accurate definition of literacy is impossible given literacy's close relationship to literature and economics, as well as to religious and political structures. Rather than searching in vain for one, therefore, I will highlight how value became an inextricable aspect of literacy as it came into its modern form.

The multi-faceted aspect of literacy is discussed in the chapters which follow in which I examine literary texts, sermons, textbooks and government documents, all of which, rather than attempting to illustrate a common and historically consistent model of literacy, reflect the ever changing and endlessly complicated nature of literacy.

4) As a value laden term, it has direct bearing on education, and in turn helps define what education is. It is through education that literacy is propagated to society as a whole, and therefore as the concept of literacy changes so too do the aims and methods of educators. For example, Reformation theology developed around a renewed appreciation for the philological issues of biblical texts, for which knowledge of classical languages was a necessity, and so led to a renewed understanding of what it meant to be literate in the first place.

As Harvey Graff notes, "One of the great innovations of the German or Lutheran Reformation was the recognition that literacy, a potentially dangerous or subversive skill, could be employed—if controlled—as a medium for popular schooling and training on a truly unprecedented scale. The great reform was hardly an unambiguous success in its time, but it may well have contributed more to the cause of popular literacy than to that of piety and religious practice."[8] Although Graff is correct that the Reformation did refocus attention on popular literacy, the separation between literacy and religious practice is not absolute. The relationship, rather, is circular: the approaches used to reform education and literacy were modeled on Protestant spiritual and ontological paradigms which had provided new ways of conceiving of texts and meaning, which were themselves inspired by earlier educational reforms.

5) Finally, literacy is often used as a cover for a contradiction still found in our own society: there is a moral obligation to bring literacy to all persons; however, in practice, changing moral paradigms and technological advancements render literacy an unstable variant. By David Cressy's estimates, based upon evidence of signature literacy, Tudor and Stuart England remained "massively illiterate despite an epoch of educational expansion and a barrage of sermons. More than two-thirds of the men and nine-tenths of the women were so illiterate at the time of the civil war that they could not even write their own names."[9] Despite the fact that a "person who could read was better equipped to prepare for salvation than his illiterate fellow Christians and was more likely, in the view of protestant divines, to lead a life of duty and godliness," and that literacy prepared one for a life in an ever increasing technical marketplace,

achieving literacy on a universal level was infeasible (and for some, like Thomas More, undesirable: More denied that "having the scripture in English be a thing so requisite of precise necessity that the people's souls should needs perish but if they have translated into their own tongue").[10]

How do we find our way out of the seeming contradictions so often found in the Western exegetical tradition? This contradiction is not isolated to simple equations of secrecy and redemption, rather it serves as a foundation for the Western literary tradition. For example, Harold Bloom writes, "We need to teach more selectively, searching for the few who have the capacity to become highly individual readers and writers ... Pragmatically, aesthetic value can be recognized or experienced, but it cannot be conveyed to those who are incapable of grasping its sensations and perceptions."[11] Bloom's position serves to put a modern lens on an ancient issue. Although Bloom does not explain the difference between "recognized or experienced" and the conveyance of aesthetic experience, one might assume that the difference lies in a willingness or ability to accept the "right" method of interpretation, and ultimately, the "right" meaning, and right interpretation begins, but does not end, with "sensations and perceptions."

In *The Western Canon* Bloom suggests that not only must certain texts be read, but certain interpretations must be arrived at. Further, only certain readers are able to arrive at these interpretations. Bloom believes that "aesthetic value" can only be taught to those who already have the skill to appreciate it. To all others it "cannot be conveyed." In this passage Bloom uses terms such as "sensations" and "perceptions" suggesting that, like Medieval commentators, Bloom initially grounds aesthetics in the senses, but these sense perceptions are not enough: they must be brought into alignment with higher values. However, Bloom seems a bit evasive: does he mean "conveyed" in the sense of taught, or "conveyed" in the sense of prone to comprehend? Ironically, by bemoaning our culture's lack of appreciation for aesthetic experience, Bloom is affirming that literacy and the experience of literature are culturally influenced; by doing so he unwittingly affirms that reading and interpretation are always, and unavoidably, politicized. Bloom's democratic and secular nod toward "highly individual readers" would seem, on the surface, to contradict the movement toward controlled interpretation and contextualization, but ironically by limiting those who are "individual" enough to those who have the capacity to arrive at "correct" interpretations reflects the exegetical notion that only correct reading leads to salvation, and that such correctness lies not in the literal sensations of language but in a code or set of acceptable reading strategies.

For Bloom, however, it doesn't seem to matter: the Canon only exists in the academy anyway, and since those prone to comprehend it, either directly or through pedagogy, are an endangered species, it is sure to go the way of classics departments. Nonetheless, the Western Canon exists "precisely in order to impose limits, to set a standard of measurement that is anything but political or moral."[12] What it *is*, is the memory of what we are, were and can be as a species; in short, the few who can read correctly and carefully (enough) are saved and may fully participate in culture. Those who cannot shall suffer a life of political antagonism and resentment. In the course of this book, I argue that questions such as those raised by Bloom and other modern theorists are not simply reactionary responses to a perceived cultural decay (no matter how hard they might argue to the contrary), but are reoccurring issues in the history of Western humanism.

Bloom's concerns illustrate that once literacy is seen as one part of a larger system or context, then literacy is no longer simply concerned with the act of reading, but for the right *use* of texts. Brian Stock notes that, likewise, "to investigate medieval literacy is accordingly to inquire into the uses of texts ... to inquire into the audiences for which they were intended and the mentality in which they were received." The examination of literacy must take into consideration both the use of texts and what constitutes a correct reading of them. The various texts I will be examining in the following pages allow us some insight into what was considered the "right" way of reading texts in Reformation England. However, what constituted right reading was very complex: economic, aesthetic, and political influences often clashed with Protestant ontological and pedagogical demands. On the other hand, these same economic, aesthetic and political influences often defined Protestant ontology and pedagogy. Obviously no one book can cover all these issues, but by a careful cross sectioning of topics, I have represented how many of these facets influenced and in turn were influenced by the Protestant Reformation.

The Religion of Protestants

Given the focus of this discussion and the necessity of avoiding static definitions, the following chapters will read against the historical grain, that is, the time period under consideration avoids the problems inherent in terminology such as "late medieval," "Early Modern," "Renaissance," "Reformation," and "Restoration." This overlap in time periods emphasizes change and development. The tension between monarchy and episcopacy, for example, does not reveal itself totally in the reign of any one monarch. The subject matter of this book is, to quote Patrick Collinson in *The Religion of Protestants: The Church in English Society 1559-1625*, "the interrelation of these two creative forces in a period of sustained ideological instability ..."[13] Like Collinson, I will focus on debate, controversy, and both dogma and heterogeneity in an attempt to clarify the tensions which come to delineate what it means to be literate. Although I choose the years between 1560 and 1640, I have often gone outside this frame for the purpose of following or revealing trends. Likewise, a possible ending point could have been 1662 and the Act of Uniformity, an event which serves as a coda to the movement toward centralized control over pedagogy and literacy.

These factors remind us that it is impossible to characterize and define historical eras according to predefined chronological dates and to maintain a unity in terms of the ideas represented in and by that era. The same could be said of the time periods under consideration in the following chapters. The comparison is made all the more fitting because of the profound importance medieval texts and mentalities have on the Renaissance.

In a study of this breadth, there is also a problem of defining and distinguishing between public beliefs and private beliefs. What, for example, does it mean to be a

Protestant? "When I mention Religion, I mean the Christian Religion; and not only the Christian Religion, but the Church of England," wrote Parson Thwackum in Fielding's *Tom Jones*.[14] The equating of England with Christianity, and in turn labeling what is one type of Christianity with all of Christianity, results in a patriotic form of synecdoche peculiar to Reformation Europe. However, defining and limiting what is meant by "Church of England," as well as by "religion," are extremely difficult tasks. As Patrick Collinson, and others, have noted as an example, the English Church is not clearly defined. In fact, Collinson comes to the conclusion that what constitutes Elizabethan and Jacobean popular religion is too multi-faceted to define.[15] As he points out, Protestants and Puritans both knew that "the multitude" was not of either side. "The 'religion of Protestants' in its more intense and fully internalized form was never popular in the plain and ordinary sense."[16] Popular religion could be defined, fairly safely, as "prayer-book religion," not participating in specific doctrinal debates, and acting somewhat independently of monarchical pronouncements, especially in such matters as vestments and the use of unleavened bread during Elizabeth's reign; nonetheless, it is textual. It can also be confidently said that not all Tudor or Stuart Englishmen went to churches which were similar in all aspects, and it is equally likely that many who did go to church on even a semi-regular basis did so only after being coerced, and many never went and remained ignorant of basic tenets of Christianity. Although it is not my aim to support or refute the particulars of Collinson's generalizations, they do point to the urgency felt by monarchs and Church leaders alike for normalizing pedagogy and doctrine, and they suggest the issues which would eventually lead England to civil war.

Despite the difficulty in defining Protestantism, one generality is possible and important for the study which follows: Protestants as a rule found salvation in the literal Word of God. However, even this generalization must be tempered, and the exceptions which will be developed reveal a great deal about Reformation philology. The lens through which I will examine and delimit the Reformation is article six of the 1551 *Thirty-Nine Articles*, which states that:

> Holye Scripture conteyneth all thynges necessarie to salvation: so that whatsoever is not read therein, nor may be proved thereby, is not to be required of anye man, that it should be believed as an article of faith, or be thought requisite necessarie to salvation.

Following article six, it is clear that salvation is textual and that the Word of God should be ontologically sufficient for salvation. However, such a manifestation creates pedagogical as well as philological problems which cross many of the newly created economic, social and political margins that arose with the Reformation.

If the literal level of understanding was capable of conveying, albeit sometimes ambiguously, the spiritual meaning of the Bible, how exactly did one read literally? What did it mean to read the original Word of God? Figurative language allowed a reader to assume that the real doctrinally sound reading lay outside the material sign or signifier, but when faced with literal interpretation, the words on the page somehow had to have a direct link to meaning. With the growing use vernaculars for all forms of communication new questions arouse: how could two (or more) languages all say the same thing? Could one do so better than another? And what was the role of Latin? Although not an original biblical language, Latin existed as one in the eyes of Renaissance exegetes primarily because of the medieval Catholic Church's reliance upon it to convey doctrine. Without access to Latin, however, Protestant theologians could not engage the Catholic heresies from which they had sworn to protect their followers.

Allegory and the Literal

Debates concerning spiritual matters put a great deal of stress on language as writers searched for ways to explain the ineffable. One illustrative example of the complex relationship between literacy and the extrinsic social issues which resulted from the Reformation is found in the history of the Christian exegetical tradition, most importantly with the developing distinction between allegory and the literal. An important aspect of this grammatical understanding of spiritual meaning is Augustine's understanding of the word "Literal" in all its connotations. According to Augustine, Literal means interpretation which is in line with Catholic doctrine, be it figural or not, as opposed to the "literal" interpretations of the Manichees which focused on material, strictly denotative meanings. For Augustine, Literal could mean allegorical; likewise, allegory for Augustine could mean "supra-literal" or spiritual. For example, Augustine's *De Genesi ad litteram* does not attempt to read the book in a non-figurative manner, but rather to read the book allegorically where necessary in order to show how it embodies the teachings of the Catholic Church. "Literal" interpretation can also carry the connotation of non-spiritual interpretation, grounded as it is in purely materialistic (*materia*) language. In *From Shadow to Promise* James Preus develops the literal and Literal distinction in a way which illustrates the norming capabilities of scriptures:

> 'Literal sense,' on its two different levels, can designate both that which must be given figurative interpretation because it is unedifying, and that which need not, or must not, be interpreted figuratively, because it is normative as it stands, or one might even say, because it is already spiritual. Furthermore, the unedifying literal sense, on the bottom level, is regarded as a *figura* or *signum*.[17]

What this hermeneutics creates, according to Preus, is a *norming* of the message of the Old Testament, which must be "brought forward" in order to be equated with the New Testament message. Some aspects of the Old Testament do not need allegorical reading in order to make sense; for example, the commandments are still "right to observe as they are written," as Augustine wrote in *De spiritu et littera liber unus*.

Augustine's exegetical method may have more broadly influenced sixteenth-century allegorical invention than has been previously thought. For example, the rhetorical demonization of allegory throughout the Reformation was based upon an exaggerated claim that allegory was not based finally in the Word of God and that allegory allowed for propagandistic readings. However, what allegory actually did, traditionally, was insist upon a specific context for higher spiritual reading. The origin, purpose and rigidity of this context was one of the main sources of debate between Catholic and Reformation exegetes; Reformation suspicion of allegory lay partly in the fact that no matter what the source of the context, one had to know what the text meant doctrinally before doing an allegorical reading of it. Then as now, as J. Hillis Miller notes, in a discussion of Paul De Man's theory of allegorical reading, the irony of allegory is that "if you have the key to the allegory, then the esoteric wisdom has been expressed (otherwise), but then you would not have needed to have it said otherwise. If you do not have the key, then the allegory remains opaque. You are likely to take it literally, to think it means just what it says. If you understand it you do not need it. If you do not understand it you never will do so from anything on the surface."[18] Such is the paradox of allegory, and the reason why exegetical debates about the meaning of scripture often provided opportunities for rhetorical accusations of obscurity and propaganda; ultimately, one sect's allegorical reading is another sect's literal or heretical one. Further, since allegory calls into question how much the literal Word can communicate by itself, unadorned by external authority, a close study of the structure of allegory allows us to consider more carefully how literacy was conceived of in the early modern period.

St Augustine's allegorical interpretive model was developed, in part, as an attempt to limit and define rhetoric within his own culture. For him, allegorical interpretation was the highest form of understanding available only to those most worthy and qualified. It was Ambrose's sermons which revealed to Augustine that the text of the Bible could be philosophical and worthy of serious rhetorical study, despite the objections of the Manichees. Augustine writes that "as I opened my heart in order to recognize how eloquently he was speaking it occurred to me at the same time (though this idea came gradually) how truly he was speaking." The equation of rhetorical eloquence with Truth elevates rhetorical arts from the merely sophistic practice of Augustine's youth to the highest arbitrator of spiritual and moral value. In *The Mirror of Language: A Study in the Medieval Theory of Knowledge*[19] Marcia L. Colish notes that Augustine discovered a sense of moral and ethical behavior founded on the rhetorical arts. A person's moral state can hinder them from perceiving the truth. Despite the theological and political gulf which would open up between Protestants and Catholics in the succeeding centuries, Augustine's anchoring of salvation to cognitive signs capable of and demanding interpretation would serve as a basis for Protestant exegetical theory; "By interpreting all signs as linguistic Augustine makes it possible for himself to interpret all cognitive intermediaries between God and man as modes of verbal expression." This conception of knowledge as verbal is a significant precept in Augustine's theology, and, as Colish notes, "is one of his major justifications for having become a theologian in the first place."[20]

By embedding knowledge in the verbal, and by further embedding the verbal in higher questions of epistemology, the Reformation debate about allegory and its relationship with the literal not only reflects a long tradition of exegetical theory and practice, but also foregrounds certain paradigmatic debates still important to modern

Introduction 9

language theory. The Protestant anxieties over allegory, namely that it created unstable, obscure and transitory meaning (in opposition to the myth that literal readings were necessarily stable, clear and historically defined) are brilliantly illustrated in the words of Walter Benjamin, who sees allegory not through the eyes of anxious Protestants, but with what could be labeled a medieval Catholic lens: "For an appreciation of the transience of things, and the concern to rescue them for eternity, is one of the strongest impulses in allegory;"[21] for this reason, again in the words of Benjamin, "Allegory is responsible for establishing itself most permanently where transitoriness and eternity confronted each other most closely."[22] Obviously, one of the places where the two confront each other most closely is in scriptural exegesis; Benjamin's understanding makes of allegory a monument, but in so doing removes allegory from the propagandistic impulses which motivate many of the medieval and Protestant uses of it. Rather than spiritualizing the Word of God, Benjamin's allegory serves to materialize it: "Allegories are, in the realm of thought, what ruins are in the realm of things."[23]

Likewise, perhaps the most eloquent theorist of allegory in the twentieth century, Paul de Man, notes in opposition to some Protestant theorists that allegory "does not erase the figure."[24] Like Benjamin, de Man saves allegory from those who would dismiss it by contrasting it to the literal; in *Blindness and Insight*, he notes that in allegory a "sign [must] refer to another sign that precedes it. The meaning constituted by the allegorical sign can then consist only in repetition ..."[25] But in the course of this repetition, change, often in the form of ambiguity or distortion, occurs: allegory inevitably involves "a perpetual suspension of meaning, a detour through the various tropes, figures, and modes of oblique signification where language can never reach the point of simply saying what it sets out to say."

We can best understand allegorical representation and its relation to literacy through what Annabel Patterson labels "functional ambiguity." Annabel Patterson writes that ambiguity is a "creative and necessary instrument," one which "frees us somewhat from more absolutely skeptical conclusions about indeterminacy in language and its consequences for the reader or critic." Unlike other theories of ambiguity, Patterson's theory does not privilege "either writer or reader, or eliminate either. It is hospitable to, and indeed dependent upon, a belief in authorial intention; yet it is incapable of reduction to a positivistic belief in meanings that authors can fix."[26] In fact, the significant changes outlined in this book reveal how authorial intention is often defined as the manipulation of indeterminacy in the cause of a specific rhetorical meaning, often seen by opponents as heresy or at the very least, religious propaganda. All exegetes, Protestant and Catholic alike, see the Word of God as ultimately containing no ambiguities when read in light of doctrine, but how the seeming ambiguities are normalized is the source of endless debate.

According to Augustinian exegesis, readers who focus on clarity or self-sufficient literal meaning as an end in itself are potentially missing the true meaning of a text. This mistake is often seen in twentieth-century formalist interpretations. "Art ... is just the right way of making whatever anybody happens to be making (recta ratio factibilium)—each artifact according to its own plan, in a hierarchy, a cathedral being worth more than a cowshed, but each one right (and beautiful) in its own way," wrote

William K. Wimsatt and Cleanth Brooks in their New Critical guide to interpretation, *Literary Criticism: A Short History*.[27] The notion of art as a self-contained artifact, each object with a unique ordering and "each one [artifact] right (and beautiful) in its own way" is a reflection of one important aspect of Augustine's interpretive strategy, as outlined in *On Music*, for example, but it is only one aspect, that which he uses to support harmony and aesthetic beauty as signs of God's grace. One of the basic components of formalism is the notion of a discernible ordering of parts, each part adding to the harmony of the whole. Yet for Augustine, this ordering is only *one* aspect of the overall aesthetic pattern, since the ordered object must still be in agreement with doctrine and charity *before* it can be enjoyed.

Too much emphasis on beauty and harmony as ends can lead readers astray and seduce them in to premature enjoyment. Readers err when they remain passive and are deflected from understanding the truly virtuous aspects of aesthetic experience. So, in a humanist context, the function of poetry is to correct mistaken, earthly perceptions and notions by making them proportionate with the higher, immanent presence of truth. Good, virtuous readers make themselves worthy by active participation with the obscure lesson of poetry's often ambiguous transcendent truth. Spiritual truths, those truths which are most ineffable, are the very truths which ironically must be taught through language to all believers. For this reason, the need to "embody" ineffable and transcendent truths creates new problems in the search for an inclusive theory of language use.

For Augustine and his followers, the reader of Scripture needed to strike an ideal mean between a sheer literal interpretation which sought merely to translate the Bible, contradictions and all, into plain language, and an interpretation which, in focusing solely on poetic language, ignored the a priori system of faith, and translated the text as a system of allegorical, tropological and anagogical symbols. Both forms of erroneous interpretation diminished the authority of the Church. In the first situation, a deficiency of meaning occurs: ontologically, it becomes possible to create an infinite number of texts based upon the same basic rules of grammar, and there is no discernible way to choose one over another. In the second situation it is possible to create a false or distracting meaning, one which removes significance from the text because it ignores any message embodied in the text.

In the end, all communication and meaning is embodied in a text since all "[b]eauty transmissions are types of Truth transmissions, wherein the *logos* as the middle term is imbedded in matter but through which it shines."[28] Through this "transmission" a "transubstantiation" of sorts occurs in the sensible aspect of language in order to lead to an understanding which lies just beyond the capabilities of the original, sensible language use.[29] It is by definition Christian because this ability to read the spirit beneath the surface is only possible through Christ. Giving his followers a method for discovering the spirit in a text was Augustine's most powerful weapon against the Manichees; by replacing the Manichean anti-allegorical method of reading scripture "literally" (in the sense of non-figuratively) with a highly allegorical and rhetorical method, Augustine appropriated the notion of a Literal (in the sense of doctrinally coherent) reading for the young Christian faith.

This appropriation is perhaps Augustine's greatest legacy for future exegetes, rhetoricians and post-structuralists: after the Protestant Reformation all serious exegetes must struggle with how to negotiate between the literal meaning of a text which can be manifested in material, sensual, and sensible language and a spiritual meaning which has to be stabilized simultaneously outside of the material condition of written, sensual language. The level of spiritual understanding transcends the level of mere understanding and "use" and takes us into the realm of "enjoyment," for it is the transcendental level which most closely mirrors Truth and which is stable enough to serve as the a-priori spiritual meaning. In other words, to make the mistake some formalists do and to enjoy the letter is to miss what should be enjoyed, the spirit. Christ is the only signifier which may be enjoyed as well as used, just as He is both God and man.

As we saw earlier, Literal interpretations for Augustine did not mean that the language had to be used in its "original" sense or that clarity was the goal; rather Literal meant in accordance with Catholic doctrine. Allegory by its very nature implies a Literal truth prior to the figuration of the idea in the language of the allegory. The reader of an allegorical text must have enough knowledge to move between the "Real," doctrinally Literal meaning and the poetic figuration; allegory, therefore, is useful for teaching the "worthy" and "able." A reader becomes "worthy" of the truth when he/she accepts that the Bible as a whole must be read in accordance with the New Testament, an act of interpretation which sometimes requires reading outside the "literal" text.

Augustine's theories are important to the present study because they highlight the necessity of considering correct reading strategy in light of the relationship between sign and signifier and the manifestation of meaning. Furthermore, they do so in the context of urgent social and religious questions which can only be resolved through education. Some of these questions relevant to this study and the time period under consideration are:

- What specific ontological or philological changes occurred as a result of the doctrinal changes of the Protestant Reformation? How are these changes culturally or politically defined?
- What effect did the rise of vernaculars have on the study and dissemination of the literal or allegorical Word of God? Where does meaning "happen" when using the vernacular to manifest the Word of God? What impact does this have on the teaching of both vernacular and the original languages of the Bible?
- Finally, what influence does class have on these religious issues? If it is assumed that salvation is universally available to all members of a given church, how can one's ability to understand the written Word affect their worthiness? How could salvation, defined as textual by the sixth article, be disseminated to *all believers*, even those unable or unwilling to read?

This book not only traces literacy as a concept through several decades, but it also illustrates the importance of understanding literacy in the plural. Simply reading texts according to one paradigm, for example reading *The Faerie Queene* according to strict formalist paradigms, results in confused and distorted interpretations.

Correspondingly, relying too much upon artificial (and misleading) distinctions between Protestant and Catholic, while ignoring the important similarities, is to miss important intellectual movements and trends. Literacy, after all, is not a static paradigm, likewise, the texts which are read and the interpretations which teachers strive to impart, cannot be fully understood as the result of a single paradigm. It would be foolish to assume that even an avowed Protestant like Edmund Spenser could write a religious treatise unaffected by "Catholic" ontology.

Likewise, when considering Protestant or Catholic paradigms or models of reading, it is important to remember that those formulas do not exist independently of other reading strategies to which they are a response or earlier reading strategies to which they are heirs. As I noted above, the allegorical method popularized by St Augustine in the fourth and fifth centuries was both demonized by early Protestants and at the same time became fundamental to their own exegetical theories. Often, much of what passes as "serious" theology in the Renaissance is actually rhetorical posturing by both Catholics and Protestants. Many of the stereotypes and constructs taken as a given about various reading strategies are dispelled, or at least made more complicated, when essentialistic divisions are dismissed and the mutual dependence upon "systems" of reading, or literacies, are acknowledged.

Although this study is historically defined, we do not have to look very far for modern examples of this standard of literacy. We live in an era defined by many of these same concepts. Walter Ong's definition of reading (and, in context, literacy) as the conversion of a unit of meaning to sound, closely resembles the ancient concept of litteratus, the understanding of Latin (and later vernacular) syntax, grammar and vocabulary. E.D. Hirsch, however, in his 1987 book *Cultural Literacy*, complicates this notion by appropriating the term literacy to represent a body of texts *to be read*, not necessarily the ability to read them.[30] In Hirsch's paradigm, literacy is a form of socialization, a means toward cultural homogeneity, an understanding which precludes the written word and relies instead upon the judgment and proper utilization of received information. The question this discussion will answer, in light of Hirsch, is what is *cultural* about literacy? When did reading and literacy become "cultural" and not "personal"? Hirsch's book posits the notion that only by reading a finite set of texts can our society form a sense of homogeneity. Hirsch writes: "Only a small proportion of literate people can name the Shakespeare plays in which Falstaff appears, yet they know who he is. They know what *Mein Kampf* is, but they haven't read it."[31] Hirsch takes it as a given that all cultured persons should read (or at least know) the same things; although he never treats the topic in an ontological way, he does suggest that reading the same texts will lead to a normalization of society and culture. Similarly, Lawrence Levine notes that starting in the nineteenth century, American readers and audiences began to "approach the masters and their works with proper respect and proper seriousness, for aesthetic and spiritual elevation rather than mere entertainment."[32] Participating in culture became a way of "normalizing" and fixing one's place in society and of illustrating that position via the proper and reverential reception of "masters and their works." This "sacralization" of culture began much earlier than Levine's late nineteenth century, however; it began, ironically, with the simultaneous secularization of the sacred in the early modern period.

Augustine's theory of Biblical exegesis is an appropriate starting point for a discussion of the sacralization of literacy, for it relies on two seemingly contradictory motivations—a need for teaching and disseminating the true Word of God to a wide audience for the sake of furthering the cause of the Church (i.e. conversion and protection from competing heretical readings of the Bible), and a need for ambiguity and deliberate obscurity to insure that the audience which received the message was worthy and able to understand it. Given the Church's need to win converts by (among other things) appropriating an earlier Judaic tradition based on the Old Testament, the two motivations are simultaneous in their operation: obscurity and ambiguity allowed Augustine and his followers to interpret the Bible in ways which some new converts would understand (since they were based on familiar texts) yet which would change their belief system in favor of Christianity. Augustine found certain aspects of Neo-Platonism useful as a philosophical medium because it could also serve as an interpretive model which allows for both clarity and obscurity, based as it is on a bridgeable separation between the earthly and the spiritual.

Notes

1. John Guillory, *Cultural Capital: The Problem of Literary Canon Formation* (Chicago: The University of Chicago Press, 1993), 79.

2. Myrick H. Carre, *Realists and Nominalists* (London: Oxford University Press, 1946), 17.

3. De Trin. Xiii.iii.3.

4. Carre, 26.

5. Brian Stock, *The Implications of Literacy: Written Language and Models of Interpretation in the Eleventh and Twelfth Centuries* (Princeton University Press, 1983), 7.

6. Mark U. Edwards, Jr. *Printing, Propaganda, and Martin Luther* (Berkeley: University of California Press, 1994), 17.

7. Stock, 6.

8. Harvey J. Graff, *The Legacies of Literacy: Continuities and Contradictions in Western Culture and Society* (Bloomington: Indiana University Press, 1987), 10.

9. David Cressy, *Literacy and Social Order: Reading and Writing in Tudor and Stuart England* (Cambridge: Cambridge University Press, 1980), 2.

10. *Ibid.*, 2.

11. Harold Bloom, *The Western Canon: The Books and School of the Ages* (New York: Riverhead Books, 1995), 17.

12. *Ibid.*, 35. This "setting of limits" is paralleled in Hirsch: "The concept of cultural literacy helps us to make such decisions [regarding education priorities] because it places a higher value on national than on local information" (25).

13. Patrick Collinson, *The Religion of Protestants: The Church in English Society 1559-1625* (Oxford: Clarendon Press, 1982), 3.

14. Henry Fielding, *The History of Tom Jones, A Foundling* (Oxford, 1974), i. 131. Quoted in Collinson, 189.

15. Collinson, 189.

16. *Ibid.*, 191.

17. James Preus, *From Shadow to Promise: Old Testament Interpretation from Augustine to the Young Luther* (Cambridge: Belknap Press of Harvard University Press, 1969), 67.

18. Hillis J. Miller, "'Reading' Part of a Paragraph in *Allegories of Reading*," in *Reading De Man Reading*, Ed. Lindsay Waters and Wlad Godzich (Minneapolis: University of Minnesota Press, 1989), 162.

19. Marcia L Colista, *The Mirror of Language: A Study in the Medieval Theory of Knowledge* (Lincoln, NE: University of Nebraska Press, 1968), 19.

20. *Ibid.*, 44.

21. Walter Benjamin, *The Origin of German Tragic Drama*. Trans. John Osborne (Frankfurt: Suhrkamp Verlag, 1963), 223.

22. *Ibid.*, 224.

23. *Ibid.*, 178.

24. Paul de Man, *Allegories of reading: Figural Language in Rousseau, Nietzsche, Rilke, and Proust* (New Haven: Yale University Press, 1979), x.

25. Paul de Man, *Blindness and Insight: Essays in the Rhetoric of Contemporary Criticism* (Minneapolis: University of Minnesota Press, 1983), 207.

26. Annabel Patterson, *Censorship and Interpretation: The Conditions of Writing and Reading in Early Modern England* (Madison: University of Wisconsin Press, 1984), 18.

27. William K. Wimsatt and Cleanth Brooks, *Literary Criticism: A Short History* (New York: Knopf, 1967), 130.

28. Charles Purcell Bigger III, "The Nature of Aesthetic Judgement in Augustinian Interpretation" (Ph.D. diss. University of Virginia, 1951), 27.

29. I put the word "transubstantiation" in quotation marks to note the appropriation of the term; I do not mean the term in its fullest ontological or christological sense. Rather, I am using the word to express the powerful "symbolic meaning" which occurs when a sign is infused with the reality it refers to (see E. Schillebeeckx, O.P., *The Eucharist* (New York: Sheed and Ward, 1968)). Schillebeeckx writes, "A sign as such always refers to something else which is absent. But man's bodiliness, with its modes of expression, is the visible presence of the spirit, however inadequate this disclosure may be (as dissimulation shows)" (100).

30. Hirsch writes: "It [*Cultural Literacy*] takes no position about methods of initial reading instruction beyond insisting that content must receive as much emphasis as 'skill'", E.D. Hirsch, Jr., *Cultural Literacy: What Every American Needs to Know* (Boston: Houghton Mifflin, 1987) (1).

31. *Ibid.*, 147.

32. Lawrence W. Levine, *Highbrow/lowbrow: The Emergence of Cultural Hierarchy in America* (Cambridge, Mass.: Harvard University Press, 1990), 146.

Chapter 2

Augustine and Early Modern Literacy

> I am supposing that in every society the production of discourse is at once controlled, selected, organized and redistributed according to a certain number of procedures, whose role is to avert its powers and its dangers, to cope with chance events, to evade its ponderous, awesome materiality.
>
> (Michel Foucault, "The Discourse on Language"[1])

Two definitions of "literacy" and reading reflect two facets of contemporary thinking regarding literacy, theories which have their roots in the broad historical period under consideration in this chapter. The first comes from Father Walter Ong: "'Reading' a text means converting it to sound, aloud or in the imagination, syllable-by-syllable in slow reading or sketchily in the rapid reading common to high-technology cultures.[2] Ong's conversion of texts into sounds bears at least a family resemblance to the conception of language as a "transubstantiation" of sensual impulses to meaning which I will be examining in later chapters. Likewise, his emphasis on "technological cultures" also reminds us that literacy must be considered in relation to cultural standards and that technology and other "economic" factors play important roles in defining literacy.

E.D. Hirsch, on the other hand, reminds us that "literacy" can be cultural as well as "graphic": "To be culturally literate is to possess the basic information needed to thrive in the modern world."[3] Hirsch reminds us that there are multiple "literacies" and that how and what one reads dictates how one will "thrive" in society. In other words, the ability to read, or to convert texts to sounds, is no longer enough. I would argue that this concept of literacy is not modern; rather, its roots are first medieval in the concept of embodied meaning, and Reformation in the importance put upon understanding such embodied meaning as a requirement to full participation in society. Literacy provides a historical continuity to these otherwise arbitrary temporal demarcations. In the words of Joan Simon, "it was at the Reformation ... that state intervention in English education began; to recognize this is to see all subsequent developments in a new light."[4] The fact that the state intervention came just as the Catholic Church's centralized influence over the medieval world was coming to an end created a need for new ways of controlling and disseminating the "true" Word of God. More urgently, it engendered a need to reconcile various reading strategies into a coherent ontology, one which both replaced the previous Catholic medievalism and built upon it.

What is Literacy?

Is it enough to say, as Walter Ong does, that changing definitions of literacy are simply an end result of a changing culture and development of new technologies of information transmission? This is an important question, for it problematizes what constitutes knowledge in a hermeneutical sense, and thereby problematizes rhetorical communication and interpretation. The ontological shift I will discuss in the following pages constitutes nothing short of the beginnings of a modern concept of literacy. By examining this shift we can better understand our preconceptions of literacy and what it really means to us.

The ability and opportunity to interpret signs, the most basic attribute to any understanding of literacy, is dependent upon two conditions which are themselves external to the sign: 1) the material condition of the sign, i.e. the formal conditions which define the sign's presence to the interpreter, and 2) the ontological conditions which regulate the context for interpretation. For example, it is a commonplace that the printing press allowed for more widespread and cost-effective access to the written word, thus opening up the need for more readers. Walter Ong's subtitle to *Orality and Literacy*, "The Technologizing of the Word," affirms the materialistic nature of language and literacy.

The second condition, the ontological context for interpretation, specifically allegorical exegesis, will be examined in a later chapter. It is important to note here, however, that Augustine always interpreted scripture in light of various controversies. Besides the Manichean controversy, Augustine also found himself involved in an ongoing argument with the Donatist sect. Of this controversy Augustine writes:

> If you cling most firmly to what I urge you ... then you will in no way desert the threshing-floor of the Lord on account of the chaff which either is now being dispersed beneath the blast of the wind of pride, or will be separated by the final winnowing; ... nor will you separate yourselves by an impious secession, because of the mixture of the tares, from the society of that good wheat whose source is that grain that dies and is multiplied thereby, and that grows together throughout the world until the harvest. For the field is the world–not only Africa; and the harvest is the end of the world–not the era of the Donatists. (C. Litteras Petiliani Donatistae, III 3)[5]

Three things are noteworthy in this passage. First, the metaphoric and allegorical description of the scriptural images of the chaff, great House of the Lord, Good Shepherd and the divided flock, and the field and harvest of the world serve as an example of the sort of metaphoric language Augustine so often employed in interpreting and teaching the Bible. Second, is the use to which these images are put—to interpret, and more importantly, to *philosophize*, Old Testament images. This interpretation is done in light of the New Testament in order to validate the Old Testament stories. The third and most important use to which Augustine puts these images is to persuade those who follow the Donatists to convert back to

Catholicism. "The field of Africa" and "era of the Donatists" is the allegorical context in which Augustine is forced to make his rhetorical stance. Although Augustine is responding to a specific and particular rhetorical situation, his interpretive context widens as he moves through his argument—first it is the "society of that good wheat," then the "grain that dies and is multiplied thereby, and that grows together throughout the world." This example is a clear illustration of the fact that Augustine was attempting much more in his rhetorical discussions than the stated education of Christian readers; he needed to teach a new generation of Christians to read in such a way as to defend their faith.

Augustine served as a suitable model for the sixteenth-century theorists dealt with here because, like them, he faced a time of great societal and spiritual instability, and he sought to control that instability through interpretation. Likewise, this discussion covers a large amount of time, and the changes which occur during this time are both obvious and profound as well as subtle. My end however, is not to suggest that Augustine originated a concept of literacy which allowed reading to be dominated by powerful cultural paradigms, although I believe he did, but to trace the particulars of the evolution of literacy throughout the sixteenth and seventeenth centuries, a subject to which I now turn.

Given the strong religious and economic forces which influenced literacy patterns, it is important to question how those factors influenced what reading was and how it was to be most effectively taught. These figures remind us that the printed word and its dissemination were dependent upon many external factors, none more important that the printing press, which reinforced the concept of the Word of God as manifested in material signs and signifiers. The printing press ushered in an era in which ideas were channeled into published treatises, the result of which was a breaking of control from centralized authority, i.e. the Catholic Church and its control of textual production, and a simultaneous emphasis on meaning as contained in a single, self-sufficient entity, i.e. the *book*. Now writing could be theoretically made available to anyone able or willing to pay for it. Likewise, the proliferation of texts after the printing press resulted in a need for judging, cataloging and sorting, which further made it necessary to control *what* was read and *how*.

Since the Middle Ages and the invention of the printing press, each century has moved toward the goal of universal literacy, i.e. the universal skill of reading and writing. When we look away from stated educational goals and benign pedagogical methods and look at wider social and cultural movements, it becomes increasingly clear that as more and more people learn to read, the definition and association of what constitutes a "literate" person changes. These changes almost always result in a more select number of persons who are considered literate while the number of people who can *translate text to sound* continues to grow. Simultaneously, the necessity and importance of literacy is redefined to suggest that it is necessary in order to participate in the exchange of useful information. One of the cultural aspects which best illustrates this delineatation is religion and more specifically, exegetical understanding. To comprehend these forces I will be looking closely at a key moment in the development of Western concepts of language use and acquisition, the fourth and fifth centuries of Augustine of Hippo.

As Walter Ong has noted, all written language implies a materiality of words, a "fixity" in space and time;[6] it is at this moment that literacy became even more dependent upon the ability to differentiate between material and immaterial meanings for words and utterances, and forever split literacy from mere comprehension of grammar, syntax and vocabulary. In other words, litteratus comes to mean the search for spiritual meanings. Mere material understanding was equated with evil, with premature closure not guided by proper discernment and mediation. Strictly literal understanding was unacceptable for truly civilized and educated discussion. Immaterial understanding, understanding grounded in transcendental Truth, was on the side of good, of completeness and acceptability. Literacy, in short, became equated with value. No longer was the ability to differentiate between letters and words enough to constitute understanding; one must be able to participate in a matrix of understanding, in a system of proper and improper discourse. Textual understanding became dependent on a binary system of material/immaterial manifestations of meaning.

Augustine and the Roots of Modern Literacy

The foundation of this educational theory is Augustine's belief that secular reading could be morally damaging if not supplemented with catechism. By returning to one classical/humanistic source or authority for this concept of reading, one with particular relevance to Protestant England, we can explore the opening which occurs in our understanding of literacy when meaning is removed from the material letter and replaced by something more universal and transcendent. This need for supplement suggests that the late classical period did not simply equate literacy with litteratus, instead depended upon a concept of understanding which relied upon extra-verbal judgment. This concept of reading is dependent upon viewing texts as manifestations of spiritual truth, but manifestations in a very specific way: not as obvious literal truths but as figurative truths. This reading strategy, as we have already noted, owes a great deal to the exegetical strategies popularized by Augustine.

Central to Augustine's theories of language use and interpretation, as well as his theories of creation and morality, is the Neoplatonic concept of hierarchical progression, progression which moves at each level to new levels of knowledge with God as ultimate knowledge.[7] As Peter Brown points out, the Manichees presented Augustine with a notion of a "knowable" and supra-sensible world, the "Kingdom of Darkness," and a higher, more orderly but unsensible world, the "Kingdom of Light." The problem for Augustine, however, was that this system did not reflect "wisdom" in the way that Augustine had come to think of it from his reading of Cicero.[8] Augustine wanted a system of learning which would value *effort* and enlightenment, as well as systematic and orderly thinking. He also wanted access to the higher, "unsensible" world of order and wisdom. Thus, an accentuation on effort was necessary because of the sometimes veiled nature of the Truth. He wrote, "And to the extent that we in this life enjoy Him 'through a glass' or 'in a dark manner' we shall sustain our pilgrimage with more tolerance and more ardently desire to end it" (*On Christian Doctrine*, I.xxx).

Literal interpretations for Augustine did not mean that the language had to be used in its "original" sense or that clarity was the goal. Allegory by its very nature implies a Literal truth prior to the figuration of the idea in the language of the allegory. The reader of an allegorical text must have enough knowledge to move between the "Real," doctrinally Literal meaning, and the poetic figuration; allegory, therefore, is useful for teaching the "worthy" and "able." A reader becomes "worthy" of the truth when he/she accepts that the Bible as a whole must be read in accordance with the New Testament, an act of interpretation which requires the ability to read outside the "literal" text. The development of an alternative "literal" understanding had a strong influence on Augustine's later, anti-Manichean, theology since it is to this level of non-contradiction and clarity that Augustine hoped to arrive through the type of careful reading learned from Ambrose. The dissociation of sense from sound and appreciation of the spiritual meaning of a given text would also serve as the foundation for his allegorical method.[9] Augustine writes that "as I opened my heart in order to recognize how eloquently he was speaking it occurred to me at the same time (though this idea came gradually) how truly he was speaking." Augustine goes on:

> I had thought nothing could be said for the Catholic faith in the face of the objections raised by the Manichees, but it now appeared to me that this faith could be maintained on reasonable grounds—especially when I had heard one or two passages in the Old Testament explained, usually in a figurative way, which, when I had taken them literally, had been a cause of death to me.[10] (*Confessions* V. xiv)

The Manichee's dependence on the "literal" interpretation of the letter led only to contradiction and an unattainable spiritual truth. The figurative reading of the Old Testament, however, allowed for seeing the spiritual truth as present in the letter. For Augustine, the figurative reading of the Bible allowed for a sense of societal homogeneity, a norming of two seemingly diverse cultures into one prolonged Christian revelation. Peter Brown writes of the Bible's role in providing unity in the Mediterranean world of the fourth and fifth centuries: "The Bible itself, with its seemingly endless layers of meaning, was a microcosm of the societal and intellectual diversity to be found in the Christian Churches."[11] Religious controversies were the subject of endless debates by all classes of society: "If you ask about your change, the shopkeeper talks theology to you, on the Begotten and the Unbegotten; if you inquire the price of a loaf, the reply is: 'The Father is greater and the Son is inferior;' and if you say, 'Is the bath ready?' the attendant affirms that the Son is of Nothing."[12] Often, these discussions turned violent, with the Donatists controversy of North Africa one of the most violent.

An understanding of the history of allegory is essential to recognizing the historical changes which have occurred to literacy, for the study of its history reveals that allegory was appropriated as an important reading strategy at key moments when a crisis occurred to the dominant paradigm, resulting in a need to make renewed sense of the culture's understanding of the world and worldly texts. The writings of Philo and Origen reveal that allegorical interpretation seemed to develop, at least partially, from a need to make sense of cultural and historical stories and myths for a changing culture and society. For example, in explaining the need for allegorical understanding, Philo wrote, "How is it possible to derive the multiplicity which we see from the absolute unity which we believe to lie at the summit of the world?"[13] Philo's question serves as a summation of the problem at the center of Neoplatonic hermeneutics, and a question which Augustine set out to address with his allegorical interpretive strategy. This question serves as a summation of the cultural and religious issues which arise when any two philosophical systems come into conflict, which is the situation in the fourth and fifth centuries when Augustine is called upon to develop his interpretive system.

Augustine used allegory as a means of understanding the Old Testament in terms of the New Testament; in fact, syncretism and typology would become the main allegorical methods for both medieval and (perhaps even more so) Renaissance poets and interpreters. Augustine saw the signs and metaphors of the New Testament as literal signs which could be used for interpreting the ambiguous signs of the Old Testament. For Augustine the problem with the Old Testament of the Jews was that it was "blind" to the concept of Christ as the truth and spirit of the text:

> But their [the Jews'] senses were made dull. For, until this present day, the selfsame veil, in the reading of the old testament, remaineth not taken away (because in Christ it is made void). But even until this day, when Moses is read, the veil is upon their heart. But when they shall be converted to the Lord, the veil shall be taken away.[14]

The "veil" Augustine was referring to here is the veil of allegory which is only lifted, and the text therefore made understandable, through knowledge of the New Testament Christ.[15] Specifically, Augustine believed that all interpretations of both Testaments required knowledge of "charity." For Augustine, no matter what the interpretation, all interpretive roads eventually had to lead back to the notion of charity. Augustine writes that "Scripture teaches nothing but charity, nor condemns anything except cupidity, and in this way shapes the minds of men" (*On Christian Doctrine* 3.10.15).

It was a common complaint that Augustine was in the habit of looking for obscure meanings in Scripture, which sometimes caused him to ignore what looks like the obvious, original intent. The reason for this asperity lies in the rhetorical situation which he marked out for himself as Bishop of Hippo. Augustine's classical education and social and cultural circumstance (i.e. his rhetorical position in opposition to the Manichees) caused the book of Genesis (and the creation story in particular) to pose special difficulties for him. If he accepted the story as a poetic fabula then the beliefs of the Catholic faith came under attack; if he accepted them as literal statements of truth, then the Manichees were given strength.[16] Also, Augustine writes, again in relation to the language of the Book of Genesis, that we should not take the Genesis story "in a childish way, as though God exerted himself by working. For he spoke, not with an audible and temporal word, but with an intellectual and eternal word, and the things were done" (*The City of God* XI 8). Note the connection of "intellectual" and "eternal", as well as Augustine's insistence on interpreting "work" in a figurative sense. Augustine equated intellectual with eternal as a way of insisting on interpreting a work in a figurative way.

For Augustine, the polysemus nature of signs in the Book of Genesis was what potentially separated fit from unfit readers—the "rough outer husks" of the text would repel unfit readers, but exhort the good to learning and effort.[17] With Augustine we see the early formation of an interpretive ontology in which meanings can be hidden with the sole intent of stimulating a reader towards divine understanding; in other words, through the act of doctrinally correct reading, creating "fit" readers. For an early Christian apologist attempting to defend the Scriptures from contradictory yet *logical* interpretations (and unfit readers), allegory provides the best defense, bridging as it does the logical and the rhetorical.

This emphasis on the norming ability of careful reading is a key aspect of Augustine's notion of literacy, and one which leads to the necessity of effort and, sometimes, struggle. That which is learned through struggle, Augustine writes, is remembered more completely. In *On Christian Doctrine* Augustine writes: "And the obscurity itself of the divine and wholesome writings was a part of a kind of eloquence through which our understanding should be benefited not only by the discovery of what lies hidden but also by exercise."[18] Kenneth Burke writes in *The Rhetoric of Religion* that in chapters V and VI of the *Confessions* Augustine observes that the Bible tries to express itself in "'words most open' while at the same time preserving the 'dignity of its secret.'"[19] This understanding of scripture as simultaneously both "open" and "hidden" creates a deliberate disorientation on the part of the reader, leading her to search for some stabilizing force, and it is this stabilizing force which becomes the object of debate between Catholics and Protestants. Since it is the mysterious level which is most important to salvation, the need and desire for an authoritative understanding, and correspondingly a *way of reading*, is made all the more urgent.

Allegorical interpretation was primarily utilized as a rhetorical tool to persuade other sects that the Catholic understanding of the Bible was the truly Literal one, thereby putting the Church in control of the proper interpretation of the Bible. The early Church turned to a highly systematized concept of ambiguity and obscurity in the form of allegorical interpretation to achieve the desired effect of rendering the audience dependent on the authority of the church for the Literal meaning of the text. To further strengthen its position, Church fathers such as St Augustine affirmed that an understanding of the Literal truth was a prerequisite for salvation.

A specific example of the utilization of literacy for the sake of contentious rhetorical suppression can be seen in the debate between Augustine and the pagan Manichees, Donatist and Pelagian sects. Augustine, a convert from Manicheism, needed a rhetorical method which would allow him to interpret the Old Testament in ways which would oppose the Manichees. The Manichees posed a threat to the homogeneity of the early Catholic Church because they employed "literal" interpretation of the Bible to point out the Bible's logical contradictions. The

Manichean system of interpretation (as well as their philosophic foundation in general) was too gnostic for Augustine, based as it was on a closed system of knowledge relying on purely empirical observation as the basis for literal interpretation. While Augustine believed strongly in knowledge and guided speculation as a basis of faith, the Manichees devalued the activity of speculation and inquiry. As Peter Brown writes, "the Manichees would never concede that their picture of the universe was a 'Myth' symbolizing some deeper truth. The waxing and waning of the Moon, for instance, was not merely the distant image of some spiritual event: it was, quite literally, caused by the influx of released fragments of 'Light' flowing upwards from the world."[20] What is revealed in the Manichean belief in the waxing of the moon is an essentialistic and empiricist philosophy in contrast to the more idealistic and "mythic" system of belief of the Platonists, a system with profound influence on Augustine's later interpretive system.

Since Augustine's conversion away from Manichean belief occurred in the context of a philosophical and moral debate of no small consequence, the act of rhetorical interpretation takes on the added dimension of being a persuasive rhetorical act, i.e. an attempt to "persuade to action" (convert) the Manichees and Donatists. "Conversion" is the attempt to bring a subject to a higher, and presumably more morally correct, level of belief. All correct reading and understanding, according to Augustine and the early Church Fathers, was ideally a form of conversion. With conversion, however, comes acquiescence to a new paradigm; literacy thus leads not simply to learning to read again, but to a new form of domination, and for those not converted, a lost means to their salvation.

Augustine's *Confessions* further illustrates the redeeming power of literacy. Brian Stock notes that early in his education Augustine began to differentiate between "the activity of reading" and "the content of the text" as well as between "reading for pleasure and reading for self-improvement," the prior being an "aesthetic" impulse and the other an "ascetic" one.[21] Prior to his own conversion, Augustine had little motivation to search out his own interpretations of the Bible because its style was not "literary." He writes in the *Confessions* that "when I studied the Scriptures then I did not feel as I am writing about them today. They seemed to me unworthy of comparison with the grand style of Cicero" (III. v).[22] Augustine would come to view parts of the Scriptures as exemplifying the grand style, but only after noting the possibility of allegorical interpretation and the "literary" quality of its rhetoric. The Manichees, on the other hand, were fiercely anti-allegorical, believing that a logical reading of the Bible was the only way toward real faith. This logical reading often lead to contradiction and ambiguity, and for the Manichees this ambiguity was used to point out the Bible's, and by extension Christianity's, failures. The Manichees then attempted to replace the Christian belief system with a seemingly more morally strenuous system.

During the process of his conversion, Augustine began to see the Bible as a system of highly metaphoric language constructions which contained philosophical ideas which needed interpretation. Augustine set out to do nothing short of providing a new way of reading, and more importantly, of believing and teaching the Bible. For example, in the sixth book of his *Confessions* Augustine describes the effect produced on him by the sermons of St Ambrose, in which the veil was removed from the letter:

> And I was happy when I heard Ambrose in his sermons, as I often did, recommend most emphatically to his congregation this text as a rule to go by: 'The letter killeth, but the spirit giveth life.' So he would draw aside the *veil* of mystery and explain in a *spiritual* sense the meanings of things which, if understood *literally*, [i.e. according to the letter] appeared to be teaching what was wrong. (6.4; emphasis mine)

I noted earlier that Augustine learned from Ambrose the possibility of silent, personal and meditative reading. Here we see Augustine learning that a "deeper," more enigmatic level of understanding, gleaned either from careful personal reading or from well-educated sermonizing, can lead to salvation. The notion of a spiritual sense as opposed to a "literal" sense is the important distinction between an incorrect reading and a philosophical and intellectual one. The spiritual and redemptive understanding of a text is arrived at only after the text is examined in light of its figurative (and therefore non-"literal") meaning.

This last point is perhaps Augustine's most profound legacy to Western concepts of reading and interpretation: for Augustine, the spiritual is present in the letter. What Augustine learned is a way of bridging the discontinuity between the lower, material realm of knowledge (which the Manichees saw as the only knowable realm) and the higher, spiritual realm. Such a distinction is central to both Protestant and Catholic exegetical theories, and for both it is the role of a teacher or authority figure to lead readers away from the merely sensual toward the spiritual.

For medieval exegesis, the analysis of the letter meant grammatical analysis, which for St Augustine meant the study of the correctness of translations and the proper pronunciation of a given word, especially in the case of words meant literally but which cause ambiguity. However, grammatical analysis alone has serious limitations: "When words used literally cause ambiguity in Scripture, we must first determine whether we have mispronounced or misconstrued them. When investigation reveals an uncertainty as to how a locution should be pointed or construed, the rule of faith should be consulted as it is found in the more open places of the Scriptures and in the authority of the Church" (*On Christian Doctrine*, III, 2).[23] The emphasis on "open places of the Scriptures" would come to be of particular importance to later Reformists. Gradually in the Western Christian tradition, both Catholic and Protestant, grammar would come to be equated with an understanding of "open places" in scripture since grammatical analysis often focused on the level of sense, or the obvious or surface meaning of a text. (There are important exceptions, as we shall see, most notably found in discourse on the Eucharist, where grammatical paradigms are used to understand the spiritual level of meaning. This development will mark the culmination of grammatical understanding in the Christian tradition.) The spirit (or sententia) of a text, however, is what the text really means, the level at which understanding occurs as a result of effort and intellect. The sententia could be thought of, at least for

Augustine, as the doctrinal or "higher" meaning. All texts (when read as texts) have a letter, but some texts have only the literal sense (for example, the ten commandments), without a need for further study or interpretation. However, Augustine's interpretive strategies rely upon knowing the difference between texts which fulfill their potential meaning at the level of sense and those texts which need further study to arrive at the level of spiritual understanding. All levels of interpretation, by definition, work at the level of either sense or, in the case of the allegorical, analogical and tropological, the level of sententia. In short, the purpose of exposition is to arrive at the level of sententia. However, a complete humanistic education is still important because the reader of the Biblical text must be assured of having enough information to understand even the letter of the text: "He [the reader of Scriptures] is assisted by the accuracy of texts which expert diligence in emendation has procured. Thus instructed, he may turn his attention to the investigation and solution of the ambiguities of the Scriptures" (*On Christian Doctrine*, III. 1). The "ambiguities of the Scriptures," as Augustine sees them, are open only to the more diligent and knowledgeable reader (in this case, a reader trained in Church doctrine). By emphasizing the spiritual level Augustine is both proposing a new standard for reading the Bible, and dismissing the previous competing interpretive rhetorics of the Manichees.

The struggle inherent in attempting to understand the True Word of God as revealed in His words is virtuous. Obscurity as a means of persuasion and as an element of Augustine's interpretive strategy has a clear ethical component. A person being taught is either passive in regard to the subject matter, in which case clarity is foregrounded and becomes an end in itself, or active, in which case obscurity is foregrounded. In Book XII of the *Confessions* Augustine writes that if "had been Moses then" and if he "had been given by you the task of writing the Book of Genesis" he would also write according to the capacity of his hearers so that "those who cannot yet understand how God creates would still not neglect my word as being beyond their capacity" yet those who "already have understanding" would find in his words "every true opinion which they had reached themselves in their own thinking."[24] He would allow for meanings at all levels of understanding, but would reserve the final meaning for those worthy and willing to struggle. For Augustine, the Truth of scripture is not self-evident in the literal, unannotated text; however, for those who can only read according to the "carnal sense," they are kept safe by the "words of your book, words so lofty in humility, so copious in brevity."[25] It is important to note that Augustine never trusted obscurity or ambiguity in the material or formal aspects alone (i.e. he expected correct and regular poetic meter and correctness of Biblical translation), rather he felt that obscurity and ambiguity were important so as to lead to intellectual scrutiny. Augustine always saw true harmony and order (that is, in alignment with Church doctrine) as the final stage in any understanding; if the harmony and order were not prevalent at the formal/sensory stage, then they were discernible at the level of the spiritual and truthful.

Just as the Bible should be read in such a way that its unvarying theme of "charity" is discerned, all creation should be seen as in some way "ordered." Such formal elements as order, form, and unity are inadequate to explain what beauty *is* (a question at the center of Augustine's concerns) in relation to such concerns as Truth and enlightenment. It is necessary to look at another, "higher" level of judgment, the level of illumination and understanding. When we consider the necessity of order, and the ultimate insufficiency of order (considered separately from the whole Truth), in understanding God's Word, the dialectic between clarity and obscurity seen above becomes focused. Clarity and order are sufficient to imply that transcendent truth can be captured in the immanent, but obscurity reminds us that we cannot possess, but at best can glimpse, the truth. Augustine's uses of obscurity and allegory are in fact foregrounded in a desire to explicate and disseminate the true meaning of the text.

Augustine's model puts forth the notion that reading carefully and "correctly" (i.e. according to Church doctrine) mirrors the order of the world and God's creation. Thus, reading not only makes one aware of creation, but by allowing one to understand the mysteries of creation, makes one worthy and "valuable."

Elizabethan Literacy and the "Arts of Rhetoric"

With this ever-deepening understanding of literacy comes the question as to how universally literacy can be allowed to spread and by what methods. Who is valuable, and who can become valuable, via access to the true Word? If all persons are potentially allowed to be saved and therefore to become fully participating members of society, what is a person's salvation measured against? To what extent are all persons potentially redeemable? Can anyone fully understand the Word of God as put forth in the literal level of understanding, or must they be aided by faith or inherent intelligence? These questions must be put in the context of the continual social, economic as well as religious, campaigns toward broader literacy. It could be argued that when viewed historically, it becomes clear that as more and more people became adept at reading, at transforming texts into sound, the very definition of literacy changed. After Augustine, for example, literacy becomes more and more essential to society and salvation. Walter Ong writes in *Orality and Literacy* that literacy, "is absolutely necessary for the development not only of science but also history, philosophy, explicative understanding of literature and of any art, and indeed for the explanation of language (including oral speech) itself." In other words, literacy is what makes a human a participant in his or her world, which allows one to write and potentially change history. In short, literacy designates not only those who can read, but highlights the importance and urgency of the ability to read against the backdrop of those who cannot. What this designation suggests is that for literacy to have a value, it must *not* be universal.

As was noted earlier, Walter Ong's definition of "reading" serves as a functional definition of literacy. However, the ability to convert a text into sound only suffices to "anchor" the word in the reader's comprehension and/or perception; it does not explain how (or if) the sound undergoes further apportioning into contextualized meaning. For most modern and unreflective uses of the word "literacy" all that is assumed is that the reader is able to identify "text" (an equally under-determined term) as belonging to some sort of mutual system of sounds. More difficult to pinpoint is exactly where and how such identification becomes meaning; in fact, "meaning" is perhaps the most difficult term of all to define. Augustine's reading methods suggested that meaning occurs as a result of a-priori Truths which exist intrinsic to the letter only after they are understood.

In order to define when and how meaning occurs in written language it is necessary to first divide the question into two parts. Since I am interested in literacy in England, I will first briefly consider the historical condition of education in England during this time period. Such an understanding reveals the stated goals and methods used to teach not only reading but written communication. However, widespread methods suggest only broadly how language was understood to function. Also, such educational treatises do not necessarily suggest successful methods. We need only look at our own theories of education to note that even the most commonly accepted method of education can be only marginally successful.

Therefore the second area of consideration is broader still, but by being more theoretical allows for more specific examinations of how meaning is manifested in language. By analyzing various pedagogical texts, both Renaissance and modern, it is possible to begin to see how language was viewed ontologically and, in turn, how reading and interpretation were taught.

During the time under consideration here, "petty" schools spread basic literacy beyond the reserve of the privileged. By the 1630s perhaps as many as half of all adult males, or one third of all adults in England, could read. By the mid-seventeenth century England was one of the best educated societies in the world.[26] Partly as a result of the Protestant Reformation, reading literacy had become important to the labor class as well as the upper classes and clerics. As early as 1478 the Goldsmith's Company had a rule that no apprentice be taken "without he can write and read,"[27] an affirmation that literacy, at least literacy defined, according to Walter Ong, as "converting [words on a page] to sound, aloud or in the imagination, syllable-by-syllable in slow reading or sketchily in the rapid reading," had already become important to technological advancement.[28] Reading and writing were by then essential components of the mercantile middle class. Although it would be possible to attribute the literacy requirement to the practical needs of communication and accountability, these skills were balanced with the advancement of literary studies. For example, libraries became more important and plentiful, and the following school ordinance of 1529 is typical of the spread of literacy and access to books:[29]

> A library shall be erected not far from the school and the lectorium, wherein all books, *good and bad*, which shall be acquired for this purpose in this city, shall be assembled; they shall be orderly arranged, especially the best, each near others of its kind; keys thereto, one or four, should be in the hands of some, as with the rector and sub-rector and superintendents, that no damage may be done. [Emphasis mine]

This ordinance, from a liberal standpoint, seems ideal: there is no differentiating "good books" from "bad": all books are made available. The "best" books may warrant extra attention, but the only real "control" put upon access (seemingly) is to prevent damage. The books are "orderly arranged," thus illustrating a commitment to utility. Further, placing like books close to each other seemingly encouraged comparison of ideas. Ultimately, however, this openness was limited. The same principles which resulted in libraries and access to books soon led to renewed attempts at restricting the publishing and reading of books found to be heretical or politically dangerous. Despite attempts at controlling them, however, printing presses allowed for dissenting ideas to continue being disseminated. This is most clear in the numerous works published by and about Martin Luther throughout the first half of the sixteenth century. These conflicting impulses would define much of the exegetical and literary theory of the next hundred years (and well beyond).

The new learning of the Protestant Reformation had its origin in important religious questions, and the purpose of learning was to arrive at doctrinally sound judgments about these various issues. The first fifteenth-century foundation for seculars at Oxford, endowed in 1429, was specifically intended to combat Lollard ideas; the "College of the Blessed Mary and All Saints of Lincoln" was designed to defend "the mysteries of the sacred page against those ignorant laics who profaned with swinish snouts its most holy pearls."[30]

At the foundation of most late medieval and later Renaissance education was the teaching of grammar, which as the basis of education became the main weapon against the "ignorant laics." As early as 1505, Erasmus, in *Valla's Annotations on the New Testament* insisted that theologians must be sound grammarians since testament could not be interpreted by divine inspiration but by careful study.[31] At the same time, Erasmus spoke of the necessity of spreading literacy so that the common man might have access to the scripture in their native tongue. The notion that reading is a form of redemption is modeled carefully on the classic Christian understanding of redemption as available to all, but only with effort and true understanding. As a result of this development, the middle of the sixteenth century saw a sudden increase in grammars and poetic treatises meant for the complete education of a general audience.

Perhaps the most popular text of the first half of the sixteenth century was Richard Sherry's *A Treatise of Schemes and Tropes*, published in 1550. In Sherry's words the treatise was "very profitable for the understanding of good authors, gathered out of the best grammarians and orators." The text was appended to Erasmus' very influential treatise on educating children ("a declamation that children ... should be well and gently brought up in learning"), thus creating a one volume guide to a child's complete education.[32]

The work was fully titled "A Treatise of schemes and tropes very profitable for the better understanding of good authors, gathered out of the best grammarians and orators, by Richard Sherry." This utilization of classical authorities is typical of education treatises of this period and led to one of the most debated issues to result from the Reformation: is the vernacular equal to classical languages, especially Latin, or is it necessarily subordinate to it? The Renaissance marked the "victory" of the vernacular for English speakers, still, the source for most knowledge was classical; Sherry, for example, makes it clear that the terms for the various tropes and schemes "are not bred in our Englishe tongue, neither bene they Englyshe wordes." In defense of using such terms, Sherry relies upon an argument, which, as we shall see, would have importantly ramifications for literacy throughout the Renaissance: we are to be thankful for scholars for enriching the native tongue, since it "is not unknowne that oure language for the barbarousness and lacke of eloquence hath been complayned of." The purpose of Sherry's treatise is to civilize language by the addition of classical paradigms of eloquence. This utilization of classical writers for the sole purpose of enriching English culture and language would become a key component to Renaissance education theory, both to theories of vernacular communication and the study of classical languages themselves. In true Augustinian fashion, pagan writer's and orators can civilize (and "redeem") our own culture, and classical writers, in this case Quintillian, Cicero and Erasmus, who for Sherry had classical status, are not read for themselves, but for what they connote and represent.

The body of Sherry's book is far from revolutionary. True to his word, Sherry deviates very little from classical sources and modes of representation. For example, he divides his discussion of schemes into figures, and figures into types of figures (figure of sentence, word, diction, etc.). The text does not provide a great deal of theoretical material as to the utilization of these tropes and schemes. Sherry provides brief, and often insightful, definitions of key terms (metaphor, for example, is defined as "translation, that is a worde translated from the thinge that it properlye signifieth, unto another which may agree with it by a similitude"),[33] but for the most part depends upon a reader or student utilizing and practicing the various tropes and schemes.

Thomas Wilson's *Arte of Rhetorique for the use of all such as are studious of Eloquence* was published in 1553 and quickly became the most commonly used textbook for the rest of the century. A main difference between Wilson and Sherry lies in Wilson's use of preaching and his attention to biblical interpretation, a combination and emphasis undoubtedly influenced by Augustine's *On Christian Doctrine*. Although the next chapter will focus on matters of biblical exegesis, it is noteworthy that Wilson writes as much for preachers as for clerkes. "Seeing God hath raised suche worthe Preachers in this our tyme, that their Godly, and learned dooynges may be a moste juste example for al other to folowe: as well for their lyving, as for their learning."[34] It is when Wilson discusses rhetoric both in terms of planning an effective sermon and in terms of exegesis that his text reveals much of interest to the present question. When discussing narratives, Wilson writes:

> Some [Preachers] do use after the literal sense to gather a mystical understanding, and to expounde the saiynges spiritually, makying their narration altogether of thynges heavenly. Some rehersing a texte particularly spoke, applie the same generally unto all states, enlarging the narration moste Godly by comparing wordes long ago spoken, with thynges and matters that are presently done. Not withstanding the aunctient fathers because they did onely expounde the Scriptures for the moste parte, made no artifical narration: but used to followe such order as

> the plaine text gave them. So that if every sentence were plainely opened to the hearers, they went not much farther.[35]

I quote this passage at length not only to introduce the debate which will be examined later, but to note the importance of rhetoric not only for communicative purposes, but for interpretation of spiritual matters. For Wilson a good scriptural oration made spiritual connections between "wordes long ago spoken, with thynges and matters that are presently done" (i.e. typology and/or allegory). Wilson is clearly putting a Reformation spin on his understanding of the Church fathers when he notes that they "did onely expounde the Scriptures for the moste parte, made no artifical narration: but used to followe such order as the plaine text gave them," i.e. that they only used allegory in a clear and "literal" way: his attempt to use the Church fathers as authorities reminds us that the theories the fathers put forth were still of relevance in the mid-sixteenth century. Note, for example, the Augustinian strain in the following from Wilson's discussion of how to interpret scripture:

> There be Lawes uttered by Christ's owne mouth, the which if they be taken according as they are spoken, seme to conteyne great absurditie in them. And therefore the mind of the Law maker must rather be observed, the bare words taken only.[36]

In order to understand difficult or seemingly contradictory passages, the reader (or preacher) must find "other places in the Scripture" where the message is clearer.[37] This search for parallel passages is the primary method for arriving at consistent and thorough understanding.

Like Sherry, Wilson calls figurative language "translation," and explains that the source for it is to be found in the words of learned and wise men who sought "first to enlarge their tongue."[38] They did so by using words which were "of lyke nature", yet different in meaning. He uses as his example of translation that if speaking against a Pharisee, rather than calling them "unwise" he would say they are "crooked" in judgment, or their "wits are cloudy." It is clear why Wilson uses the term translation, since he sees a distinction between the material signifier and its ultimate signified, and he believes that meaning occurs in the act of making a transference from one to the other: "when a thing full ofte can not be expressed by an apt and mete word, we do percieve (when it is spoken by a word translated) that the likeness of that thing which appeareth in an other word ... which we would most gladly have perceived."[39] Wilson goes on to state that words used in translation cause us to understand and remember more readily since they require some effort on our part. In short, tropes cause us to remember what we already know. Wilson is perhaps consciously (or unconsciously) adopting Augustine's concept of the "magister interior" or inner teacher, which was Augustine's description of the role of grace and faith in matters of interpretation. Given the Protestant emphasis on individual faith, it comes as no surprise that this is one of the aspects of Augustine's exegetical theory which is most influential on mid-sixteenth century rhetoric: the *magister interior* can lead readers (via the act of translation and/or interpretation) through the material outer covering of a word into its real signification.

Throughout the *Arte of Rhetorique* Wilson very slyly makes reference to contemporary religious debates. When defining synecdoche, the example used is: "All Cambridge sorowed for the death of Bucer, meaninge the most part." The full ramifications of this example will be looked at in chapter four, but suffice it to note that Cambridge contained at least some scholars who were followers of Bucer's theory of Eucharistic sacrament. Another example needs no interpretation: "All Englande rejoyeth that pilgrimage is banished, and Idolatrye for ever abolished: and yet all England is not glad, but the most parte."[40] These examples illustrate that the teaching of grammar is both an opportunity for normalizing reading and interpretive habits as well as an opportunity for more overt propagandizing. In the chapters which follow I will consider not only allegorical understanding as a form of literacy, but will note how litteratus and the study of classical languages results in a supra-textual understanding of literacy.

Notes

1. Michel Foucault, *The Archaeology of Knowledge and The Discourse on Language*. Trans. A.M. Sheridan Smith (New York: Pantheon Books, 1972), 216.

2. Walter Ong, *Orality and Literacy: The Technologizing of the Word* (New York: Methuen, 1982), 8.

3. E.D. Hirsch, Jr., *Cultural Literacy: What Every American Needs to Know* (Boston: Houghton Mifflin, 1987), xiii.

4. Joan Simon, *Education and Society in Tudor England* (Cambridge: Cambridge University Press, 1967), vii.

5. Translated in Frederick W. Dillistones, "The Anti-Donatist Writings" in *Companion to the Study of Augustine*. Ed. Roy Battenhouse (New York: Oxford University Press, 1956).

6. See, for example, Ong's "Writing Is a Technology that Restructures Thought," in *Literacy: A Critical Sourcebook*. Ed. Ellen Cushman *et al.* (Boston: Bedford/St Martin's, 2001).

7. *Ibid.*, 40.

8. The leading Manichean, Faustus, reflected the limitations of the Manichean philosophy. Augustine writes in Book V, chapter viii of *The Confessions* that "the famous Faustus had shown up so badly in many of the questions which perplexed me." Augustine, however, found himself unable to completely give himself to Catholicism; it wasn't until after his sickness, upon hearing Ambrose speak, (see below) that Augustine was finally able to separate the *manner* of speaking from the meaning (see *Confessions* V xiv), a separation

which represented his complete break from pagan rhetorical theory. However, Augustine's conversion was still not complete; "So, though the Catholic cause did not seem to me defeated, it did not yet seem to me to have won."

9. Mary Preuse, *Eloquence and Ignorance in Augustine's "On the Nature and Origin of the Soul,"* American Academy of Religion Series, no. 51 (Atlanta: Scholars Press, 1985), 23.

10. nam primo etiam ipsa defendi posse mihi iam coeperunt vider et fidem catholicam, pro qua nihil posse dici aduersus oppugnantes manichaeos putaueram, iam non inpudentar asseri existimabam, maxime audito uno atque altero et saepius aenigmate soluto de scriptis ueteribus, ubi, cum ad litteram acciperem, occidebar.

11. Peter Brown, *Power and Persuasion in Late Antiquity: Towards a Christian Empire* (Madison, WI: University of Wisconsin Press, 1992), 74.

12. Gregory of Nyssa, *De deitate Filii et Spiritus Sancti: Patrologia Graeca* 46:557. Quoted in Brown, *Power and Persuasion*, 90.

13. Anthony Meredith, "Later Philosophy," in *The Oxford History of the Classical World*, John Boardman *et al.*, eds (Oxford: Oxford University Press, 1986), 703.

14. 2 Cor. 3. 12-16.

15. For more on this notion of allegory as a "veil" to those unworthy, see Michael Murrin, *The Veil of Allegory: Some Notes Towards a Theory of Allegorical Rhetoric in the English Renaissance* (Chicago: University of Chicago Press, 1969).

16. *Ibid.*, 189.

17. For linguistic background and support for this concept, see George Lakoff and Mark Johnson's *Metaphors We Live By* (Chicago: University of Chicago Press, 1980), especially chapter 26.

18. Augustine, *On Christian Doctrine*, trans. with intro. by D.W. Robertson, Jr. (New York: Macmillan, 1958), 123 (IV.4).

19. Kenneth Burke, *The Rhetoric of Religion: Studies in Logology* (Berkeley: University of California Press, 1970), 61.

20. Peter Brown, *Augustine of Hippo: A Biography* (Berkeley: University of California Press, 1967), 57.

21. Brian Stock, *Augustine the Reader: Meditation, Self-Knowledge, and the Ethics of Interpretation* (Cambridge: The Belknap Press of Harvard University Press, 1996), 26.

22. non enim sicut modo loquor, ita sensi, cum adtendi ad illam scripturam, sed uisa est mihi indigna, quam Tullianae dignitati compararem. Note that Jerome, in *Ep.* xxii 30, also found the prophets "rude and repellent" after reading the classics (John Gibb, editor, *Confessions of Augustine*, Cambridge Patristic Texts (Cambridge: Cambridge University Press, 1908), 61).

23. On logic, Augustine writes that "a knowledge of inference, definition, and division aids the understanding a great deal, provided that men do not make the mistake of thinking that they have learned the truth of the blessed life when they have learned them" (*On Christian Doctrine* II. 37). This statement serves as a clear argument against the system of logical interpretation put forth by the Manichees. And finally, on rhetoric, which Augustine here specifies as "eloquence," Augustine writes: "There are, moreover, certain precepts for a more copious discourse which make up what are called the rules of eloquence, and these are very true, even though they may be used to make falsehoods persuasive" (II. 36). All of these uses of the trivium point to the fact that the *letter* of the text is not enough–there must be more beyond to help guide the reader. The quadrivium, however, was of assistance in understanding the spirit (see below) of the text. It seems that the most important discipline in the quadrivium for Augustine was music. "An ignorance of some things concerning music also halts and impedes the reader" (*On Christian Doctrine* I.16), but the nine muses are not to be considered, for "they were refuted by Varro" (I. 17). In various places throughout *On Christian Doctrine* Augustine emphasizes the importance of numerology in understanding some of the more obscure passages of Scripture.

24. Book XII, chapter 26. Ed. and trans. by Rex Warner (New York: New American Library, 1963).

25. Book XII, chapter 30.

26. Graff, 98.

27. Simon, 15. See also *The Rhetoric of Leviathan*. David Johnston (Princeton University Press, 1986).

28. Ong, *Orality and Literacy*, 8.

29. Frederick Eby, *Early Protestant Educators: The Educational Writings of Martin Luther, John Calvin, and Other Leaders of Protestant Thought* (New York: McGraw-Hill Company, 1931), 211.

30. J. Wells, *Oxford and its Colleges* (1897), p. 133. Quoted in Simon, 43.

31. Simon, 70.

32. Facsimile reproduction from the copy in the Huntington Library (Folger Library STC 22428).

33. *Ibid.*, 89.

34. Thomas Wilson, *Arte of Rhetorique for the use of all such as are studious of Eloquence* (1553), 103.

35. *Ibid.*, 102.

36. *Ibid.*, 116.

37. *Ibid.*, 117.

38. *Ibid.*, 192.

39. *Ibid.*, 193.

40. *Ibid.*, 196.

Chapter 3

The Control of the Word: Renaissance Exegesis and the Education of the Reader

> Holye Scripture conteyneth all thynges necessarie to salvation: so that whatsoever is not read therein, nor may be proved thereby, is not to be required of anye man, that it should be believed as an article of faith, or be thought requisite necessarie to salvation.[1]
>
> (Article VI, Thirty-Nine Articles, 1551)

The warning over the door in the house of Busyrane in Spenser's *Faerie Queene* to "be bold ..." but "be not too bold" (III.xi.54) can also serve to remind Renaissance readers of the inherent restraint and limitations put upon them by the Articles of Faith, while the charge to "be bold" could serve as a reminder of the seeming autonomy that the Protestant reformation allowed for in the first place. This dichotomy is likewise reflected on the inscription carved above the door at the former Lady Chapel at St Albans:

> The chapel which once bore St Mary's name
> Under Elizabeth a school became;
> Why not? When faith and learning are combined
> Then only do we true religion find.

This inscription illustrates one of the sources of these boundaries: the Elizabethan union of church and state. The school was founded with the following prerequisite: "No man shall take upon him to teach but such as shall be allowed by the ordinary and found to meet as well for his learning and dexterity in teaching as for sober and honest conversation and also for right understanding of God's true religion."[2] The reference to Elizabeth as patron of the school serves as a reminder that Elizabeth is the head of the one true religion (and Mary as the head of the false one); the basis of "true religion" in "faith and learning" serves to optimistically reflect the aims of the Reformation. However, as Joan Simon writes in *Education and Society in Tudor England*, "the 'right understanding of God's true religion' was the matter most in dispute"; as a result, the school's founding prerequisites suggest some of the more restrictive and controlling impulses of the English Church.

During the reign of the Tudors, the Church of England was affected by two methods of normalizing and controlling religious discourse: first, by making the political head of the nation the spiritual head of the church, and second by centering biblical exegesis around doctrinally literal interpretation, as characterized by article six of the *Thirty-Nine Articles*. However, such attempts at control did not go without controversy. As we have already seen, the Church was often divided by debates concerning the role of secular leaders in spiritual matters. A major problem facing the establishment of widespread religious homogeneity in the middle of the sixteenth century was the historically vague distinction between Church and State. After Henry VIII's assumption of the role of King and *supremum caput* of the Church of England, the relationship between Church and State became fundamentally blurred. The question of who had power over spiritual matters stimulated debate about issues both substantive and symbolic, and this debate is seen most clearly in the various attempts at educating English readers in the proper interpretation of scripture.

Elizabethan Church and State

If there is a single agent behind these controlling impulses (and the complex and often contradictory structure of the English Church would suggest that there is not necessarily a single agent), it would be Queen Elizabeth, who in the guise of the *supremum caput* of the Church of England was probably instrumental in revising the *Thirty-Nine Articles* in ways which invested her with more ecclesiastical power. At the same time, however, she was probably also responsible for noting in Article XX of the Articles of Religion that "the Church hath power to decree Rites or Ceremonies and authoritie in controversies of fayth."[3] By defining and seemingly limiting the State's power to "decree" and to settle controversies, Elizabeth was allowing for what appears at first to be some level of religious autonomy. But the crown still reserved, by divine right, the power to define what was controversial, and therefore a matter of Church authority, by defining what was catechism. As a result of this seeming autonomy being put into the service of larger forces of homogeneity, the agencies of control were diffused throughout the network of religious, pedagogical and political institutions. As Stephen Greenblatt has noted of Renaissance self-fashioning, "There is always more than one authority and more than one alien [to that authority] in existence at a given time" and "if both the authority and the alien are located outside the self, they are at the same time experienced as inward necessities, so that both submission and destruction are always already internalized."[4] Internalized (and in the case of the subjects under consideration here, textual) submission and the threat of destruction are even more evident when the experiences have redemptive, spiritual connotations.

As Patrick Collinson has noted in *The Religion of Protestants*, the overall debate concerning the separation of Church and State was manifested clearly in matters of episcopal appointments. Even though the Church had the right to "decree Rites or Ceremonies," Elizabeth reserved the right for her government to make episcopal appointments. Most often, questions of episcopacy were fixated on questions of title and pedigree. However, for Anglican apologists the very existence of episcopacy, let alone the uses to which it was put, was questionable.[5] In short, Elizabeth had to find a way of controlling religious entities which many of her subjects felt should not exist in the first place.

Like Luther, Elizabeth came to realize that religious liberalism, however, did not allow for easy control over the masses. In fact, it was Luther who first called for centralized authority over education. Luther's desire to control religious, and by extension secular, education lies in stark contrast to the pronounced Protestant trend toward universal access to the interpretation of the Bible. The Catholic Church's response to Luther's decentralizing of doctrine likewise reflected a deep fear that its effects would be too universal; Petrus Sylvius predicted that the "Lutheran common folk":

> will cultivate division, unrest, war, robbery, [and] murder, not only against true Christendom but also against each other. [They will do this] all on account of the many-sided and self-contradictory, wicked Lutheran teaching and their wicked lives, as Luther teaches ... that one can and may freely practice and commit every vice ... even of the whole world and it would be no sin if one only had mere faith. But one should only protect oneself from good works for although they are done in the best way, they would nevertheless be nothing more than horrible sins.[6]

As Mark Edwards notes, "All the elements of the Catholic view are presented in this one summary statement." Although Sylvius' statement is an example of Catholic propaganda, English reforms were equally concerned with how to control society as a result of breaking with not only the medieval Church but with continental reform movements as well. Specifically, Elizabeth had to concern herself with many of the same tensions and concerns as the Lutheran reformers. The fact that a Catholic apologist would see such a widespread cultural threat in a reformation of exegetical interpretive practices and the decentralization of Church hierarchy represents how closely connected doctrine and social structure were. For Catholics, the Reformation represented a threat not only to ecclesiastical power but to all power; for Elizabeth, the double threat of Catholicism and continental reform movements required careful rhetorical handling. The tension between secular and spiritual realms was both a logical result of the cultural homogeneity desired by Luther and the new found freedoms which the Reformation promised via universal access to God's word.

Many of these controversies manifested themselves in relation to the interpretation of scripture. Despite the monarch's leadership of the official state church, who was ultimately in control of biblical interpretation? The Council of Trent (1545-63) had stressed the centrality of tradition and biblical precedent in matters of belief and had established the canonical books of the Bible, and finally had decreed that the Church alone was authorized to interpret the Bible. Such concentrated control on the part of the Catholic Church was, obviously, regarded by many Protestants as a secretive and "private" type of interpretation. Following the outlawing of Catholicism, "private" readings or ceremonies with scriptural interpretation became a preoccupation for Protestant anti-Catholic propaganda. For example, in 1583, Archbishop Whitgift prohibited "all preaching, reading, catechisms, and other such like exercises in private places and families."[7] These "private" gatherings were seen as sinful and potentially leading to schism. What really went on in these meetings is impossible to know, but the attempt at controlling religious discourse and keeping it in the realm of the public was partially a response to what was seen as Catholic traits: closure and secrecy, as opposed to openness and universal availability.

One of the ways in which these various paradigms were sorted out was by distinguishing between public and private religion. Although undoubtedly a Protestant country, Catholicism still had a place in Elizabethan society.[8] Catholicism became either a household religion or a religion far removed from the centers of power, at least until William Allen founded a college at Douai, in the Netherlands. Here Allen began training a new generation of priests with the sole aim of returning to England and working as clerks.[9] "The priest, once back in England, was left on his own: without priestly dress, without a church, without a hierarchy above or below, with no refuge in the continuity of material institutions and objects."[10] With the rise of the priestly clerk, Elizabethan Catholicism flourished only in individual estates or loosely affiliated homes with access to a priest who performed small, private masses. Often, the priest "arrived in England without either exterior signs of his priesthood or the structure of clerical order behind him; he did not appear as a priest, but as a gentleman, a soldier, or a servant."[11] Towards the end of Elizabeth's reign, more Catholics began to appear at court, most notably Lord Henry Howard.[12] On the one hand, the Elizabethan settlement allowed for some tolerance of Catholics, but at the same time the reign of Elizabeth was marked by a tendency to conceal and overlook Catholicism, except in the most general of denotations.

These tensions are illustrated in the St Albans' inscription reminding us that, "When faith and learning are combined/Then only do we true religion find," which brings to light the enormous importance of state control over education, an education more and more centered on matters of theology and doctrine; as a result, the state was charged with carefully governing biblical and doctrinal interpretation. This combination of faith, learning and statehood represents the English Church's greatest debt to the Lutheran reformation. As a result, the attempt to control or normalize the reading and dissemination of the Bible in Protestant and Catholic churches was reflected in all aspects of education.

The English Reformation, although obviously similar, differed in important ways from its continental precursor. Henry VIII had separated England from papal control but had remained, in his doctrinal views, very Catholic. On the other hand, the development of Protestant doctrines had begun over a decade earlier when Lutheranism first began to be popular at Cambridge, Oxford, and later, London.[13] Lutheranism spread at least partially due to the presence of the Lollardy movement and other localized historical factors; therefore, the English Reformation was centralized more than the continental Reformation. Another reason for this localization was the authority vested in the King. This is seen most clearly in the Act in Restraint of Appeals of 1533, which cut off all jurisdictional appeals to the Roman Church and put them into the hands of the King:

> Where by divers sundry old authentic histories and chronicles it is manifestly declared and expressed in this realm England is an empire, and so hath been accepted into the world, governed by one Supreme Head and King ... unto whom a body politic, compact in all sorts and degrees of people divided in terms and names by Spirituality and Temporalty be bounden and owe to bear next to God a natural and humble obedience.[14]

The role of an Empire is to bound diverse people, with diverse beliefs, into "obedience," and as an empire England was to be ruled by a secular leader, the King, who ruled "next to God." In this formulation the urgency of interpretive, as well as social, control and normalization, is clearly identified. Two years later Stephen Gardiner would note that the secular rule of the King had spread to the Church of England, and one type of rule quite naturally allowed for the other. To make his point he emphasized the homogeneity of English society:

> I see no cause why any man should be offended that the King is called Head of the Church of England rather than Head of the realm of England ... the Church of England consisteth of the *same sorts of people* at this day that are comprised in this word realm, of whom the King is called the Head. Shall he not ... be the Head of the *same men* when they are named the Church of England? (Emphasis mine)[15]

The implied democratic scope of this rationalization, that both England and the Church of England were composites of their members, glosses the true ontological distinction between spiritual matters and historical/secular matters. The implied conceit is that there is no difference between a Church and the nation which serves as the "home" for it. Such a collapse of the secular and spiritual realms served the purposes of Henry, and the later Tudor-Stuart rulers, namely the *via media* of religious compromise.[16]

This union of Church and State membership was the source of much tension since not all members of the English Commonwealth necessarily considered themselves members of the Church of England. Richard Hooker responded to such critics and disagreed with those who felt a tolerance for plurality and he believed that all citizens of the state were, by definition, also members of the dominant church. However, with Elizabeth's compromises of the 1580s, Catholics could, with some restrictions, claim allegiance to the Church and the crown while remaining true to their heart-felt religion. With the compromise we see a certain subordination of religious belief to matters of state. However, this compromise also led to more debate and emphasis on distinctions between Protestants and Catholics. For example, Elizabeth, who favored celibate priests in Eucharistic vestments and giving the sacrament with unleavened wafer bread in front of crosses, was in disagreement with those who wanted a more austere altar, free of vestments, crosses and "Catholic" paraphernalia. As we shall see in the following chapters, as a result of these debates, the arguments surrounding the use of images and *things* were themselves couched in language reminiscent of ontological exegesis.

Throughout her reign, Elizabeth looked for ways to unite education with matters of state and religion. During her reign churches were often used not only for services, but for lectures and education for adults, as well as gathering places for public occasions, such as thanksgivings for victory over the Spanish;[17] likewise her public image was carefully crafted to represent her as both a religious and secular leader. However, the union of Church and State under Elizabeth was still being questioned by many, including Richard Hooker, who problematized the extent to which political power participated in divine matters: as one historian put it, "Hooker virtually never thinks of royal power as participation in the divine but as an authority able to constrain people to perform their duties, something they might otherwise not wish to do."[18] In his own words, Hooker believed that "in matters of God, to set downe a form of public prayer, a solemn confession of the articles of Christian faith, rites, and ceremonies meet for the exercise of religion; it were unnatural not to think the pastors and bishops of our souls a great deal more fit, than men of secular trades and callings."[19] But the wider issue imbedded in the controversy regarding episcopal appointments, for example, challenged the source of divine power: did it reside in divinely appointed secular leaders such as the monarch, in appointed Bishops, or in individual believers? The notion that the monarch could be sole head of the Church reminded some of the abuses of the Catholic Church: Bishop George Carleton, in response to Stephen Gardiner's attempt to make the "will of the king the Church's only law,"[20] wrote that this was to take "the massie crown of Juridiction" from the Pope's head and give it to the King, "gold, silver, copper, drosse and all."[21]

The claim to sacred royal supremacy helped both to define the interdependence of politics and religion, and to obscure some of the real differences, thereby putting strain on traditional language models and rhetorical constructs. But many of these differences and controversies would remain abstract and theoretical, and therefore beyond the reach of any attempt at normalization or control, unless they were made textual debates or until their resolution was a matter of specific interpretive practice, practices which could be controlled via the interdependence of Church and State leaders. As Paul Alpers notes, "print alone could provide ... a heterogeneous group of knowledgeable readers,"[22] and reaching these readers, and influencing how they read, was the most effective method of normalizing spiritual interpretation.

Textual Redemption, Translation, and the Roots of the Henrican Reformation

Since Mary Tudor's reign had virtually wiped out an entire generation of English Protestants,[23] the Elizabethan church's continuity with its Protestant past was primarily textual, depending as it did on such texts as the English Bible, *The Book of Common Prayer*, and the Articles of Religion.[24] While these texts redefined the practice and dissemination of scripture and worship, they simultaneously influenced how reading and interpretation were conceptualized. The truths of the Bible could no longer be seen as either hidden in the catechism of the Catholic Church nor as standing alone and self-evident. A new way of teaching and reading had to be formulated which would allow for normalizing the written word while still allowing for autonomous individual conscience. This need paralleled the apparent threat to social stability and uniformity which could result from the multiplication of conflicting doctrines. King Henry, and those political and religious leaders who followed, responded to this threat by implementing laws and statutes which set out to shape society by controlling how the Word of God was interpreted and disseminated. By defining all citizens as members of a politicized Church, and by dictating how those members understood not only the text of the Bible but many other lessons as well, spiritual/political leaders insured at least partial homogeneity across class lines.

These issues and debates have been well documented in books such as Eamon Duffy's *Stripping of the Altars*, J.J. Scarisbrick's *The Reformation and the English People* and Patrick Collinson's *The Religion of Protestants: The Church in English Society 1559-1625*. However, what has not been attended to as closely is the impact these debates had on reading, interpretation, and the embodiment of meaning in the written word. For example, one of the most contested issues for Anglicans was reflected in the beginning of the Prayer Book's Communion Service, which states:

> Thou shalt not make to thyself any graven image, nor the likeness of anything that is in heaven above, or in the earth beneath, nor in the water under the earth. Thou shalt not bow down to them, nor worship them: For I the Lord thy God am a jealous God, and visit the sin of the fathers upon the children, unto the third and fourth generation of them that hate me, and show mercy unto thousands in them that love me, and keep my commandment.[25]

The prohibition against worshiping icons, repeated in numerous texts, including *The Second Tome of Homilies* (1563), was based upon two criteria: one, that such worship was a reminder of Catholic superstition, and two, that God did not reside *in* images, nor, by extension, in any man-made object. This two-pronged attack exhibits two concerns found in many of the texts which follow: first, that those things which are Catholic are to be treated suspiciously *because* they are Catholic and, second, that the embodiment of spiritual entities in material signs is a topic with the most urgent ramifications for all aspects of Reformation ontology, most importantly the question as to how the literal text of the bible can contain the spiritual meaning of the entirety of God's Truth.

Much of this debate was initiated with the publication of Erasmus' paraphrase of the New Testament, translated by Nicholas Udall in 1551. Although not literally a translation, Udall's introduction suggested that Erasmus' paraphrase was interested in questions of translation and access: he notes that, "What thynge hath the whelpes of the Romishe Antichrist so fiercely always barked against, as at the translating of Scriptures and other bookes concerning matters of religion into the vulgar tongue for the use of the people." Both translation and paraphrase allowed exegetes to remain consistent to the a-priori meaning of text as defined by doctrine while reformulating it for more universal access and specific rhetorical and exegetical purposes. As we shall see, for many later exegetes, versification and summation serve as a form of translation, one which is in opposition to "Catholic" allegory, which was often portrayed as preserving the same words, but finding different meaning.

Unlike many exegetes, however, Erasmus did provide some original interpretation, usually in the form of brief introductions to each book. The following, from his introduction to John's Letter to the Ephesians, is typical:

> And although it might be justly answered unto me, that it is not the onely lacke of the translated paraphrases, wherby the common people commonly continue still in ignorance; but much rather the lack of as well and good will as habilitie in the priests and curates, that reade the good homilies alreadye set forth, and the Scriptures, with cuttyng, hackyng, hummyng, choppyng, and mincyng after such sort, as the people are in most Parishes not only brought unto great tedious wearines because of the unsavery and impersise readyng, pronoucyng, and pointyng of those good thyngs, but also into a certayne contemptuous loathsomness and hatred therof, seeing their curates beare so little good will and so untoward to the futheraunce of gods worde and glory ...

All of this incompetence leads the parish "to popish *private* masses" and "straunge tongue service" (my italics). Like Wastell and Clapham, Erasmus was concerned first and foremost with the quality of literal understanding. The Bible is understood as long as it is read clearly. Precision and pronunciation were the main concerns for Erasmus, and one of the ways these were manifested was in public displays of scripture, which he equated with honesty. Bad public displays could lead the masses to private worship, something usually equated with "straunge tongue service" and secrecy. Throughout his introductions Erasmus was concerned with historical accuracy and proper understanding of the places and *auctores* of the various New Testament books; rarely did he attempt deep scriptural exegesis. Likewise, what we shall see in the treatises looked at in this chapter is an emphasis on access to the written word and the public *utilization* of it for persons of all social and economic ranks.

The real social impact of the Reformation can be found in article six of the *Thirty-Nine Articles*, which reminds us, like Erasmus, that salvation is textual–it is based upon text and is found *in* the literal, unadorned Word of God. By focusing on Article six we can better understand how literacy was central to the aims of the English reformation and some of the social tensions which resulted from these revised notions of literacy. If what John Donne said is true, that "most ministers in England usually shoot over the heads of their hearers,"[26] then how was the Word to be delivered to the mass of Englanders who had little time or understanding of print-based catechisms? How could salvation, defined as textual by the *Thirty-Nine Articles*, be disseminated to those unable, or unwilling, to read? Finally, how could the social equality cited by Simon be based upon a written text?

One of the main complications which faced Reformation exegetes and spiritual leaders alike was that not all facets of society could be reached in the same manner. Joan Simon summarizes the impact this linguistic movement had on social equality: "Protestantism in all its varieties not only satisfied long, latent anti-papal and anti-clerical feelings but gave expression to a social and moral outlook which had hitherto lacked recognition; moreover, proclaiming men's freedom to make their own terms with their God without the intervention of a priesthood, it inferred a new equality on the social plane."[27] For example Frances Inman wrote in his introduction to *A light unto the unlearned* (1622) that:

> There be many poore servants and laborers; many that are of trades and manuall sciences; many aged persons of weak and decaied memories. Of those, some never learned so much as to reade, some very little and the most of them have or will have small leisure to learne long discourses: the world, or other vanities, taking up their thoughts and cares. Yet all those have immortall soules, to remaine after a few daies in eternall ioye or in endless paines.[28]

Treatises such as this one, the full title of which was *A light unto the unlearned: Or, the principles of the doctrine of Christ set downe most briefly for the use of yong and ignorant persons*, suggested both the need and urgency for getting the spiritual lessons to all people. The focus of popular interpretive treatises, as we shall see, was often not on the act of reading, or how to *read*, i.e. make meaning from the sound of letters, but rather on *what* to read and *how* to make in mean what it always already means.

Protestant reformers were themselves often guilty of the same type of propaganda they accused the Catholics of spreading. Given this fact, the important difference was that Protestants had to redefine the act of reading, much as Augustine had, in order to mask their use of exegesis as anti-Catholic. Various methods were utilized in this effort, from outright censorship to subtle didacticism. In order for a given exegesis to be used to control the beliefs of a populace, it had to reach all citizens, including those "poore servants and laborers; [those] that are of trades and manuall sciences [and those many] aged persons of weak and decaied memories," not just those privileged enough to be able to understand John Donne's sermons.

One thing that was universal in texts such as Inman's was the focus on the Bible as the unified and uncontradictory Word of God. For that reason, when reading the Bible, it was of the utmost importance to treat it as a whole and complete text. As Inman's title suggests, it was not always necessary to even read the text, as long as one knew what the text said. Further, all writers agreed that the literal level was the obvious source for the unadulterated text, free of Catholic dogma and interpretation. We see the roots of both of these concepts when Cranmer wrote in the introduction to the "Great Bible" in 1540 that:

> The Holy Ghost hath so *ordered* and *attempered* the scriptures that in them as well publicans, fishers, and shepherds may find their edification as great doctors their erudition; for those books were not made to vain-glory like as were the writing of Gentile philosophers and rhetoricians, to the intent the makers should be had in admiration for their high styles and obscure manner of writing, whereof nothing can be understood without a master or an expositor. But the apostles and prophets wrote their books so that their special intent and purpose might be understood and perceived of *every reader*, which was nothing but the edification or amendment of the life of them that readeth and heareth it. [Emphasis mine]

"Every reader" is able to receive edification from scriptures since it is "ordered" and "tempered"; it is the order of the scriptures which creates the level playing field necessary for universal literacy and salvation. Yet, despite this democratic impulse, Cranmer, like Inman, went on to declare that by reading and memorizing the Bible, "princes learn how to govern their subjects ... husbands, how they should behave them unto their wives; how to educate their children and servants." In short, the Bible will remind everyone of every station what they ought to believe and how to behave toward others, and that order was mirrored in the "grammar" or conformity of the testaments. Cranmer found an example of social conformity in how God "hath so ordered and attempered the scriptures." What is most important to Cranmer is that the Word of God be memorized, and as we will note, memorization and salvation were made easier by emphasis on the "order" and "tempering" of God's Word. From Cranmer's Great Bible of 1540 to Inman's treatise of 1622, we see a steading focus on the normalizing power of scriptural interpretation.

The interdependence of literacy, literal interpretation, and social conformity is clearly seen in the attempts and ensuing controversies which surrounded the issue of scriptural translation. The proposed aim of translation was to provide access to the Word of God to all, not just those trained in Latin. However, it had long been assumed that Hebrew, Greek, and, to a lesser extent Latin, through the "divine" work of Jerome, were the "languages of God." This raised the issue as to how vernaculars could reflect that spiritual word. Henry's own call for a new translation was both an attempt at censoring earlier ones while providing a more universal access to the Word of God. However, the particular circumstances of the English Reformation complicated the goal of universal access to the word of God. Whereas writers like Inman desired to make the literal text of the Bible available to all readers, this effort was possible only after exegetes had made sense of the literal word of the Vulgate. Focusing on the literal word of God also allowed reforms to wrestle it away from Catholic propaganda. This essential aspect of the English Reformation was also exhibited when in September, 1538, a royal injunction was issued that required every parish church to purchase an English Bible and lay it in the choir. That same year Cranmer issued an injunction calling for all clergy to own both an English *and* a Latin Bible within a year and to study a chapter daily working through from beginning to end. This suggests, on the one hand, a desire to disseminate the English Bible, while also reaffirming the importance of the Vulgate.

It is the issue of translation which most closely identifies the English Reformation with the Lutheran. Vernacular translations were central to the Reformation's move away from the medieval Catholic Church. In "To The German Nobility" Luther called for a turn away from "doctor decretorum" and instead prays for a "Doctor of Holy Scripture," which can only be given by God, for the Bible says "They shall all be taught by God" (John vi. 45).[29] Luther writes: "[W]e should verily be forced to act according to our title, and to teach the Holy Scriptures and nothing else." By emphasizing "nothing else," Luther was objecting to and scorning Peter Lombard's *Sentences*, which Luther equated with Popish control of doctrine and which he saw as a diversion from the true Word of God.

On the other hand, Luther was greatly affected by the lack of good education in his native Germany, and undoubtedly came to feel that relying entirely on the laity to correctly understand a text such as the Bible was dangerous to the religious homogeneity he sought.[30] Because of this fear, and despite his reliance upon the Word for all knowledge, Luther later recanted and called for a reliance upon his Catechism as the best method for teaching the masses. Luther wrote that "The Catechism is the right Bible of the Laitie; wherein is conteined the whole Summ of Christian Doctrine, necessarie to bee known of every Christian to Salvation."[31] Luther's transformation from strict literalist to writer of catechism mirrors a central dilemma found in Protestant models of literary understanding, one found clearly in Inman's text: how do you educate *all* citizens to become free and independent readers and create homogenous beliefs?

Luther's democratic views were seen as direct threat to the power and control of Henry VIII. In response to the spreading of heresy, Henry called a conference in May 1530 which resulted in the censoring of all printed "heresy," which included all translations of the Scriptures, including Tyndale's. In June of the same year, Henry called for a new translation to be done, and added that he would cause the New Testament "to be by learned men faithfully and purely translated into the English tongue to the intent that he might have it in his hands ready to be given to his people as he might see their manners and behaviors meet, apt and convenient to receive the same."[32] Henry was attempting, first, to cleanse the country of falsehood, and second, to redeem them with the Truth, while at the same time loosening the hold and dominance of Papal authority. However, we should not forget that in that same year and month Henry was also assembling those friendly to his cause in order to write a letter to the Pope demanding a quick solution to his marriage "problem." With this letter and proclamation the Protestant Reformation in England produced a new focus on the role of state controlled education in the life of all citizens, and it was inevitable that education would become the mechanism by which doctrine and learning would be regulated.

The Catechisms: "The Reduction of the Law"

For the remainder of this chapter I will examine some exegetical treatises and how they were products of this new interdependence between religion and politics as well as a response to Calvinist, Lutheran, and of course Catholic beliefs. When examining these texts, it is important to remember that at the confluence of faith, education, and politics, several controversies arose as a result of the new learning, controversies which needed resolution, or at least control, in order for the "true religion" to dominate all facets of society. However, not all facets of society could be reached in the same manner. John Donne's desire, as stated in sermon 8:331, to "deliver people out of that ignorance" serves to remind us that the central motivation of this debate was educational reform.

The attempt to "deliver people out of that ignorance" was approached in two ways. Many Elizabethan writers of catechisms believed that a "trickle down" theory seemed to work best: use the catechisms to teach learned adults (usually males or heads of households), and they will take on the responsibility of teaching wives, children and servants. In so doing the treatises simultaneously reinforced the social order, a fact which has important implications for the discussion which follows. On the other hand, some catechisms were so simple that practically any semi-literate person, including "poore servants and laborers; many that are of trades and manuall sciences; many aged persons of weak and decaied memories," to use Inman's distinctions, could use and learn from them. Many of these simplified catechisms relied upon charts and other graphic methods to teach the consistent and interrelated lessons of the Bible and survived not only into Elizabeth's reign, but for long after. However simplistic these treatises might seem, they remained steadfastly committed to the notion that salvation and redemption were textual, and that "reading" the Bible was often a matter of understanding relationships between various lessons found in it more than the actual free and active interpretation of it. Furthermore, these graphic elements served to highlight the literal level of exegesis by emphasizing the materiality of words as units in a higher system of organization—first words as units in sentences, then sentences as units of meaning in a unified system of scriptural doctrine, and finally the testaments as the unified Word of God. The fact that almost all the treatises discussed here did both—highlighted societal order and emphasized the material/literary nature of scripture—serves to illustrate the importance which writers during the English Reformation put on the Word *as* written language governed by the rules of grammar.

I chose as the focus of this discussion various exegetical texts so that I can investigate the nature of Renaissance exegetical theory. Following Patrick Collinson I will look at both catechisms meant for those less educated as well as those who were capable of handling complex and subtle arguments. Unofficial catechisms of the time were plentiful, and seemingly very popular to all classes, but as the scarcity of surviving texts suggest, the books were often cheaply made and therefore "ephemeral."[33] These texts tell us a great deal about the manner in which spiritual discourses could be used to normalize and control the social order. For instance, John Donne's sermons, looked at more closely later, represent what could be considered "high" literacy, with their reliance upon sophisticated biblical allusions and dense metaphoric treatments of complex and subtle religious controversies. On the other hand, many of the texts I will be looking at are similar to *A light unto the unlearned* in that the audience represents what could be considered "low" literacy, those who do not have such sophisticated access to either church doctrine, the Bible, or poetic sensibilities. The distinction between "high" and "low" literacy is not meant in a patronizing way, rather, it reflects the actual educational and class differences which the writers addressed.[34] In fact, the similarities between texts and audiences reveal that the various texts under consideration here have much in common rhetorically and linguistically.

Allegory was the "courtly trope" during the reign of Elizabeth, as Spenser's *Faerie Queene* suggests, and allegory, despite its demonization, did occasionally play a role in biblical exegesis and religious debate. A fine example of overt Protestant allegory is *The Hunting of the Romysh Wolf* (1557), written by William Turner, doctor of Phisik, a thinly disguised allegorical debate between a Hunter (a member of the Protestant Church) and a Dean (a member of the Catholic Church), on matters such as preaching in "strange tongues" (Hunter: "thy [tongues] are not so necessary unto the congregation, as the declaring of Scripture is, and that tongues are not to be allowed in the Church"), the use of tropes in the New Testament (the Hunter is against it, except for the "moral level") and the return of Church property to local municipalities. The allegory *The Hunting* is so thinly disguised it almost ceases to read as an allegory. Note for example the following from the Preface:

> About ten years ago, I hunted a certayne Romyshe Fox, father to all the foxes in England, and with him another fox, as great as hys father, with divers other lesse cubs, which dyd much harme.

The equating of Foxes with bishops, and the continual reference to foxes as in disguise or undercover, does not leave much room or need for interpretation. This text seems to define allegory as a *literary* mode invoked at particular times for special reasons, much like typology.[35] In fact, one could read *The Hunting* as a warning *against* allegory; readers of the text are warned to be very careful of not accidentally being convinced by devious Catholic rhetoric. The warning to heed words carefully and to avoid hasty interpretations is essential to Protestant exegetical theory.

What is at the root of this suspicion of allegory at a time when, as Barbara Lewalski points out, the understanding of God and the Bible was becoming more "literary"? It is important to emphasize that this was not simply a manifestation of anti-Catholic feelings, rather, there are many similarities between Protestant and Catholic paradigms of signs and manifestation of the Word which suggest that much of the suspicion is fallacious. For example, whether Protestant or Catholic, to interpret means to control. The nature of scripture renders this necessary. The composition of the Bible, two testaments of differing cultures and histories, several "auctore" and one "Truth", made prevalent questions of consistency and accuracy. Pascal noted that "If one takes the law, the sacrifices, and the kingdom as realities, it will be impossible to coordinate all passages (of the Bible); it is therefore necessary that they be mere figures."[36] The attempt at proving that the two testaments do not contradict each other has been a motivating factor throughout the history of biblical exegesis, and there have been traditionally two ways of proving it: first, through allegorical interpretation, and second, by emphasizing that there is no real contradiction between the two texts, instead, there is a clear order to God's revealed message. In a commentary by John Calvin, entitled *Harmonia ex tribus Evangelistis composita, Matthaeo, Marco et Luca: adiunto seorsum Iohanne, quod pauco cum aliis communia habeat* (1560), Calvin wrote that "it is not possible to comment skillfully and intelligently on one Gospel without comparing the other."[37]

Given the Protestant suspicion of allegory, many exegetes dealt with it up front, problematizing the use of allegory both as a Catholic trope and as a sometimes necessary means of interpretation. The discretionary use of allegory is seen, for example, in *Three Partes of Solomon his Song of Songs, Expounded* (London, 1603), where Henoch Clapham wrote that in explicating the Song of Songs he wanted to avoid "on the left hand, in making Religion an Allegorie: so, to [slight] the error on the right hand, whereby some would have Religion without all Allegorie." If we assume that the theme of the Songs is love, he writes, then "Solomon's daughter must be the Church of Gentiles and Christ is Solomon." An extensive discussion of the allegory of Church and Christ follows, reminding us why the Song of Songs has been treated allegorically since the early Middle Ages, and Clapham's discussion never veers far from traditional medieval interpretation. For example, in interpreting verse 5, "Respect me not because I am blacke, for the Sunne hath looked uppon me," Clapham states that the Church of the Gentiles doth herin offer up first, a Petition to the Synagogue of the Jewes, "Regarde me not because I am blacke." For Clapham, this statement reflects the humility and imperfection of the early Church. Clapham's interpretation is unexceptional and traditional in all but one way: at 299 pages of close allegorical reading of a single text, Clapham is attempting a thorough and authoritative reading of a single book in the hopes of arriving at a doctrinally complete exegesis in alignment with Protestant doctrine. For Clapham, Protestant doctrine can be summarized by his praise for King James: "Henrie the eighth (like a sacramental eighth-day) did cut off the fore-skin of our Corruption. Edward succeeding, reformed much. Then (the firie Paren-thesis of Mary past over) our late Deborah Eli-shebet, added to the Father and Brothers blessing." Although Clapham is somewhat apologetic for his allegorical treatment, the peculiar nature of the Song of Songs requires the use of allegory. It is also worth noting his "figurative" use of grammar (in this case, parenthesis) to emphasize the relationship of syntax and religious homogeneity. He defended the use of allegory because through it God teaches the wise: "And the more wise (Gentle Reader) thou covets to bee, doe the more hunger every forme of divine knowledge, embracing Moses and Christ, Historie and Mysterie, Shadow and Substance, Signe and Thing signified." These dichotomies reflect the traditional distinction between the literal and spiritual sense of scripture, with "Moses," "Historie," "Shadow," and "Signe" all representing the literal level. The last dichotomy, between "signe and thing signified," is the most important for our purposes and reminds us that allegory was fundamentally, like all exegetical methods, philological. The attempt to "embrace" both the sign and the thing signified defines Protestant exegetical theory.

As we can see from Clapham's text, allegory was considered useful in certain situations where the sign could not easily be aligned with the signified, instances which highlight the ambiguous and obscure nature of analogical discourse. Often, however, allegory was understood to involve the invention of fictions, or a system of symbols, to represent spiritual truth. Allegory differed from typology, according to Erich Auerbach, because the latter was a "mode of signification in which both type and anti-type are historical, real entities with independent meaning and validity, forming patterns of prefiguration, recapitulation, and fulfillment by reason of God's preordained control of history." But, as Henri De Lubac notes, "Scriptural allegory gives sanction to typology, it gives it its foundation, it contains it in itself."[38] Like allegory, the correspondence between two different entities is a prior truth in harmony with "God's preordained control" of reality. Although many Reformation exegetes were unwilling to acknowledge the prior nature of allegory to typology, and the resulting ontological dependence of typology on allegory, many of the same exegetes made room at least rhetorically for allegory. For these same exegetes, however, the basis for scriptural understanding is a verifiable and material referent. By briefly considering typology as an acceptable form of allegory, I would again like to assert that allegory had certain unavoidable rhetorical uses which even the most suspicious preachers and interpreters could not avoid. As Auerbach suggests, typology was an acceptable subspecies of allegory because it relied upon specific passages of the Bible in relation to other specific passages; in other words, its meaning was still grounded in the text, i.e. was rendered material and "positivistic," and was confined to historically specific contexts.

Generally, typological interpretation relied upon a highly sophisticated understanding of the literal level of a text. Likewise, such a literal and historical understanding made necessary at least partial understanding of the literal meaning of the Hebrew Testament. Calvin, in his *Institutes of the Christian Religion*, is clear to affirm how typology is aligned with the literal sense and how both can be used to exemplify doctrinally sound interpretation. He writes how Isaiah can and should be read as a precursor to the New Testament Jesus without the use of allegory: "the Prophet speaks in the same manner as Saint Paul spoke from him" and all that needed to be done to understand Isaiah was to "join what is proposed in Saint Matthew with what the Prophet Isaiah wished to affirm."[39] In other words, Isaiah spoke clearly and literally, as did Matthew and Paul, and the centuries which separate them are negligible given the spiritual nature of God's Word.

One of the methods used to reach those who did not possess highly literate skills, or whose tastes did not prompt them to search out complex and subtle theological debate, was a simplification and/or spatialization of God's Word. This spatialization took many forms, but one of the most characteristic was the concordance or catalog of scripture and doctrine. A perfect example of both the spatialization of scripture and the political problems which faced those who wrote such treatises was John Marbeck's 1550 *Concordance,* the full title of which was, *that is to say, a worke wherein by the order of the letters of the A.B.C. ye may redely finde any worde conteigned in the whole Bible so often as it is there expressed or mentioned.* This text clearly illustrates the constraints put upon writers of exegetical texts written for wider, less educated and potentially more easily persuaded audiences. Marbecke's concordance is dedicated to Edward VI, and in the introduction he writes:

> Better, nor a more blessed thyng cannot happen to an Christian realme then a Governoure indued with the knowledge of Goddes most Sacred and holy worde, which seketh to rule all thynges accordingly, and to *order nothing*, which ought to bee ordered by the same wordes ... [and] to pry holiness from hypocrisy, and Papisticall leaven, from sincere and pure doctryne.

Further, Marbeck calls for Edward to follow the lead of King John in "destroying their images and pulling downe their Altars." Finally, Marbeck claims he was not lettered but "altogether brought up in your highnesses College at Wyndlose in the study of Musike and playing on Organs, wherin I consumed vainly the greatest part of my life."

The concordance was based upon a Latin work he had "heard" about, a work in which "any man having but competent learning, might safely turne to the original place thereof, and without study, although he remembered but one worde of the sentence, which he desired to find." Clearly Marbeck is primarily concerned with the original literal Word of God and its proper placement, and this method of interpretation led many of his contemporaries to similar "reductions" of the written

Word to alphabetized words and sentences. Further, Marbeck is very clear that he is not treading on doctrine, nor that he is in any way attempting to be original or to introduce new ideas to the scripture. His is, simply, a study aid, but a study aid defined by the philological paradigms of the English Reformation.

It turns out, however, that Marbeck has a story to tell, a story which reveals much about early-modern exegesis. According to the *Dictionary of National Biography* entry, on March 16 1542-3, commissioners arrived at Windsor to search for heretical books. In Marbeck's possession were found writings against the Act of VI articles and a concordance of the Bible in English. He was examined five times by Gardiner and eventually reprimanded for endeavoring to supersede the Latin language in religious worship by translating a concordance into English. His defense was that he had simply copied a Calvin epistle written before the "promulgation" of the VI Articles. He was found guilty and sentenced to die at the stake the next day, but due to Gardiner's regard for his musical talent, he obtained a royal pardon. Three of Marbeck's friends, however, were executed the next day. (As the *Dictionary of National Biography* notes, Fox mistakenly assumed that Marbeck was also executed and lists him as one of the Protestant martyrs.)

Marbeck waited until July 1550, and the accession of King Edward, to publish his *Concordance*. Although abbreviated, the final document reaches nine hundred folio pages, with each page divided into three columns. In deferment to the Vulgate and the privileged place of Latin, every word is followed by its Latin equivalent. In the Preface Marbeck explains why he has "joined" every English word with the Latin— first, because "either of the tongues addeth to other a certain light, and peradventure also, an occasion of learning the English of some rare and strange Latin wordes," and second, so that no man "might cause of suspect that I had altered or added any worde in the most Holy Bible, which I have not." Marbeck's experience suggests that in 1550, Latin was still very much the privileged language of scripture. Therefore his book "must neded be clere from all erroneus doctrine, yea, or suspicion thereof, which hath caused me the more boldier, to dedicate it to your most excellent Majesty."

He writes in the preface that as he completed his "greate and huge volume," he came in the:

> troublesome net of a lawe called the Statute of vi articles, where by the meanes of good workers for my dispatche, I was quickly condemned and judged the death, for my copying out of a worke, made by the greate Clerke Master John Calvin, written against the same articles, and this my concordance was not one of the least matters, that then they alleged, to aggravate the cause of my trouble: but the same tyme was my greate worke, emong others, taken fromme and bitterly lost, whiche (believe my labor) I had spent no small tyme in.

To make a long story short, he felt God saved him by having King Henry grant him a pardon, and a "friend" was in the process of having the King grant permission for the next draft to be published when "God tooke hime to his mercie" (i.e. his friend died), leaving the book unpublished. Assuming that Edward would want what was

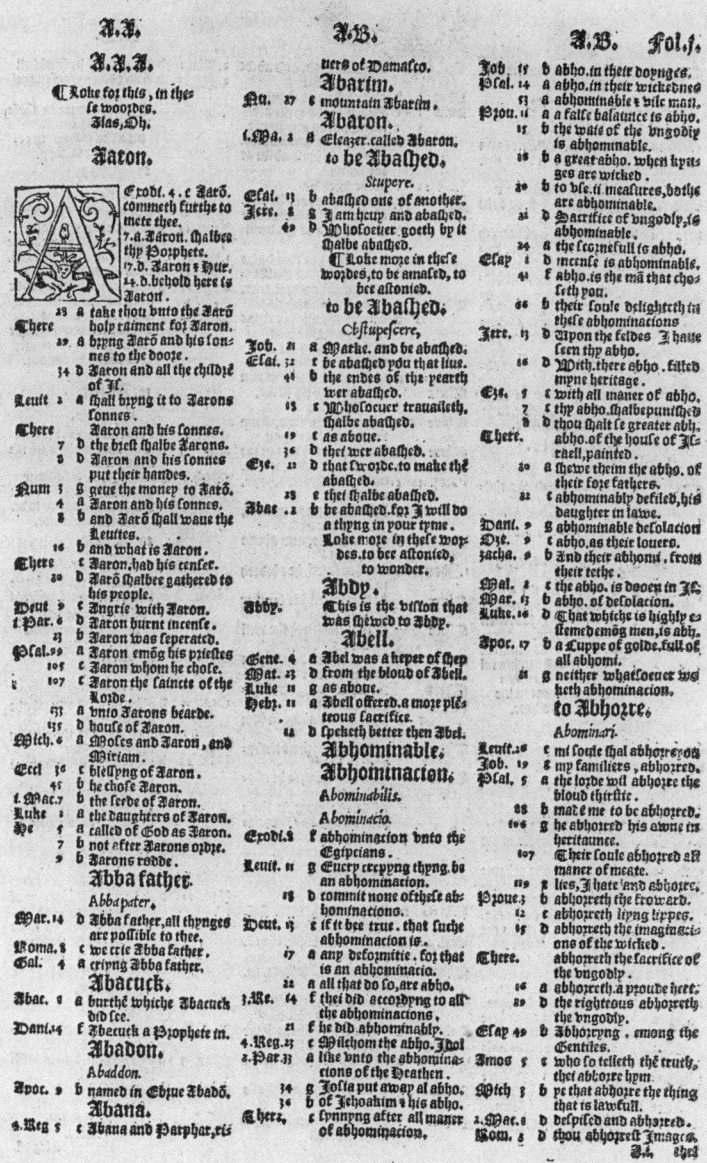

Figure 1 John Marbeck, *Concordance*, 1550. Reproduced by permission of the Folger Shakespeare Library.

best for the country, Marbeck further assumes the King's permission and finds a printer for the book who tells him the "great and huge" book will cost too much for the king's populace to afford, and thus comes the final draft.

At 900 folio pages, what he finally produced was the earliest concordance in English of the whole English Bible (Thomas Gibson had published a concordance to the New Testament in 1536). The struggles and obstacles which he had to endure, as well as his own apologetic tone, remind us of the prohibitions put upon scriptural dissemination during the English Reformation. In the end, Marbeck's *Concordance* is a very practical book which allowed readers to do basic textual comparisons. As promised, Marbeck's book contained little original exegesis, rather it treated the Bible at the most literal level: as a compendium of distinct phrases and useful aphorisms.

By defining the Bible as a catalog of wisdom, and avoiding the often confusing narrative elements which highlighted inconsistency, Marbeck did not need to "interpret" the message of the Bible. By placing all of the Bible in a concordance, Marbeck's alphabetizing suggested its own kind of harmony and consistency. This consistency was arrived at by summation and ordering as opposed to overt interpretation (see Figure 1).

The "reduction" of the Bible to a system of moral and ethical behavior is typical of "lower" literacy. Dogmatic questions were avoided through a form of typology which compared Bible texts to other Bible texts in an attempt to suggest that the whole of the Bible provided a stable and consistent Truth. Concordances, like the other kinds of "reductive" treatises looked at below, suggested that the Bible was harmonious when considered as *a whole* and that its Truth could be found easily and without a lot of prior knowledge. Thus, it was possible to propagate its message to all (or most) semi-literate and literate persons. The pressures and limitations put upon Marbeck remind us that during the reign of Henry the means for producing such potentially widely disseminated treatises was ideally to remain in the King's hands. A similar attempt at directly controlling the production of Latin primers was for the same end–to make certain that all the King's subjects gained access to the written word in a way that was in line with Protestant doctrine and not socially or politically threatening to the Queen or her country. Whereas concordances provided a graphic way of seeing the uniformity of scripture, summaries and paraphrases also allowed for more easily understanding the Word of God. To that end, in 1596 Henoch Clapham wrote a treatise vastly different from his Song of Songs allegorical study looked at earler. In *A Briefe of the Bible, Drawne first into English Poesy, then illustrated with apt annotations*, he writes that he wishes to allow "for giving a taste of that large Truth, in short speach" and for aiding in memory so as to not be persuaded by Catholic arguments. What he provides is a versified summation of the whole of the Bible, in correct chronological order, reduced for easier memorization. Graphic elements also play a role; for example, Clapham utilizes a two column page at the point where Judah and Israel split (in 1 Kings). Here Clapham splits the texts into two columns to better aid the memory and represents the tribes of Judah and Israel in two different columns, and he writes: "Here we must beginne a double account, because of this double Regiment, which after that Schisme or Rent, was never united or made One" (see Figure 2).

76 A BRIEFE OF

ting Tinker-like fellowes (such as we haue a number) for sacrificing Priests. By this meanes, as they had Schized from the true Church, so now likewise from the true worshippe to a false. Neither after this did the kings of *Israell* better, of whom therfore still the holy Ghost saith, *He followed Ieroboam the sonne of* Nebat, *who caused Israel to sinne*. This Supreame head of Idolatry sprung out of *Ephraim*, and begun his Raigne with *Rehoboam* of *Iudah*.

The age of the *Olde* and *New-world* here, was 3030. yeares. Of the New-world, 2344. from the Promise. 1917. From AEgypt, 516. From former Iudgeshippe hitherto, 120. And from the Temples structure, 36. yeares.

Heere we must beginne a double accompt, because of this double Regiment, which after that Schisme or Rent, was neuer vnited or made one. And it may be a figure of Romish Idol-people (moe by a great many then *Iudah* the orderly people) who will neuer returne to the vnitie of true Faith: but rather couet to die in that Papisme-apisme, *Babel*, Confusion.

IVDAH.	*ISRAEL.*
1 *Rehoboam* raigneth ouer *Iudah* and *Beniamin*, 17. yeares.	1 *Ieroboam*, King of *Israel*, (or ten Tribes) stretching out his hand against the Prophet that denounced Iudgement against the Altar in *Bethel*, that hand of his withered. He beseecheth the prayer of the Prophet: who praieth vnto God, wherevpon the hand was healed. At this
2 *Abiam*, called also *Abijah*, *Rehoboam* his son he succeeded & raigned 3. years: wicked he was, as was his Father: but for *Dauids* sake, G O D gaue vnto him a Light, (that is, a Son) to Raigne after him. He begun his	

Figure 2 Henoch Clapham, *A Briefe of the Bible's Historie*, 1596. Reproduced by permission of the Folger Shakespeare Library.

For the second part, the one which predictably deals with the New Testament, Clapham combines the separate Gospels into one narrative, thus emphasizing their commonality and consistency and using reduction to gloss over any doctrinal or scriptural inconsistencies. For example, Christ's last supper is described thusly:

> Great wonders, he
>   did worke in every place:
> But Dragon still
>   pursues him to the end.
>
> He institutes,
> A Supper full of grace;
> Which to his Church,
>   for ay he did commend.
>
> That done, he wends
>   to pray in Olivet
> Iscariott hither his foes did fret.[40]

"A Supper full of grace," i.e. the Eucharist, is a common topic for these exegetes who, despite an announced intention not to deal with complicated doctrine, seldom miss an opportunity to emphasize their anti-Catholic opinions of the last supper. Here Clapham emphasizes that the Eucharist is a ceremony grounded in Christ's wishes, not a carnal sacrifice, thus emphasizing its existence as a metaphor rather than a literal transubstantiation.

Clapham, like many of his contemporaries, treated the Word of God as one continued narrative, albeit one which often had to be read in an extra-literal way. However, the emphasis on the singularity of doctrine and narrative removed any suspicions that they were practicing allegorical exegesis. Clapham takes a slightly different approach to Biblical exegesis, one which foregrounds the philological methods of the Protestant exegetes, with his *A Manual of the Bibles doctrine, for law and gospel, letter and spirit, signe and thing signified: reduced to the first chapter of Leviticus*, Published in London, 1606. By examining the "sign and thing signified", Clapham illustrates how complex "literal" interpretation could be. He states his argument in verse form (note his use of "Types"):

> From Tabernacle
>   doth Jevoha speake
> To Moses, and
>   and he speaks to Israel.
> And for that Moral
> justice was too weak,
>
> He unto them
> doth preache the Evagell,
> Of Christ in Types,

he better things doth tell
In Beasts, birds, bread
& drink-oblations tedred,
Is Jesus Christ
and all His merits rendred.

Clearly Clapham is privileging typology, but a typology which finds all of the scriptures prefigured in Leviticus. In the preface he calls his text a "Reduction of the Law, Gospel, letter and spirit, Shadow and substance, into Leviticus, chapter 1." Clapham notes that in the Hebrew, Leviticus opens with the letter V. Such philological insight suggests that Clapham had at least some knowledge of Hebrew and reminds us that despite the simplicity and practicality of these texts, they often contain real philological insight. According to Clapham, the same letter opens Genesis, Exodus, Numbers and Leviticus. The comparison of "sign" with "thing signified" is for Clapham an emphasis on how one testament fulfills another—the sign is Leviticus, while the "thing signified" is Christ and the New Testament. By making Christian, i.e. New Testament, referents the stable signified, which brings meaning to the Hebrew sign, Clapham essentially normalized the Hebrew scriptures by foregrounding their place relative to the New Testament. Although what Clapham is doing here is cloaked as standard Christian exegesis, his emphasis on a close sign/signified relationship reminds his readers that he is not reading solely according to the literal level. Clapham used the same phrase, "sign and thing signified," in his treatise on the allegory of the Song of Songs. Clapham strongly suggests that this treatise is not allegorical. However, Clapham's text is a clear example of the debt typology owes to allegory: by placing the two "texts", in this case Leviticus and the New Testament, side by side, an interpretation can be made which simultaneously normalizes the Hebrew Testament and reaffirms the order and unity of both testaments.

Throughout the book Hebrew sacrifices are seen as types of Christian ones. Other examples of note: Exodus opens with generations of Israel, while Matthew opens with generations preceding Jesus; Leviticus opens with sacrifice imposed upon Levi, and Luke begins with Zacharie, a Levite, sacrificing; Numbers opens with the counting of the Heads of Israel, while Mark opens with the heads of the Church.[41] The text primarily focuses on the types of sacrifices outlined in the text of Leviticus and how those sacrifices are represented throughout the Bible, and how they present a continual and historical narrative. Sacrifices must be "perfect," but perfection is only possible through Christ. The blood of sacrifices is to be sprinkled on the altar in Leviticus, which "very clearly" means, or signifies, that the nation of Israel and "the whole earth (or nations) around Israel"[42] would receive the blood of the Messiah (Clapham notes a reference here to Revelation 7).

These writers all believe that any part of the Bible could be compared and "normalized" with any other since all parts of the Bible have Moses as a base and in following his words, they build upon them. Thus, one can look for consistency and agreement in the whole Bible. However, with Christ the older methods of sacrifice and cleansing are modified. For example, the Lord's Supper substitutes for the meat offerings of Leviticus.[43] The ancient fathers knew this, says Clapham, and had anyone suggested that upon eating the sacrifices they had actually eaten the "real carnal nature of the Messiah,"[44] they would have been "stoned to death." This reference to the Eucharistic debate again illustrates that theological opinions could be supported by this type of literal exegesis and that literal readings were not value free, however much the writers suggested that they were not interested in scholarly (or scholastic) theological debates which were over the heads of their readers. In fact, Clapham's text is essentially 259 pages of typological theological exegesis which is itself a gloss upon the Geneva Bible's argument for Leviticus, which reads, "without the blood of Christ the innocent Lambe there can be no forgiveness of sinnes." In this sense, each argument in the Geneva Bible is, in essence, a Protestant exegetical *and* theological treatise.

Summarization and careful "ordering" of texts in the aid of memorization of the Bible is again seen in the *Microbiblion, or The Bibles Epitome*, by Simon Wastell, "Designed according to the Alphabet, that the Scriptures may be more happily remembered and things forgotten may be easily recalled," which was printed in 1629. It was printed for Robert Mylbourne, "and [was] to be sold at his shop at the signe of the Greyhound in Paules Churchyard" (see Figure 3). The author writes his *Microbiblion* so that "the simplest Christian may reape the greater benefit, when all things are done to edification." Although some biblical treatises may attempt more in the way of exegesis, Wastell's book is "brief and Alphabeticall, and metricall, for the better and surer memorie. Plaine also it is because the pure and spiritual word needs not the mixture of mans depraved braine." Wastell's text sets out to reduce the Bible to simplified verse summations which aid the memory not only due to their brevity, but through alphabetization, rhyme and meter. The reason for doing so is made clear early in the book: "most men now content themselves to live in this our Church which hates Idolatry and popish superstition, and think this will bee sufficient to [get] them to heaven after death whereas (poor souls) they ought as well to look to the truth of their prosession ..."; it is then necessary, necessary a priori, that they first know what it is which God commands: "now this is revealed unto the world." What is revealed, however, is not literally God's Word, but a versified and condensed version of it. However condensed or modified this literal word might be, it still passes as "literal." Note the first two stanzas of his summation of the opening words of Genesis:

> At first Johovah with his word,
> > did make heaven, earth and light:
> > The firmament, the moone, and starres,
> > the glitterng Sunne so bright.
> By him, the earth was fruitfully made
> > and every creature good:
> > He maketh man like to himself,
> > and doth appoint his food.

Not only is this a radical reduction of the original scripture, but by alphabetizing it Wastell makes it even easier to memorize. In essence, Wastell has versified scripture, and thus made it easier to remember, but he has also ordered it through alphabetization. By doing so Wastell doubly emphasizes that scripture is "materially" manifested in the English alphabet and as such is clear to the senses. This method

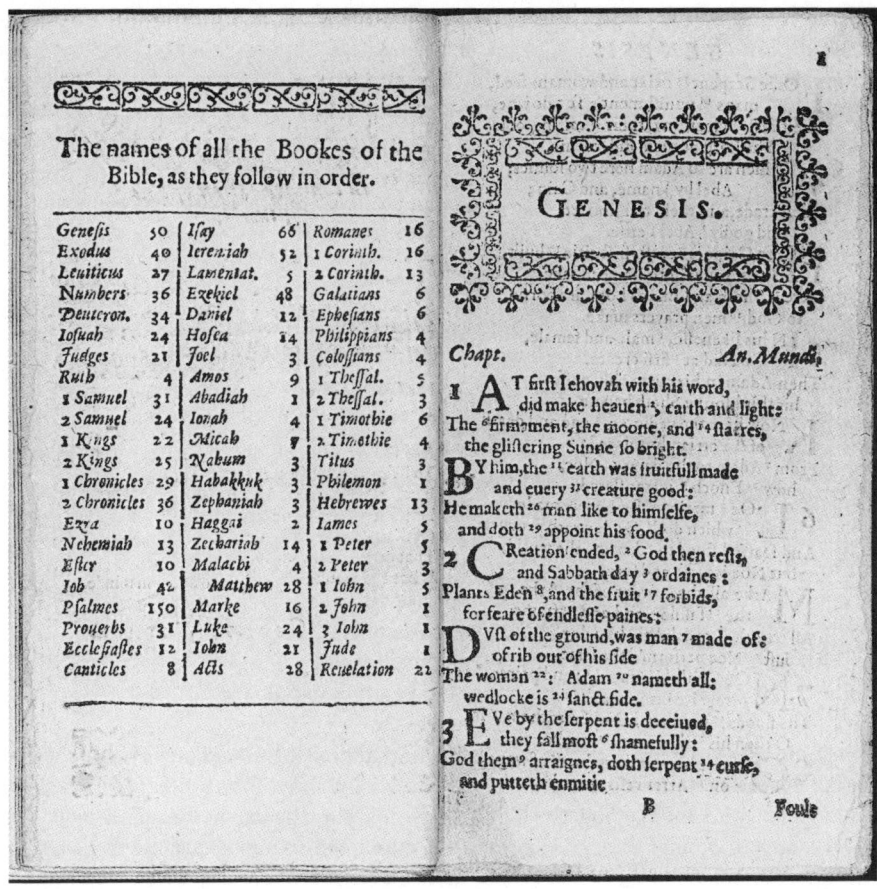

Figure 3 Simon Wastell, *Microbiblion*, 1629. Reproduced by permission of the Folger Shakespeare Library.

allows for order, historical continuity, and, by extension, legitimacy, while shading more difficult questions of allegorical embodiement.

Wastell's position is a common one: arguments about minute points of doctrine are a product of man's imagination and reason, and serve no real purpose in terms of spiritual edification. There is no attempt at considering any possible contradictions or problems as a result of careful reading. In fact, Wastell's text is not even a compendium, it is, rather, in his own words, an Epitome, or summary. He writes in his introduction:

> And are not now compelled to goe seeke
> The hard phrased Hebrew, nor the copious Greeke,
> For, God speaks English to us, and assayes
> To worke true knowledge in us divers way.
>
> Some men interpret, some again expound:
> And this our Author here, a meanes hath found
> To helpe the Memorie: And not in vaine
> If others adde endeavor to his paine.
>
> Peruse it Reader. And so mindful be
> Of that, whereof this Booke remembers thee;
> That others in thy life, may copyed finde,
> What thou art hereby taught to beare in minde.

Some authors faced contradictions and textual problems head on, and in so doing wrote revealing treatises which make even clearer how the desire for exegetical homogeneity dictated exegetical philology. Arthur Broke, in his discourse *The Agreement of Sundry Places of Scripture*, attempted to show that "such places of Scripture as seeme to disagree" do not in fact disagree when they are read in light of doctrine. However, elaborate allegorical readings are not necessary; simple, literal readings will suffice. For example, Exodus' "An eye for an eye, tooth for tooth" could be seen to contradict Matthew 5, "If any man strike thee of the right cheak, give him the other." The explanation, according to Broke: the book of Exodus is meant for magistrates, while the message of Matthew is to suffer your condition, for we are "not to overthrow the law appointed" by our Fathers. Again, historical continuity lends credibility to the literal interpretation of scripture at the expense of allegorical exegesis. At the same time, Broke is using the textual contradiction to reaffirm the status quo while simultaneously avoiding any dependence on extra-textual, analogical or allegorical interpretation; Broke turns to the original historical context of each book in order to arrive at his explanation.

The interpretation given by Broke does not rely upon allegory, or even overt typology; there is no attempt to explain away the seeming contradiction by noting that Christ tempers the Old Testament, for example. Rather, it suffices to note that the same law applies to both Testaments, but in differing ways. Broke likens the search for precise meanings in the literal sense to "dead letters." In explaining John 5, "search the scripture," against John 6, "They shall be taught by God," Broke takes the opportunity to slight Catholics, who "said they had the life in them, and yet thy meddle only with the dead letter." Broke condemns anyone who will "go awry from the natural meaning of them and to put the light of life by perverse opinion."[45] "Natural meaning" is that which is clear in light of church doctrine, i.e. the denotative, and not the product of "interpretation," i.e. artificial connotative meaning. Broke's entire reading of the Bible rests upon the doctrinally sound literal level of interpretation.

Conclusion

For English Protestants, following Paul's words in the First Epistle to the Corinthians, obscurity became an end in itself—there are some things in scripture which we will never know while on the earth and to strive to know them is a dangerous undertaking. This leads to a seeming contradiction: inner knowing (faith) and guidance from the Word leads to faith, and faith in turn allows for participation with the divine in the form of the Word. By placing the understanding and dissemination of God's Word in the literal text, the Word of God came to meaning as part of a larger whole. This coming-to-meaning is not metaphoric for these exegetes but real and material—it can be sensed, and therefore represented to the senses: it is metonymic as opposed to metaphoric. Of course, remembering what we have learned from post-structuralist theory, we need both the metaphoric and the metonymic for meaning to be manifested in language, and therefore the two are not exclusive. Rather, as these exegetical treatises remind us, interpretation can be "controlled" as long as they are conceived of separately, yet when utilized, the metonymic and literal must be kept prior to the metaphoric and allegorical.

Richard Hooker wrote that those who followed the Church Fathers were merely led astray, but "the heresies of the Church of Rome ... what one man among ten thousand did ever understand?"[46] Hooker's desire to separate Catholics who might have participated in Catholic rituals without understanding them from those Church Fathers who were intellectually responsible for the doctrines illustrates the tendency to separate intellectual positivism from matters of faith. To this end perhaps the most representative and interesting text from this time period is James Warres' *Touchstone of Truth*, "wherein Veritie, by Scripture is plainely confined, and Errour confused. That one of meane capacity, by helpe of this Booke, may be able to argue with any Papist, and confuse him by Scripture." Printed in London by Augustine Mathews in 1634, the text is a remarkable example of both literal exegesis of the scriptures through comparison (the book is simply a listing of various topics and passages in the Old and New Testament, with no comment on them), and a compendium of the most urgent issues defining English Protestantism and Catholicism. Dedicated to King Charles, the text promises to tend to the "maintenance of true Religion and the most ancient Faith." Also dedicated to the "Christian Reader," Warre promises that the text will correct the errors "our Fore-Fathers were subjected unto by Raging Rome." In the pages which follow, Warre lists judgments, such as "Adoring of Images unlawful," "Against Prayer and Service in an unknowne Tongue," "Against Popish

Transubstantiation," and "The Pope is not above the Scriptures." He then lists Bible passages which seemingly favor his opinions. He does not, however, explicate or explain the passages. The assumption is that the passages are clear enough once doctrine is established, clarified, and duly noted.

An example of Warre's explication aims is seen in the entry, "Popish Transubstantiation." Warre cites John 6, 26 as an example: "Jesus answered them, and sayd, Verely, verely I say unto you, ye seeke me not because ye sawe the miracles, but because yee ate of the loaves, and were filled." Warre also cites verse 63: "It is the spirit that quickeneth: the flesh profiteth nothing: the words that I speak unto you, are spirit and life."[47] Clearly, these two passages are not directly about transubstantiation, and would require some knowledge on the part of the reader of very specific facets of the Eucharist debate. These passages from John suggest that the Eucharist functions as a sacrament not because of a miracle inherent in the bread, but because of a miracle which occurs in the eating of the bread which becomes a symbol of Christ at the behest of Christ.

Another example Warre cites is Matthew 26.27: "Also he tooke the cup, and when he had given thankes, he gave it them, saying, Drinke ye all of it." Warre is following the lead of the gloss in the Geneva Bible, which states that "they which took away the cup from the people, did against Christ his institution." In other words, the cup does not belong to the Pope, rather, the cup belongs to those who receive it in faith.

Throughout this text Warre's intent was not the development of Protestant doctrine by close analysis of the two scriptures of the Bible, nor was it to develop an interpretive method which bridged the contradictions between the two testaments (Warre simply juxtaposed the two books spatially, suggesting they were equal representatives of God's true Word). Rather, Warre's foundation was the incorrect dogma of the Catholic church. For Warre, and the Protestant exegetes studied inn this chapter, literal meant "not Catholic."

Warre represents a tendency found in many Protestant exegetical treatises to replace Augustine's a-priori reading of the Bible with its inverse; interpretation needs no further explanation to uphold it other than its opposition to Catholic doctrine. Obviously, behind these interpretations are very profound and consequential theories of embodiment and spirituality, but in keeping with Luther's (and Calvin's) insistence that doctrine be made available to all people, those theories are not brought forth into the debate. What this suggests is that while there are very important ontological changes occurring, the general public was not necessarily privy to them.

Sometimes literal scriptural interpretation and simplification were utilized in doctrinal and theological debates. Pierre Du Moulin, whose tract on the Eucharist will be examined later, wrote, "But our adversaries, which in other controversies relie upon tradition, hiding themselves in the obscurity of the unwritten word, here do change their manner of fight ... they would seeme desirous to stick to the words of the Gospel."[48] Du Moulin was writing about Catholic doctrine of the Eucharist, which turned to scripture to defend its position. Clearly, the issue was a textual one, with close readings of the Bible needed to support both sides. It is a literal reading of these various texts which comes under fire in this debate, and in the course of it the very nature of what it means to do a literal reading becomes questioned.

Notes

1. Article 6, *Articles of Faith* (London: Richard Jugge and John Cawood, 1571).

2. Joan Simon, *Education and Society in Tudor England* (Cambridge: Cambridge University Press, 1967), 299.

3. Stephen Buick, "'A leaden mediocrity': Competing Views of the Elizabethan Settlement of Religion in *The Stripping of the Altars* and *The Seconde Tome of Homilies*." In *Renaissance Papers, 1996* (Columbia, SC: Camden House).

4. Stephen Greenblatt, *Renaissance Self-Fashioning From More to Shakespeare* (Chicago: University of Chicago Press, 1980), 9.

5. Patrick Collinson, *The Religion of Protestants: The Church in English Society 1559-1625* (Oxford: Clarendon Press, 1982).

6. Quoted in *Printing, Propaganda, and Martin Luther*, by Mark U. Edwards, Jr. (Berkeley: University of California Press, 1994), 157.

7. E. Cardwell, editor, *Documentary Annals of the Reformed Church on England* (Oxford, 1844), i. 468.

8. John Bossy, "The Character of Elizabethan Catholicism," *Past and Present*, no. 21, April 1962.

9. Bossy, 130.

10. *Ibid.*, 46.

11. *Ibid.*, 51.

12. *Ibid.*, 53.

13. A.G. Dickens and John Tonkin, *The Reformation in Historical Thought* (Oxford: Basil Blackwell, 1985), 59.

14. Quoted in Dickens and Tonkin, 59.

15. *Ibid.*

16. *Ibid.*, 63.

17. *Ibid.*, 325.

18. Deborah Kuller Shuger, *The Renaissance Bible: Scholarship, Sacrifice, and Subjectivity* (Berkeley: University of California Press, 1994), 136.

19. *The Works of Hooker*, iii, 410. Quoted in Collinson, 4.

20. *Ibid.*, 13.

21. Carleton, *Jurisdiction: regall, episcopal, papall* (1610), pp. 6, 13. Quoted in Collinson, 13.

22. Paul Alpers, "Pastoral and the Domain of Lyric in Spenser's *Shepheardes Calendar*," in *Representing the English Renaissance*, ed. by Stephen Greenblatt (Berkeley: University of California Press, 1988), 174.

23. Buick, 23.

24. *Ibid.*, 23.

25. *The Book of Common Prayer 1559: The Elizabethan Prayer Book*, ed. John Booty (Charlottesville: The University Press of Virginia, 1976), 248. Quoted in Buick, 27.

26. Quoted in Collinson, 233.

27. *Ibid.*, 130.

28. Quoted in Collinson, 233.

29. Frederick Eby, *Early Protestant Educators: The Educational Writings of Martin Luther, John Calvin, and Other Leaders of Protestant Thought* (New York: McGraw-Hill Company, 1931), 40.

30. John Calvin (1509-64), meanwhile, had a more systematic approach. His *Institutes of the Christian Religion* were extremely hostile to allegorical approach, except when demanded by the text. This response to the allegorical method was at least a partial response to Catholic medievalism and the use of allegory. Allegory was demonized as a tool of the Popes to render the message of scripture dependent on the Pope's will. It was seen, by both Calvin and Luther, as needlessly obscure and ambiguous.

31. Eby, 97.

32. J.J. Scarisbrick, *Henry VIII* (Berkeley: University of California Press, 1969), 253.

33. Collinson, 232. Collinson notes that the earliest version of Stephen Egerton's *A brief method of catechizing* had reached its forty-fourth edition by 1644, yet only a single copy of its sixteenth edition (1610) survives. We can assume, therefore, that we have access to only a fraction of the texts actually produced during the period.

34. For a discussion of "high/low" cultural distinctions in relation to the "sacralization" of culture, see Lawrence W. Levine's *Highbrow/Lowbrow: The Emergence of Cultural Hierarchy in America* (Cambridge: Harvard UP, 1988). Although Levine's focus is on nineteenth and twentieth century American culture, his analysis of the process of sacralization and the resulting distinction between "high" class and "low" is relevant to the present discussion.

35. Barbara Lewalski, *Protestant Poetics and the Seventeenth-Century Religious Lyric* (Princeton, NJ: Princeton University Press, 1976), 122.

36. Quoted in Stephen Greenblatt, ed. *Allegory and Representation* (Baltimore: Johns Hopkins University Press, 1981), 13.

37. Quoted in Jaroslav Pelikan, *The Reformation of the Bible, The Bible of the Reformation* (New Haven: Yale University Press, 1996), 127.

38. Henri De Lubac, *Medieval Exegesis*, Vol. 1. Trans. By Mark Sebanc (Grand Rapids, Michigan: Williams B. Eerdmans Publishing Co.), 259.

39. Quoted in Pelikan, 31.

40. Henoch Clapham, *A Briefe of the Bible, drawne first into English Poesy, then illustrated with apt annotations* (1596), 15-18.

41. *Ibid.*, 146.

42. *Ibid.*, 234.

43. *Ibid.*, 232.

44. Folger manuscript, STC 3811, *The Agreement of sundry places of Scripture*, Arthur Broke, 1563.

45. Broke, 87.

46. Hooker, "A Learned Discourse of Justification," in *Of the Laws of Ecclesiastical Polity*, intro. Christopher Morris, 2 vols (New York: Everyman Library, 1969). XI.

47. All citations from *The Geneva Bible*, a facsimile of the 1560 edition. With an intro. by Lloyd E. Berry (Madison: University of Wisconsin Press, 1969).

48. Pierre Du Moulin, translated by Edward Skipwith, *An Apology of the Holy Supper of the Lord Against the Corporeal Presence, Transubstantiation, Masses Without Communicants, The Communion Under One Kind, Together with Certayn Analytical and Orthodox Propositions upon the Lord's Supper*, London, 1612. 62.

Chapter 4

The "Real" Word of God

> For I affirm that with slight qualification the whole attainable knowledge lies enclosed within the literary monuments of ancient Greece.
>
> (Erasmus, *De Ratione Studii*)

On April 8, 1546, the Council of Trent provided the Catholic Church the opportunity to evaluate, correct, and otherwise render doctrinally sound, the Vulgate. The Council decreed that "from all Latin editions of the sacred books which are in circulation" the Vulgate was the "authentic" scripture. However, the council also decreed that "hereafter the holy scripture, particularly this ancient Vulgate edition, shall be printed after a thorough revision." Forty years later, Pope Sixtus V would appoint a commission for the production of a final and authentic edition of the Vulgate.[1] The product of this first commission was published in 1590, and was quickly found defective and was withdrawn. The Jesuit Cardinal Robert Bellarmine helped create the *Biblia Sacra Vulgate Editionis Sixti Quinti Pont. Max. jussu recognita atque edita*, published 1592-3. This edition remained the officially sanctioned edition until 1943, when Pius XII issued his *Divino afflante Spiritu* encyclical, encouraging new translations from original languages.[2] The search for doctrinally "accurate" versions of the Vulgate, itself a translation of the original language of scripture, ironically resulted from the various theological debates and religious factions of medieval Europe and reminds us that understanding the "literal" Word of God is a very complex and intellectually challenging proposition. Likewise, what can be defined as the definitive and final Word of God is the product not of direct apprehension but of interpretation and approximation.

Both Protestants and Catholics directed their attention to controlling and disseminating philologically and doctrinally accurate Latin translations. Protestants began their search for sound translations with Robert Stephnus Estienne's two-volume edition of the Vulgate, which appeared in Paris between 1527 and 1528. This volume was considered to be the first attempt at a philological critical edition of the Vulgate.[3] However, as with most attempts at doctrinally sound translations, the volume met with criticism. The Theological Faculty of the University of Paris tried to control publication in Paris and condemned the volume because it was "scattered with things that are erroneous, conductive to scandals, favoring Lutherans, and breathing heresies long ago condemned."[4] At this time, "Lutheran" was a convenient label for all seeming "heretics", and one of the most heretical acts of Luther's was the translation of the Bible into the vernacular. However, even Luther, who in general despised Jerome, relied heavily on the Vulgate in his own translation.[5]

Because of the canonical status of the Vulgate, Latin was elevated almost to the level of an original Biblical language. As we saw in chapter three, the status of the Vulgate and its centrality to the Catholic mass led Protestants to attempt to render it obsolete, and the dissemination of the Word in vernaculars was one way of doing so. However, many exegetes turned their attention to learning the truly original languages of the Bible in order to bypass the Vulgate altogether. This emphasis on "original" languages led to a renewed focus on Greek and Hebrew as well as Latin and on the interrelation between those original languages and vernaculars.

The rationale for learning both Hebrew and Latin, for example, was often framed by questions of authority and accusations of opportunistic and propagandistic translations, most often aimed at the Catholic Church. A closely aligned question, and a question with some basis in real scholarly interest, asked, what if Jerome's translation was faulty? What if Jerome duped all of us reliant upon his translation? Worse, what if *Jerome* was duped? For example, Sebastian Munster (1489-1552) explained to Henry VIII that patristic scholarship was inadequate:

> In our era we are assisted by the multitude of books, which we know were unavailable in earlier ages. For St. Jerome himself had no help in interpreting the Old Testament except a naked Bible and an uneducated (and untrustworthy) teacher: no Aramaic translation or Targum, no commentaries, not even a Hebrew grammar—without which many places of Scripture cannot possibly be accurately explained, no matter what some people say. (6:ii)[6]

Munster's reference to "a naked Bible and an uneducated teacher" suggests the extent to which biblical exegesis had come to rely upon scholarship focused on the straight literal level of interpretation. Munster is reaffirming the importance of humanistic education for the full understanding of religious doctrine, and his suggestion that education equals trustworthiness should serve to remind us of the importance of extra-literal knowledge in spiritual matters. "[N]o matter what some people say" is an elliptical statement pointing to the debate not only between Catholics and Protestants (Jerome's appropriation as a "Doctor of the Church" by Roman Catholics was fodder for the suspicion against him), but between various Protestant sects as well.

The need for greater access to Greek, Latin and Hebrew was a direct result of both the Protestant suspicion of allegorical interpretations and a suspicion of Catholic interpretations of the Bible. Those who followed Luther, most notably Calvin, would also make the learning of classical languages essential to understanding fully the redemptive truth of scripture. Calvin, like Beza, was trilingual, utilizing Latin, Greek, and Hebrew in his biblical commentaries. More so than Greek and Latin, the Hebrew language became essential to understanding the historical sense of scripture which was the basis for literal interpretation.

Vernacular translations of the Bible reflect the fact that simultaneous to the development of a sense of origination came a search for definitiveness. As we shall see in the following pages, originality and definitiveness were often conflicting goals which existed alongside rich cultural and religious movements. One of the basic tenets of Reformation humanism was that residing in the perfect past were truths with urgent applicability to modern readers and that the modern (Christian) world was a better place for retrieving those truths. However, the Reformation had also called into question many of those classical sources and truths, suggesting that the medieval church had based its lies on Latin and Greek culture. Humanistic philology was partly based on a return to less barbarous times and more stable language use in order to fully understand the literal meaning of texts.

The "Left Hand" Tongue

What was at stake in the search for linguistic stability was the existence of an original, and therefore totally incorruptible, language of God. Due to its historical existence as both a classical/pagan language and the favored language of medieval Catholic exegetes, Latin was, unfortunately, corruptible. It is not surprising that Hebrew began to grow in importance as more readers and exegetes saw in it a purity not available in Latin and Greek. Predictably, of the few Hebrew pedagogical texts in existence in the sixteenth and seventeenth centuries, most required a knowledge of Latin, which remained the linguistic pre-requisite for deep philological understanding.

Hebrew teachers and primers were nowhere near as prevalent as Latin (and to a lesser extent Greek) teachers. Hebrew was the "lefthand tongue," as it was called by Edward Hopkinson, the London gentleman to whom Lancelot Andrewes turned to learn Hebrew. Andrewes had to travel to London to learn Hebrew since it was unavailable to him even at Cambridge.[7] John Udall's *The Key of the Holy Tongue* (1593) was one noteworthy exception.[8] This text was subtitled "A short Dictionary containing the Hebrew words that are found in the Bible with their proper signification. All Englished for the benefit of those that (being ignorant in the Latine) are desirous to learn the Holy Tongue." This textbook opened with Proverbs 1.7, a citation which could serve as the manifesto for Christian humanists: "The feare of the Lord is the beginning of knowledge, but fooles despise wisdom and instruction." A glance at the "Table containing the principal heads of the Hebrew Grammar" reveals that Udall did not treat Hebrew any differently than the typical breakdown of Latin treatises: words and syntax were the first parts, with nouns and verbs further categorized by types and genders. There was little information on the particulars of Hebrew syntax. Clearly the purpose of this layout was to make those already familiar with Latin pedagogy comfortable in this more exotic (and difficult to learn) language.

For many reasons, philologists made sound arguments for Hebrew as *the* original language. Luther wrote of Hebrew that it "above other languages is very plain, but therewith it is majestical and glorius, it conteineth much in simple and few words, and therein surpasseth all other languages."[9] In *The Bible in the Sixteenth Century*[10] David Steinmetz mentions Johannes Reuchlin's *De rudimentis Hebraicis*, published in 1506, as one of the first Hebrew grammars available to English readers. In this text Reuchlin asked, "what if one discovers that Jerome and Lyra, on occasion misunderstood the Scripture?" For example, Jerome made numerous errors:

In these matters relating to the method of interpretation and the art of grammar as well as the truth of the idiom, why may I not set forth what I have gleamed from the most learned Hebrews—those very people to whom Jerome himself testifies that he had recourse whenever he was troubled by a question in the Old Testament. For though I venerate Saint Jerome as an angel and reverence Lyra as my teacher, I worship the truth as God.[11]

Two details are important in this statement. First, the writer equates the art of grammar with the "method of interpretation," suggesting just how closely related the two disciplines were to the founders of Renaissance philology. Second, "truth" is the object of all studies, and "truth" is clearly not a mortal construct; it is the guiding principle behind, yet separate from, all humanistic studies. Both of these notions equate grammar with interpretation, while simultaneously "disembodying" understanding from strictly material language.

When scholars write of Renaissance Latin education, they often think exclusively of William Lily and the many texts influenced by him. Although Lily is undoubtedly a major influence on Latin studies in the late sixteenth and early seventeenth centuries, he is by no means the only influence. The various texts which precede and influence Lily are themselves important objects of study if only because they reveal a great deal about how the study of Latin changed and the various debates surrounding its role in society. Although Lily's grammar was clearly the most influential text, it is too easy to see it as the only text through which Latin was taught. On the contrary, there were numerous texts, both obscure and popular, which suggest the religious and social context of Reformation pedagogy. By briefly examining both the texts themselves as well as the audiences for them, we are better able to understand the tension between vernacular language use and classical. Furthermore, there is an important development in the history of the texts to be studied. As the vernacular grew in influence, so too did the audience for Latin primers and dictionaries. Part of this growth was undoubtedly due to the refinement of the printing press as well as the expansion of mercantile classes and the spread of wealth. However, a close analysis of these texts suggests that the spreading interest in Latin learning was the result of a change in how classical languages were seen in relation to the most important type of knowledge, knowledge which led to salvation.

With the renewal of the use vernaculars for spiritual issues, and the renewal of classical languages, new models for understanding how language functioned were necessary. Richard Waswo notes that vernaculars point to the contradiction between treating words as semantically constitutive and conceptualizing them as merely cosmetic.[12] For language to be "semantically constitutive" would imply that language functions fully and completely without any argumentation. If vernaculars are capable of conveying spiritual meaning as well as classical languages, and if both languages can be equally "right" and "accurate," how (and where) does "right" meaning embody itself? Following the Reformation, the English educational system focused a great deal on litteratus, the learning of Latin grammar, which created a new way of speaking and understanding shared experience, one which Marc Bloch notes "forced [those who used it] to resort to perpetual approximations in the expression of their thoughts."[13] As a perpetual second language, the usual rule-oriented study of grammar resulted in an approximation and "improvisation" of otherwise pre-existing and a-priori thoughts. While Latin (primarily as a *grammatical* language) served the purpose of stabilizing legal and religious communication among the well-educated and professional classes, it also decentralized the importance of the newly energized vernaculars for all students of Latin.

Despite the rise of vernaculars, Latin remained the stable textual referent for most academic and legal resources, with vernaculars marginalized to the spoken and everyday. At least one-tenth of all published works in England before 1640 were in Latin; in addition, almost half of all books published in England before 1640 were works of philosophy and religion.[14]

The Early Latin Primers

According to Eric Auerbach, after the eleventh century Latin began to again rise in importance, but it never again became a "non-literary" language; it was always a second language, one read but not often spoken, and marginalized for very specific interpretive and rhetorical roles. This is an important point: as a purely literary and "second" language, Latin's worth became a matter of how the language could be utilized as opposed to how it *functioned* in relation to the world. With the loss of this sense of function came the problem of how to view language in relation to verity and ontological truth. Meanwhile, vernaculars took up the function once occupied by Latin, namely as a culturally defined *written* language.

The fact remains that Latin was *the* literary language for the Renaissance. Although it was not literally seen as an original Biblical language, like Hebrew and Greek, its position as the original Romance language and primary conduit of scripture gave it the stability necessary to serve as a basis of linguistic development. Richard Waswo quotes Castiglione's Cardinal Bembo on the "natural" superiority of Latin and Greek, a superiority disputed by Lazaro who compares Latin to a decayed and rotten relic "made into an idol for the superstitions."[15] Bembo asserted that neither language was truly dead for both could produce effects in living persons. These effects, however, could be literary, i.e. secondary to the everyday use of the vernacular. Protestantism, by emphasizing textual revelation, treated the Bible as a text with "literary language," i.e. language which was in need of interpretation. This emphasis is important to Protestant exegesis since no matter how artistic or learned the translation, the text of the Bible was still a translation and therefore at least once removed from the original. In this way Latin can be seen as the ultimate vernacular: for Protestants, the Vulgate *qua* translation was not a perfect representation of the Word of God, why, therefore, could not German or English just as accurately reflect the Word of God? Historically Latin held a special place, and even Luther had relied a great deal on it for his own vernacular translation, especially of the Hebrew scriptures. As we shall see, this dichotomy was influential on how Latin education was reformed in the early modern period.

The dual nature of Latin pedagogy is evident in the various Latin treatises published between the second half of the sixteenth century and first half of the seventeenth century, which typically reflect a variety of audiences and approaches to the teaching of Latin. Likewise, the purposes for teaching Latin vary greatly, with some revealing historical parallels. For example, one of the earliest types of Latin primer in England was the vulgaria, so called because of the everyday subject matter of the examples used for translation.[16] These primers were firmly rooted in social situations and were very practical, reminding us that the subject matter was not necessarily literary or historical. The vulgarias focused on phrases such as "Sit away or I shall give thee a blow" and "Would God we might go play,"[17] suggesting that the students spoke Latin on the school premises and used it for "real life" situations. These everyday situations were supposedly situations familiar to a young schoolboy of any class, as the primer *A Fifteenth Century School Book* from a manuscript in the British Museum (MS. Arundel 249)[18] demonstrates:

> "What say you, ploughboy, how do you do your work?"
> "Oh, dear sir, I must work very hard. I go out at dawn, drive the oxen ..."
> "Oh, your tasks are very hard."
> "Yes, sir, they are heavy, for I am not a free man."[19]

The implied lesson here is that learning Latin will protect you from the drudgeries of hard labor. Although written for a general audience, at least anyone able to afford a printed book in the first quarter of the sixteenth century, these treatises suggested to the reader that the effort necessary for mastering Latin was nowhere near the effort inherent in *not* learning it.

Often, the vulgaria centered on Latin phrases to illustrate grammar rules, and this led to a fierce objection from John Colet, who felt that the first step in Latin training was composition, not simply translation. Colet's opinions would greatly influence Lily and led to a fundamental debate: should students learn to compose Latin or merely read it? As these examples illustrate, the earliest Latin treatises were grounded both in practical exercises and in grammar, and in both cases it would be hard to argue for a strong humanist focus. However, by utilizing harsh, daily situations to remind students of their subordinate roles as students, such primers strongly emphasized the urgency of learning Latin and to see it as central to their daily lives.

It is interesting to note that there were no new vulgaria written after 1520, and the last two published reveal a great deal about changing tastes in Latin studies. One of these was William Horman's, published in 1519, which followed Erasmusian subject headings, thereby giving at least a partial introduction to classical writers.[20] The last new vulgaria was published by Robert Whittinton in 1520. This book was much more colloquial than Horman's and again relied upon "everyday" situations, much like the earlier vulgaria. However, it was still focused on repetition and reading, as opposed to composition, and for these reasons Whittinton meant for his text to be a direct challenge to the Horman edition, which was supported by William Lily, the writer of the most influential post-medieval Latin grammar.[21]

The Horman–Whittinton competition led to one of the most unusual literary debates of the time and reminds us of what was at stake in publishing Latin primers. Whittinton, after Luther, reportedly nailed verse invectives against Lily on the door of

St Paul's, presumably so that all who passed by would see them. In response, Lily wrote the *Epigrammata*, which was appended to Horman's *Antibossicum*. For some reason Whittinton had taken the pseudonym "Bossus" ("Bos" and "Sus"); Lily, however, accuses Whittinton of taking the pseudonym because he had fallen in love with the "Bosse" (or water-tap) in Billingsgate; the bosse/water-tap was built by Richard Whittington (no relation), the Lord Mayor of London, and its sign was in the form of a bear. Because of these details, the *Antibossicum* was decorated with woodcuts representing a bear baited by six dogs. In essence, in a series of overtly ad-hominen attacks, Lily was calling for the metaphoric baiting of Whittinton.

The text of the *Antibossicum* consists of the preface by Lily, a rejoinder by Whittinton, and a pointed criticism, in prose, of Whittinton's grammar. Beatrice White, in her edition of *The Vulgaris*, claims that there is reference to Whittinton's *Opusculum*, a "collection of laudatory verses" addressed to Henry VIII, Wolsey, Brandon, Duke of Suffolk, Thomas More, and John Skelton, published in 1519. This list suggests the broad nature of the pedagogical debate; in fact, Skelton sided with Whittinton in the *Antibossicum* controversy, presumably, according to John Bale, writing a *Carmen inuectiuum in Guilhelmum, Lilium poetam lauretum, lib. I, A Urgeor impulsus tibi, retundere dentes*,"[22] ("John Skelton ... wrote an invective poem against the laureate poet William Lily, a single book beginning 'One struck, Lily, I am bound to knock your teeth in.'"[23]) Whittinton praised Skelton, Skelton supported Whittinton, and Lily, not to be putdown, writes of Skelton:

> Quid me, Scheltone, fronte sic aperta
> Carpis, vipereo potens venemo?
> Quid versus trutina meos iniqua
> Libras? dicere vera num licebit?
> Doctrinae tibi dum parare famam
> Et doctus fieri studes poeta,
> Doctrinam nec habes, nec es poeta.[24]

> [With face so bold, and teeth so sharp,
> Of viper's venome, why dost carp?
> Why are my verses by thee weigh'd
> In a false scale? May truth be said?
> Whilst thou to get the more esteem
> A learned Poet fain wouldst seem,
> Skelton, thou art, let men know it,
> Neither learned, nor a Poet.][25]

By suggesting that Skelton was neither poet nor learned, Lily was illustrating the tone of the entire debate. What this controversy epitomizes is the importance and centrality of Latin pedagogy and the central role its pedagogues potentially had in society; it also points to a seeming need on the part of the authors to limit the number of texts available to students. Although the tone of the argument is personal and vindictive, and the impetus probably was personal, it is quite probable that Lily's and Horman's disagreement with Whittinton was over sincere differences in pedagogy, differences which they felt could not be ignored or compromised. The tone of the argument suggests that there was no room for compromise or heterogeneity; ultimately, all students were to learn Latin in the same, state-sanctioned way.

Whittinton's version began to lose its hold over Latin studies by the late 1520s, when Cardinal Wolsey, at Cardinal College, prescribed that one grammar be used in all schools, so that boys would not have to learn a new method when they changed schools.[26] Wolsey's proclamation was the first example of the movement toward more overt control over humanistic education. The first official grammar was Leonard Cox's revision of Lily's grammar. Cox was a follower of Cromwell, and it was Cromwell who helped see to the publishing of it in 1540.[27] This textbook became the standard for many years. King Henry's royal proclamation, prefacing the English introduction to Cox's text, proclaimed that all:

> schoolmasters and teachers of grammar within this our realm and other our dominions, as ye intend to avoid our displeasure, and have our favour, to teach and learn your scholars this English introduction here ensuing, and the Latin grammar annexed to the same, and none other, which we have caused for your ease and your scholars' speedy preferement briefly and plainly to be compiled and set forth.[28]

The true impact of this proclamation will be examined in chapter eight, but it is important to note here that for the first time we see an overt attempt at centralized control of Latin pedagogy. Since the "our" in "as ye intend to avoid our displeasure, and have our favour" is the Court of Henry, this proclamation is particularly heavy-handed and severe. There is very little within the actual text which would suggest why this text, "and none other," would be chosen for official recognition, except for its unique approach to Latin as simultaneously a classical and "modern" language, continuing the legacy of the earlier vulgarias in presenting Latin as both a living and historical language.

Lily's grammar was revolutionary for its focus on translating from English to Latin, in other words, composing in Latin as opposed to merely reading it. Although the earlier vulgarias focused (at least partially) on imitation, Lily's *Rudimenta* was concerned with rules and advice on the *composition* of correct and stylistic Latin. This rather simple syntax existed in many editions and predated the final version of the grammar, with the earliest probably printed c. 1509.[29] The syntax begins with the statement, "Whan I have an englysshe to be tourned into Latin I shal reherse it twyes or thries and loke out the verbe." By turning from English to Latin, Lily suggests that English can be prior to Latin in terms of stable ideas. It is not just that Lily focuses on the translation from English to Latin that makes this textbook revealing or interesting, but rather that he does so within the context of a general humanist education. Colet in the introduction states:

> When these Concords be well knowen unto them, an easy and pleasant payne, if the foregrounds be well and throughlye beaten in, let them not contynue in learnyng of their rules orderly all as they lie in their Syntax, but rather learne some preaty book, wherin is contayned not onely the eloquence

of the tongue, but also a good playne lesson of honesty and godlyness, and
thereof take some little sentence as it lyeth, and learne to make the same Arte
Out of English into Latine.

As Lily makes clear, eloquence is based on the ability to turn from one language to another, to find a verbal equivalent of an idea in two languages. Clearly the main purpose of learning Latin was not virtue, for virtue may lie in English texts: a "pretty book" in English was just as likely to express virtue as a Latin book. Languages are not themselves conduits of virtue, rather, they reflect virtuous meaning which exists outside of language, and any language can, therefore, reflect this meaning. As the introduction states: "A great helpe to further this readiness of makyng and speakinge shal be, if the master give him an englishe booke, and cause him ordinaryly to turne every daye some part into Latine. This exercise can not be done withoute his rules, and therefore doth establysh them and grounde them surely in hys mynd for readinesse, and maketh hym more able to speake sodaynelye whensoever any present occassion is offered for the same." Colet is emphasizing the practical and immediate needs of conversation as opposed to the more literary classical and written Latin; furthermore, true understanding of Latin comes not from knowledge and use of rules, but when the student is "withoute his rules."

The King's Grammar

Unlike the older vulgarias, Lily's grammar taught Latin not by emphasizing its priorness, but by suggesting that it could only be completely learned as a companion to English, and that it could only be truly learned if it was made useful. As Vincent Joseph Flynn pointed out in 1939, we need to be careful of what we call "Lily's Grammar." Flynn notes the revisions and appropriations of Lily's various works on Latin by writers such as Colet, Erasmus and Cardinal Wolsey. "First of all, people sometimes speak of Lily's Grammar when they mean an accidence by John Colet and a syntax by Lily, both in English, published together in one small volume, the text later taken up by Cardinal Wolsey."[30] More often they mean a syntax in Latin written by Lily and later revised by Erasmus. These two treatises, plus a set of Latin verses by Lily, were put together after his death and became what was commonly known as "Lily's Grammar." (Since I am interested in the influence of this text on questions of literacy and literature, and not in questions of authorship, I will refer to the document as a whole, including the various introductions and prefaces to the various editions, as the work of Colet–Lily, and the English syntax as the work of Lily, but I do not wish to perpetuate any errors by doing so. Following Vincent Joseph Flynn, I am aware of the complex authorship of the text, and the probable presence of not only Colet and Lily, but of Erasmus, etc.)

There is no doubt as to the popularity of this text. From the first edition in 1527 the grammar continued to appear well into Elizabeth's reign in a variety of formats. King Edward VI gave official recognition to it on December 2, 1547, and Elizabeth continued it in 1559. Watson notes that 10,000 copies were allowed to be printed annually (when 1,250 copies of a book was considered an ordinary edition).[31] Many other Latin texts were in circulation by the second half of the sixteenth century, but Lily's grammar remained one of the most popular. It was so popular, in fact, that as late as 1675 a bill introduced into the House of Lords to remove Lily's official status was dropped after one reading.[32] As early as Edward's reign Lily's grammar came to be called "The King's grammar."[33]

According to T.W. Baldwin in *William Shakespeare's Small Latine and Lesse Greeke*, it was Erasmus' idea to write a text book which would have the "minimum essentials to memorize." Students using Lily first memorized the Accidence (declensions and conjugations) in English for about a quarter of a year. Then the students memorized the "concords," again in English. At this point in the student's education memorization by rote ceased. Now the students "learne some pretty book wherin is conteyned not onely the eloquence of the tungue, [but] also a good playne lesson of honestee and godlynesse." This is where Lily's grammar is unique: students learned to translate *from* English into Latin, using any of the previously memorized rules which might apply. Once the student completed his or her translation, they were to "take the booke and construe it, and so shall he [be] least troubled with the parsyng of it, and easilyest carry his lesson in mynde." All of this was to prepare the student for the "redynesse of makyng and speakyng." With Lily, students spend considerably less time memorizing and more time using Latin.[34]

Colet, specifically, was concerned that many students could translate Latin into English, i.e. understand Latin, but "they cannot speake" it, and when they are away from their books, "they can not contrarywise tell you for the English the Latine agayn, whensoever ye will aske them." The inability to speak Latin, as opposed to simply reading it, is a shortcoming for many Latin students, students who were supposedly taught with a different text. Colet made an argument for making this text a prominent one because it would allow students to truly *utilize* Latin rather than simply learn it. Furthermore, English could represent ideas prior to their figuration in Latin. Such a step was important for it suggested that Latin was not necessarily an a-priori language, rather, it was a mutable language capable of "carrying" vernacular thought. This in no way de-emphasizes the position of Latin as a classical language, rather, it reflects the English Reformation's position as a combination of older Catholic values and newer Protestant ontological paradigms.

Flynn notes that the earliest surviving printing of the Lily–Colet grammar, dated 1527, is appended to Colet's catechism, articles of faith, short explanation of the seven sacraments, and a reference to the importance of the Eucharist: "If I fall to synne I shal anone ryse agayne by penaunce and pure confessyon. As often as I shal receyue my lord in sacrament, I shall with al study dispose me to pure clennes and deuocyon."[35] Also included: resolutions concerning sickness and death, 49 precepts of living, the Apostles Creed, the Lord's prayer and the Hail Mary. Cardinal Wolsey's famous edition of 1529 was intended for use in all schools in England, "institutae, quam omnibus aliis totius Anglie shcolis prescripta." Whether this particular prescription came from Henry can only be conjectured; however, one year after Wolsey's grammar was published, Henry refers to a regulation in the Convocation of Canterbury on March 8, 1530:

> Octavo die Martii (sess. LIII) de reformatione scholarum grammaticalium actum fuit: quia multiplex et varius in scholis grammaticalibus modus est docendi grammaticam, visum fuit necessarium, quod una et eadem edatur formula auctoritate hujus sacrae synodi, in qualibet et singula schola grammaticali per Cant. proviniciam usitanda et edocenda.

As Vincent Flynn notes, "When we consider the date of what is probably the first edition—June 4, 1529 (that of the preface is August 1, 1528)—we can sense the connection: obviously there was a movement afoot to regularize instruction, and 'Wolsey's grammar' was chosen as a text. But we are ignorant of further details."[36] Joan Simon suggests that Wolsey's grammar may not have circulated widely due to his disgrace in 1529, the year it appeared.[37] Whatever the reason for the lack of success, clearly Lily's grammar, without Wolsey's stamp, went on to be the official grammar, and the use of the resolutions, 49 precepts of living, the Apostles Creed, the Lord's prayer and the Hail Mary, suggests that there was a strong connection between religion and Latin studies. It is revealing that a Latin grammar could be a suitable place for inclusion of this information.

In July of 1546 Henry handed down a proclamation calling for the burning of all heretical books. Richard Cox, writing to his friend Paget, complained that in many places people burned testaments and Bibles as well as primers "which now be utterly despised and not used nor taught to youth ... They teach the old Latins with the old ignorance and would that printers should print them again."[38] The various injunctions led to a new attempt at controlling all facets of education. This control had particular effect on the teaching of Latin, for after the mid 1540s there would be many attempts at prescribing official texts.

The move toward a regularized grammar culminated about 1540 when a new text, based on the *Aedito-Rudimenta*, the *Liberllus*, and *De Generibus Nominum* (a short Latin poem by Lily), was put forth with the following preface:

> Henry the VIII ... to all schoolemaisters and teachers of grammar within this his realm greetynge ... to the intent that herafter they [English children] may the more readily and easily attein the rudymentes of the latyne toung, without the greate hynderaunce, which heretofore hath been, *through the diuersitie of grammers and teachynges*: we will and commounde, and streightly charge al you schoolmaisters and teachers of grammar within this our realm, and other our dominions, as ye intend to auoyde our displeasure, and haue our favour, to teache and learne your scholars this englysshe introduction here ensuing, and the latyne grammar annexed to the same, and none other, which we have caused for your ease, and your scholars spedy preferment bryefely and playnely to be compyled and set forth. Fayle not to apply your scholars in lernynge and godly education.[39] [Emphasis mine]

The two references to "this our realm" suggests the extent to which the study of Latin had become a matter of national interest and defined by political boundaries. The stated purpose of an official grammar was to avoid confusion as students moved from one school to the next, or as one schoolmaster took over from another. However, another purpose seems to be suggested in the following from the printer's preface: "And as his maiesty purposeth to establyshe his people in one consent and harmony of pure and tru relygion: so his tender goodnes toward the youth and chyldhode of his realm, entendeth to haue it brought vp vnder one absolute and vniform sorte of lernynge." The equation of uniform learning and "harmony of pure and tru relygion" suggests the mutual normalizing of both reading skills and religious belief. Although there is nothing in the actual text of the Colet–Lily grammar which would suggest specific Protestant doctrine, the approach taken to teaching Latin does reflect Protestant paradigms of textual manifestation of meaning, and reflects the complex relationship of vernaculars and classical languages in the context of a post-Catholic Reformation. More specifically, this approach suggests an attempt to control the teaching of Latin, with the stated goal of homogeneity in pedagogical matters.

Colet's edition ends with a reproduction of the royal coat of arms.[40] The preface to a 1557 printing makes clear the text's position in Post-Reformation society: "Like as there is nothing more necessarie for the prosprous estate and preservation of a good commune wealth, than the godlie bringing up & training of youth in good letters, the which, not having some taste of vertue and godliness, grassed as it were, within them by diligent teaching in their tender age, but left unto their own . . . in that rudeness and natural corruption, wherin all flesh is borne, runne for the most part headlong into unhapppiness." This inevitably leads to "utter ruine of the commun wealth." For these reasons, the preface states, the author has written the present guide to the Latin tongue. By combining religious practice, ease of learning and nationalistic pride, Colet had accounted for most of the needs of his society and for these reasons his text was given official sanction by religious and political leaders.

The Latin Grammar School

Nothing exemplifies the centrality of Latin to early modern culture more than the fact that England had an official Latin grammar, Lily's grammar, ten years before an official English Bible. This fact alone does not suggest that Latin supplanted scriptural studies, rather, it reminds us that Latin was, if not a prerequisite for a vernacular scripture, at least a necessary component in the development of one.

In the aftermath of the Reformation, Erasmus and Vives both championed the establishment of publicly supported schools in every township, and they both agreed that Latin would be the best medium for teaching. Greek should also be taught, but only after Latin was begun. Ideally, the two tongues could be taught concurrently through most of the student's education.[41] The teaching of foreign tongues also focused attention on grammar and vernacular rhetorics. For Richard Sherry and Thomas Wilson, it was the outward facets of the language, i.e. tropes and schemes which could be utilized in English, which gave it its stabilizing power. These tropes and schemes were rooted in Latin and Greek, and, as we saw in the previous chapter, the study of them often entailed reading classical writers. However, among many humanists Latin and Greek were seen as the depository of all wisdom, as Erasmus wrote in *De Ratione Studii*:

> It is true, of course, that in reading an author for purposes of vocabulary and style the student cannot fail to gather something besides. But I have in mind much more than this when I speak of studying 'contents.' For I affirm that with slight qualification the whole attainable knowledge lies enclosed within the literary monuments of ancient Greece.[42]

Erasmus is privileging the "attainable knowledge" available from the study of languages over the sheer act of learning to read *that author*. Although Erasmus is a "pure" humanist who sees knowledge as "literary monuments," as opposed to those Christian humanists who saw Greek and other languages as pragmatic tools to scriptural understanding, he shares with those Christian humanists a sense of spiritual urgency in the learning of languages.

Vives, in *Introductio ad Sapientam*, emphasized the more utilitarian, and for Renaissance pedagogues, the more influential, nature of language study: "Retell in Latin whatever you have read or heard to your fellow-students. Speak in the vernacular to others unskilled in languages, endeavoring to repeat the matter with no less grace than when you first heard or read it. In doing this, you will have to exercise both your wit and your tonque." It is important to note that since "grace" is manifested in both the vernacular and Latin versions of the matter, neither language has final priority over the other. Because of this, students move beyond simply acquiring a second language; rather, they explore the nature of language and linguistic embodiment, and participate in the simultaneous dissemination and normalization of classical culture.

Like Sherry and Wilson, Vives and Erasmus were concerned with how one *understands* the structure and ontological aspects of language in addition to how one *writes* and *reads* it. Such concerns were a logical product of Reformation theology. Whether it is a concern with tropes or classical language, language is best understood when its power to embody meaning is exercised to its fullest. For Vives this meant repetition of read or heard phrases in both vernacular and Latin, and for Erasmus it meant searching the classics for "attainable" and pertinent knowledge. From a practical standpoint both writers viewed the classics as contemporary sources of wisdom and education.

Since Latin (as opposed to Greek and Hebrew) was both secular and religious, and since it provided access to Hebrew, and finally since the purpose of reading texts was both literary and practical, the question of how Latin was taught and how it was conceived of in the Renaissance is pertinent to both literary history and to understanding Reformation exegetical theory.

John Bird in *Grounds of Grammar Penned and Published* (1639), noted that if anyone "were to learn the Greek and Hebrew Grammar, we should not have the Rules set downe in Greek of Hebrew, but in Latine." Bird set out to "correct and amend some errors in our old [Lily's] Grammar." Bird acknowledged that many had set out to accomplish the same thing, but he took exception with them for four reasons: first, they did not include the Rudiments of Grammar, which Bird thought were essential so that teachers did not "have boyes runne, before they can creep or goe." Second, Lily did not include adequate discussion of "Derivation and Composition, two speciall Acciendts of every part of speech, and season all the rest with delight and profit."

Third, they did not include enough examples, and fourth, they too often turned English into Latin, when they should "not be mixed together, nor one comprehended under an other." In a reversal from earlier, pre-Lily grammars, Bird emphasized that English was the "foundation of the Latin tongue." Bird's criticism of Lily's grammar was a common one, and his insistence upon Latin's preeminent place was likewise a familiar argument for revising it.

As we have already noted, the literal understanding of scripture was most often approached via grammar, the study of "the Art of writing and speaking rightly."[43] This definition was utilized in the vast majority of texts looked at in this chapter, and it raises important questions. For example, the way grammar was often taught in Latin treatises was as a *prescriptive*, as opposed to *descriptive*, art. Students were given the rules and paradigms by which to read and *compose* Latin, as opposed to guidance in the stylistic particulars of ancient writers. The study of Latin was a very practical and utilitarian subject; as a result, Latin writers were often read according to (and as examples of) English grammar rules. Not all writers let this seeming dichotomy go unnoticed. Joseph Webbe, for example, the writer of *An Appeal to Truth* (1622) wrote that "Grammar (an Art whereby Languages are now commonly held to be sufficiently taught in every Nation) was not in use among the ancient Romans."[44] What Webbe means is that classical writers were not *constrained* by grammar rules, and therefore grammar rules taken from the ancient writers are *descriptive* of those writers while being made *prescriptive* for modern students. Webbe was against the emphasis on grammar and instead called for a more "natural" and intuitive method of teaching Latin, one which we will return to later in this chapter.

Webbe's opinions about the place of grammar in a child's education can also be seen in the opinions of John Colet, who became dean of St Paul's in 1505, and who wrote in the preface to the school's Lilian grammar that students should:

> busily learn and read good Latin authors for chosen poets and orators, and note widely how they wrote and spake, and study always to follow them, desiring none other rules but their examples. *For in the beginning men spake not Latin because such rules were made but contrariwise because men spake such Latin, upon that followed the rules and were made. That is to say Latin spech was before the rules, not the rules before the Latin speech.*[45] (Emphasis mine)

Unlike Webbe, Colet sees the study of grammar as the most important aspect of a child's education, namely because Latin represents for him the "perfect language," the language God seemingly spoke "in the beginning" (rather than Hebrew) and handed to mankind. Situating grammar "before the rules" suggests that it functions as the original language and as the language from which grammar rules originate. The purity of classical Latin allowed it, at one time, to serve as the unadulterated medium for God's word. This view of Latin served as an argument for humanistic studies and simultaneously suggests certain limitations to humanism; Latin is the language to study not simply to gain knowledge of the ancients but also to gain access to the source of knowledge, the Christian Word of God.

Webbe, however, is bemoaning the fact that the study of grammar, particularly Lily's grammar, quickly grew to encompass the majority of students' early education. It was through grammar that students came not only to knowledge of how to read and compose Latin, but to gain their first access to classical writers, and eventually morals and ethics. Since these texts were primarily aimed at giving students the freedom to read and interpret classical texts and Christian texts, the study of it was moral and ethical. Again, Joseph Webbe:

> But this little creeping fountain, having in time, through continuall and universall employment, gotten credit, wealth, and patronage, grew ambitious; and under the first title of entire simplicity, hath at length engrossed rivers, streames, and branches, out of *Orators*, *Poets*, and *Historians*, yea and almost all the greatest artes, and sciences; and it become a full-swollen, and over-flowing Sea, which by a strong hand arrogates unto itself (and hath well near gotten) the whole traffick in learning, but especially for languages. (A3)

Specifically, Webbe is criticizing the powerful position Lily's grammar had on Renaissance education, but his point can be made more generally since Lily's grammar was simply the most successful result of a significant cultural need: the need for a universally disseminated Latin treatise which could guarantee every student an education in Latin. Why was this need so prevalent? What was unique about Lily's grammar which gave it such prominence? Finally, what social and/or economic factors were present in Reformation England which influenced the writing and publishing of these textbooks?

"Grammatical Tyranny" and Lily's Grammar

In most of the texts to be studied in the following pages, the study of Latin was appropriated as a skill necessary for the full participation of *all citizens* in matters of the Church and State. Further, as many of these texts attest to, education in Latin was readily available, and attempts were made to simplify its learning, unlike the deserving reputation of Hebrew and Greek as scholastic, difficult to learn languages. For example, the following introduction was attached to a Latin primer written by Christopher Syms, published in Dublin in 1634:

> An Introduction to, or the art of Teaching, the Latin Speech, Which by this method may easily be taught to any boy however dull of capacity within the course of foure years. And the author doubeth not, but an intellegent man having once tasted thereof, may by himself by this method attain the understanding thereof with the help of a dictionary.[46]

The pedagogical method which follows is very standard and straightforward, presenting all the conjunctions and declension forms for memorization first, and then following up with various syntactical rules. This text is unique, however, in that its

82   *Religion, Allegory, and Literacy in Early Modern England, 1560–1640*

stated purpose, as seen above, was to introduce the art of *teaching* Latin. This, as well as the emphasis on "foure years" and dull capacities, reflects the large, multi-faceted audience for these treatises. However, the importance of learning Latin was also noted:

> Neither can the knowledge of divine and human things bee wel attained without a competent science of elegant and famous latine language in which *lyeth hid* the wisdom of the Ancients, and through the help of which, divine scriptures may be better understood. (A2. Emphasis mine)

The emphasis on "divine and human things" suggests that for Syms, Latin was the medium for all worthwhile knowledge. Just as he divided divine from human, he likewise separated the "wisdom of the Ancients" from that of "divine scriptures," yet Latin was the common medium of both kinds of knowledge. At the same time, however, the knowledge "lyeth hid" in the wisdom of the Ancients, i.e. spiritual meaning was sometimes embodied in classical languages. And just as John Donne's exegetical ontology suggests that the body exists for the sake of the spiritual, the ancients existed for the sake of bettering the understanding of divine scriptures.

In addition to this rather standard belief in the hidden secrets of scripture, this particular treatise suggested another reason for learning Latin. It opened with a riddle in Latin:

> Kings armies lead, to battle order men;
> I letters only rank and file with pens;
>   . . .
>   Here generals I hide
> In midst of battle compas'd on each side
>   With col'nels, captains, officers, and flocks
>   Of all the host, supposing now the knocks,
>   And heat of battle past, neer pressing at,
>   At each first can, unto his general.
>   Each shoulder in the impress heaves and raises,
>   As high as it can lift, great Charles, and praises,
>   There's not a letter in front, reare, or flank
>   May justly termed bee supply or blank.
>   Great C begin, change motions round about
>   From rank to file, four quarters throughout,
>   Carolo (cryeth every fourth decuria)
>   Regi magnae britanniae victoria.

Hidden within the anagram/riddle is the letter C and the word "Carolo" (see Figure 4). What is most interesting is the manner in which Syms fills the page with what seems at first glance a repeated, but orderless, series of letters. As his explanation suggests, these letters spell out "Carolo regi magnae britanniae victoria." The first four letters in each direction, emanating from the center C, produce the word "Carolo," thus, "cryeth every fourth decuria." Typically, Syms is using spatial relationships, in this case a visual metaphor for grammar and typology, to emphasize how meaning can be "hidden" within written language, and with effort, and the proper learning, how it can be understood.

Further, as Syms' explanation suggests, this anagram is meant to represent King Charles's primacy in the battlefield, but what it also implies is that classical studies, particularly Latin, were governed or centralized around secular power. At the foot of the anagram Syms wrote, "Excogitatum anno regni regis Caroli primi primo." The reference to Charles' reign and the centering of his name in Latin convey the centrality of Charles' reign to all knowledge. Before writing that "knowledge of divine and human things bee wel attained without a competent science of elegant and famous latine language," Syms praises Charles for being the "venerable patern of ... sacred virtu and religious piety." Syms finally asks Charles to "vouchsafe this little, plain, and easy door and gate to the latine" with his royal protection, and to command "the general practice thereof, and entrance thereby into the latine, may aswel as your inferior subjects, and their posterity to the worlds end reap benefits, ease, and delight thereby."

No longer was the study of Latin merely a means to social status and professional betterment. As Syms' text suggests, Latin is a necessary requirement for "posterity to the worlds end." By dedicating the book to Charles, Syms was affirming the extent to which the learning of Latin was an endeavor at normalizing how scripture was read by the general public, but at the same time proposing that King Charles was the "heart" of interpretation. How can a single, mortal being manifest truth? The answer is clear from the above examples: by controlling the interpretation of spiritual matters, and by being at the center of humanistic scholarship designated to cultivate that interpretation. As Sym's relatively late text illustrates, the teaching of Latin had evolved from an objective, highly pragmatic exercise to an attempt at normalizing and controlling how "hidden" meaning is understood. With Sym's dedication to Charles and his acknowledgment that the state was central to pedagogy, we see a culmination of a movement toward overt secular control of exegetical languages. This movement begins at the very conception of the English Reformation, and from this moment English humanism will be at least partially dedicated to the pursuit of secular utilization of Latin.

Lily's grammar was not alone in its status as an official text. In April, 1582, a textbook in Latin verse by Christopher Ocland was published. This remarkable text, entitled *Anglorum Praelia ab anno Domini 1327 nimirum primo inclytissimi Principis Edvardi eius nominis terti, usque and annu Domini 1558*, was an overt propaganda tool, containing, as the title suggests, a history of England from 1327 through the reign of King Edward. Attached to the text was a letter calling for "publike reading & teaching of this Book in all Grammar and Free Scholes within their Dioceses." Since the book was prescribed for schools, one can assume that it served as a reader, probably in companion to Lily's text. The book was written in Latin hexameters, and summarized by Hallan in *Literature of Europe* as being written in a "tame strain, not exceedingly bad, but still farther from good."[47]

Although this text was primarily meant as a Latin lesson, intended to encourage patriotism while giving somewhat advanced students practice in reading Latin, an English translation was published only three years later, *Valiant Acts and Victorious*

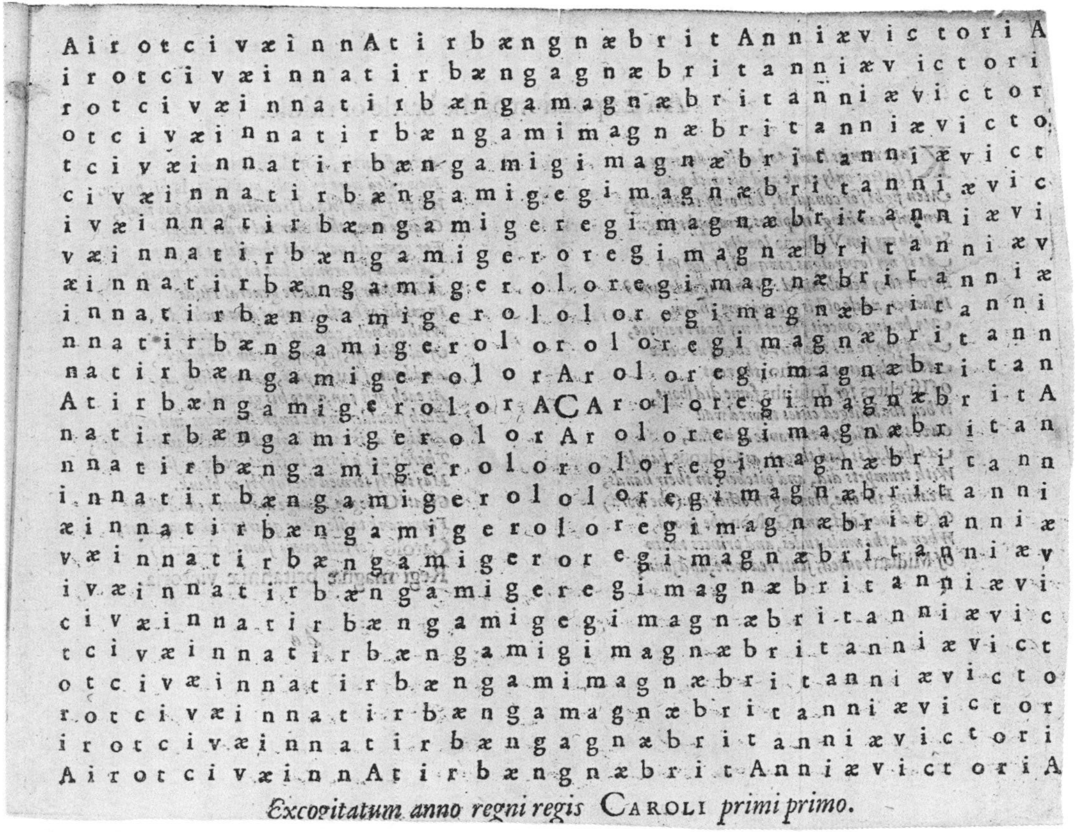

Figure 4 Christopher Syms, *An Introduction to ...*, 1634. Reproduced by permission of the Folger Shakespeare Library.

Battles of the English Nation: from the year of our Lord 1327, being the first year of the reign of the most mightie Prince Edward the third, to the year 1558. By translating this text from Latin the publisher was acknowledging that moral and ethical lessons existed prior to their figuration in language, and that whether the language was Latin or English, the same culturally normalizing lesson could be taught.

Eventually, Ocland updated the text with praise for Queen Elizabeth, entitling his revision *De pacatissimo Angliae State, Imperante Elizabeth compendioso narratio*. As Ocland suggested, his purpose in writing the text was "for the removing of such lascivious poets as are commonly reade and taught in the said grammar schooles." Since the text combined the study of Latin with praise for the ruling monarchy, and since the Latin was primarily a tool for reading about the history of the monarch, it served a purpose similar to Sym's later Latin grammar: it reminded readers that, in addition to access to the spiritual Word of God, the monarch was at the heart of the study of classical languages.

Ocland was successful in ushering in a new era, one which was a logical result of the state controlled educational policies of Henry and Edward. Under Elizabeth these policies became more overt. The privy council letter to the High Commission of schools described the book as "worthy to be read of all men, especially in common schools, where divers Heathen Poets are ordinarily read and taught, from which the youth of the realm doth rather receive infection in manners than advancement in virtues."[48] The High Commission commanded the bishops to use the text in all grammar schools and ordered a preface to the book in 1582, and in six months a reprint was needed.[49] This new text suggested the extent to which Latin primers had become tools for "normalizing" culture and supporting the status quo. Although not strictly a primer, its exclusive use of Latin in praise of an English monarch, as well as the edict calling for its public teaching in schools, suggested that it had a strong pedagogical function. As Lily's and Ocland's texts, as well as the earlier vulgaria, suggest, there arose a need to move away from a notion that the past is different to a "typological" model of humanism which made sense of its modernity. Likewise, with the emphasis on spiritual renewal and universal access to the text of the Bible came an opportunity to renew the "usefulness" of classical studies.

The grammars of the time are even more revealing of the important role Latin played in English society. Even though Lily's grammar dominated the genre, other textbooks survived under its shadow. Lily's grammar received the imprimatur of Henry VII, first in 1530 and again in 1540. However, the text's official status did not keep many writers from criticizing it or "correcting" while covertly attempting to supplant it. Some texts simply made an argument against the need for an official grammar (much as later reformers would argue against requiring an official prayer book), while many simply suggested that Lily was flawed and in need of revision or glossing. What all these texts have in common is a desire to make Latin analogous to the vernacular for the ease of teaching.

The controversies which met Lily's grammar were similar to those which confronted Whittinton's primer much earlier in the century. Unlike Whittinton's text, however, the controversy was not vicious nor personal, it was, instead, utilized to clarify Lily's text. As Joseph Webbe noted, Lily's text had become "become a full-swollen, and over-flowing Sea," and more important had the King's validation. A good example of this controversy is seen in the *Animadversions upon Lillies Grammar, or Lilly scanned. An extract of Grammatical Problems. Gathered out of the Inquiries and Disputes of the most judious Grammarians.* This text, published in London in 1625, set out to correct mistakes found in Lily. The author, Thomas Wise, while showing respect for Lily, is nonetheless pointed in his criticism of usually minor points in the text. The text is clearly meant as a companion to Lily's text, however, and the criticism is always limited to minor points of pedagogical practice and no attempt is made to undermine the writer nor the fundamental aims of Lily's method. The most pointed criticism comes early in the text, when Wise notes the difference between a "Grammaticus" and a "Grammatista": the former is "among ancients ... who did not only teach how to speak a tongue well, but also how to examine and discuss all the difficulties in Poets, Historians, Orators, Philosophers." The latter taught "the Elements of Words, Letters."[50] Lily is the latter, suggesting that his knowledge, and as a result his textbook, does not participate in larger, potentially more important topics. Ironically, the rest of the text consists entirely of questions referring either to points which Lily either left confused or mistakes he made. A majority of the mistakes concern pronunciation or accents, again suggesting that by the first half of the seventeenth century the purpose of Latin studies was the ability to speak, as well as to read, Latin.

Although none of them were very successful, there were many attempts at simplifying or altogether replacing Lily. Surprisingly, many writers agreed that the best way to teach grammar was with a universal method, but what that method should contain and how it should proceed were constant points of debate. Thomas Granger's *Syntagma Grammaticum* (1616) is a typical text which aimed to simplify Lily. Like John Udall's *The Key of the Holy Tongue*, Granger was heavily influenced by the method of Peter Ramus: Granger wanted to redesign the process of teaching Latin by distinction and method. "By distinction it separeth ... differing things. And by method it orderly disposeth and placeth all things of *the same nature and kind in order*, even as in the frame of the world" (emphasis mine). Because some students are "rudely brought up in the countrey, and afterward coming to some great place," it is mistaken to assume all students are ready to begin by translating Latin or that they are capable of understanding the rudiments of Latin grammar, especially if they have not been taught English grammar, which is "the key of Arts." Granger followed a "natural" course of study, beginning with grammar in English before proceeding to the more advanced study of composition in Latin. "Natural" seems to have the same connotation found in exegetical texts: the meaning of the word is grounded in the vernacular, as opposed to Latin. None of these texts attack the basic pedagogical advancement of Lily's method, namely that English is either prior to Latin in signification or parallel with it. Never is Latin seen as the prior language.

Of all the attempts to supplant or perfect Lily the most interesting is by Henry Edmundson, who in 1655 published *Lingua Linguarum*, or *The Natural Language of Languages*.[51] Edmundson presented a compendium of Latin/English synonyms and cognates with the hoped for result of students learning Latin by making comparisons with their vernacular. Edmundson notes in the preface that his text is "contrived and built upon" a series of analogies: 1) of one Language with another, the learned or strange tongue with the known or Mother tongue. 2) of Words with the Thing, which

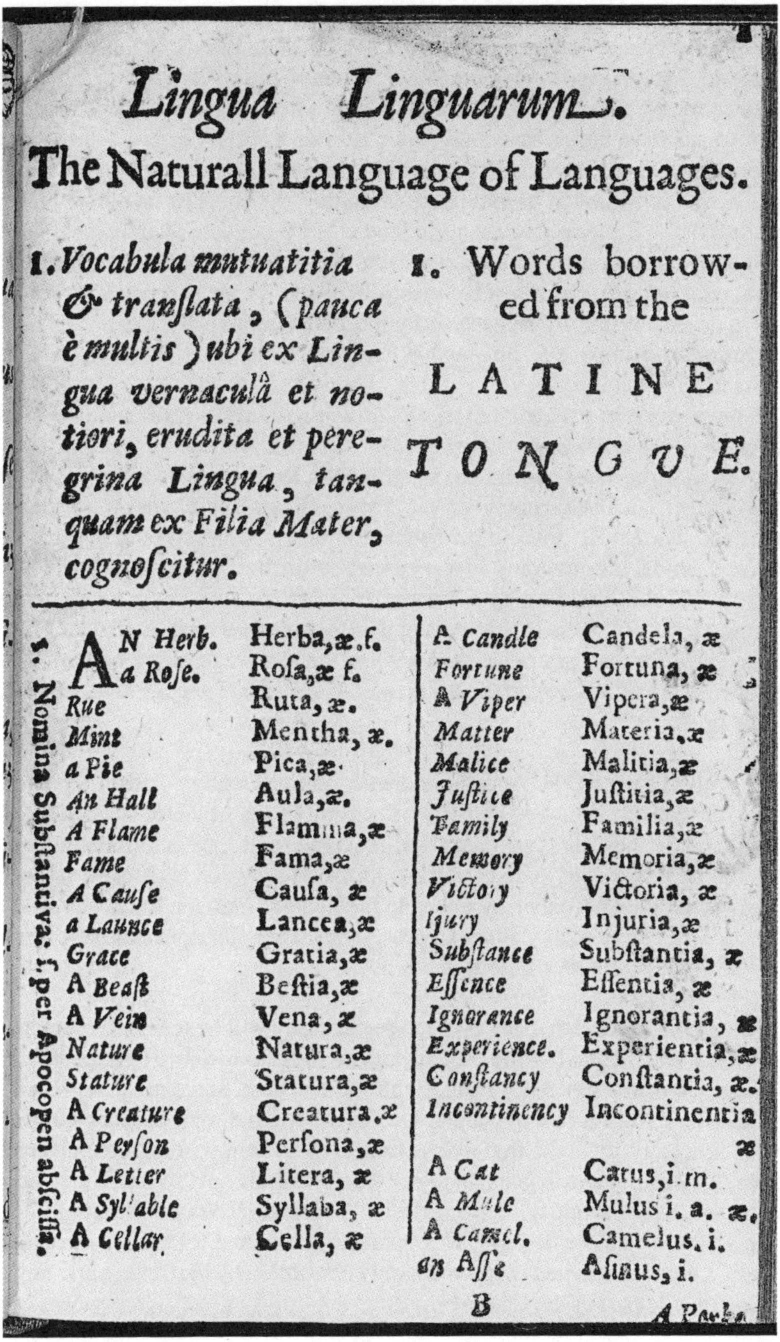

Lingua Linguarum.

The Naturall Language of Languages.

1. *Vocabula mutuatitia & translata, (pauca è multis) ubi ex Lingua vernaculâ et notiori, erudita et peregrina Lingua, tanquam ex Filia Mater, cognoscitur.*

1. Words borrowed from the

LATINE TONGUE

§. Nomina Substantiva: 1. per Apocopen abscissa.

AN Herb.	Herba, æ. f.	A Candle	Candela, æ
a Rose.	Rosa, æ f.	Fortune	Fortuna, æ
Rue	Ruta, æ.	A Viper	Vipera, æ
Mint	Mentha, æ.	Matter	Materia, æ
a Pie	Pica, æ.	Malice	Malitia, æ
An Hall	Aula, æ.	Justice	Justitia, æ
A Flame	Flamma, æ	Family	Familia, æ
Fame	Fama, æ	Memory	Memoria, æ
A Cause	Causa, æ	Victory	Victoria, æ
a Launce	Lancea, æ	Ijury	Injuria, æ
Grace	Gratia, æ	Substance	Substantia, æ
A Beast	Bestia, æ	Essence	Essentia, æ
A Vein	Vena, æ	Ignorance	Ignorantia, æ
Nature	Natura, æ	Experience.	Experientia, æ
Stature	Statura, æ	Constancy	Constantia, æ.
A Creature	Creatura, æ	Incontinency	Incontinentia, æ
A Person	Persona, æ		
A Letter	Litera, æ	A Cat	Catus, i. m.
A Syllable	Syllaba, æ	A Mule	Mulus i. a. æ.
A Cellar	Cella, æ	A Camel.	Camelus. i.
		an Asse	Asinus, i.

B A Parts

Figure 5 Henry Edmundson, *Lingua Linguarum*, 1655. Reproduced by permission of the Folger Shakespeare Library.

by Sound they are made to signifie. 3) of Words "mutually among themselves." For Edmundson the bridge between a word and thing is sound; he calls this the "Naturall Language of Languages" since languages "teach themselves." Since Edmundson emphasizes sound, the only logical result of such a pedagogy would be to read a text aloud or to speak in Latin, especially since Edmundson gives very little advice on syntax or grammar. By doing so, he effectively presents a method similar in spirit but vastly different in approach from those of Granger and Bird. The layout of this text is reminiscent of the Bible concordances looked at in the previous chapter (see Figure 5). Note the emphasis on graphic placement and the use of columns to emphasize the simplest and clearest possible relationship between words and other words in an attempt to de-emphasize differences. Edmundson's treatise is the clearest example of the "vernacularization" of Latin—as his text makes clear, the language is literally parallel with English.

The most overt and extended argument against Lily's grammar was Samuel Hartlib's *The True and Readie Way* (1614).[52] In opposition to Edmundson's use of auditory similarities between words, Hartlib calls for the use of visual cues, in the form of images, in the teaching of the very rudimentary elements of grammar, syllables and words. He notes in his epistle to Francis Rous, speaker of Parliament, that a "New Model is commonly first prepared before the old one be removed." It is noteworthy that Hartlib is turning to a member of Parliament to make his argument for a "new model." In fact, in his epistle Hartlib is clear that Latin pedagogy is politicized. More than simply a commentary on the weaknesses of Lily, Hartlib makes reference to "the Grammatical Tyranny of teaching Tongues," and tells Francis Rous that he is:

> willing to make an Appeal, and seek out an Eminent Patron for this bold Attempt, not doubting that your impartiall Judgement, not wedded to things, because they are Customary and received, will look into this thing with a more single eye, to discern the truth of what which is offered, [more than other authors do] that are either so far engaged unto the Road way, that they will not think of any better Course to be taken; or suspect all New Designes as light Projects or unsettled braines.

Hartlib makes it clear that any effort to replace Lily will be seen as impetuous, and that one must cast off slavish attention to custom in order to do so; but, as his remarks make clear, "custom" does not reside with the teachers, students or readers of the nation; rather, it resides in Parliament. On the other hand, like Edmundson, Hartlib grounds Latin learning in the student's natural senses, as opposed to artificial rules or grammar. However, Hartlib goes on to say that his aim is not "so much to overthrow what is in use, as to introduce a Better, Easier, and Readier Way of Teaching," and to do so in a way which pleases the "Honourable Committee for the Advancement of Learning." Clearly Latin pedagogy is not only controlled by the State, but is now seen as an inextricable part *of* the State.

Hartlib is less than completely honest in his epistle to Rous, for the theory which follows, if implemented, would render Lily's grammar useless and obsolete. He continues his direct attack of the "Grammatical Tyranny" by referring to the

"Dictators and Monarchs of the Schools, who crave to be heard alone touching these businesses, and in affairs of this nature; and who are of opinion, that the task of censuring is assigned to them onely."[53] He writes directly of Lily's grammar that the "common Way of learning the Latine Tongue, which hitherto used in Schools, is clogged with much labour, wearisomnesse, and difficulty."[54] A plainer and easier method is needed, and he is willing to present one. It is important to note that Hartlib's method is not itself a grammar, and so he is not technically presenting a new one, but he is presenting a more general theory of education. He notes that there is nothing in Latin, Greek or Hebrew which prevents them from being learned as naturally as one's "mother tongue," and that there is little consistency in the manner of learning, an ironic statement given that this lack of consistency is Henry's originally stated purpose for advancing Lily's grammar.

The real enemy for Hartlib is the "vulgar way of teaching Children in Schools," which includes blows and "stripes."[55] This style of teaching, often equated with Lily, focuses on memorization of rules and precepts, not on the natural manner of learning which arises from his method. Hartlib sees the weakness in Lily's grammar to be principally its emphasis on prescriptive grammar:

> For neither is it possible for these boyes hitherto to know any word of the Latine Tongue, Noun, or Verb, unlesse they know before, or together, what Figure, Case, Mood, Tense, Person, &c. every one of them is; to learn any Phrase, any Sentence, unlesse before or together they be able to give an account, by what Rule of the Syntax they may speak so after this, and not after another manner.

Lily's grammar is often slighted for its emphasis on grammar. Hartlib would, like Edmundson, have students begin with vocabulary, finding ways to make the Latin words meaningful and immediately useful to them. Not surprisingly he is also against translating from English into Latin, an important part of Lily's method: "[f]or into what Tongue any one desires to translate another tongue, and by what Tongue as an Interpreter any one hath a minde to learn any other Tongue, that Tongue which he useth by way of interpretation ought to be very well know unto him."[56] Again, Hartlib's method is more natural in the sense that it is grounded in the student's vernacular.

Hartlib would emphasize "visible Images or Resemblances ... fitted to the formes or fashions of Letters, and marked with the names of Letters."[57] This is a "natural" method because all understanding begins in the senses, preferably in the sight. The example he gives of this method illustrates an attempt at reaching all classes of students:

> As for example, the letter L not the turn'd, but the running one, as it's called by Printers, being made very exactly in wood or brasse, is represented by that Instrument wherewith we measure linned, and cloth, and other things. And that Instrument, seeing it called in our Country-Idiome or proper speech an Ell, and is sufficiently known to boyes, a man may easily bring it for to get

the knowledge of the forme of the Letter L at one showing for the first sight, and to express the naming thereof.

Hartlib is clearly emphasizing the material nature of language, and by doing so is insinuating to his readers that material and economic necessities are the reason for education in Latin. For Hartlib, prior experience should be the basis for learning, not artificial adherence to rules. We see in Hartlib one of the more widespread critiques of Lily, that by binding Latin into rules, even with the intent of translating them into English, he "deadens" the language and makes it less natural. In many of the attempts to "naturalize" language learning we see reference to spatial relationships, including the use of visual representations of letters for demonstration in Hartlib's system for teaching syllables:

> Here now in some other greater Table those Letters, together with those aforesaid Images, being set over or above to the vowels, and likewise to the consonants, may be so disposed one with another in three lines; as the consonants from b to m may be placed in the upper line; the other consonants from n to z, in the lower, and the five vowels in the middle placed between the consonants in the middle line. From which letters thus disposed or ordered, and already known to Children, School-masters shall be able to expresse any syllable whatsoever, and to shew to children all the variety of syllables.[58]

Such a graphical system emphasizes the sufficiency of placement and the material/metonymic relationship between letters (and by extension words) as central to good literal understanding. As Patricia Parker notes, "The proper 'iogning' of words and sentences ... was thus in the period [of the later sixteenth century] the foundation of the construction of order both in grammar, rhetoric, and logic and in the social and political hierarchy their ordering reflected."[59] For example, Richard Sherry in *A Treatise of Schemes and Tropes* (1550) noted that "not only must we chose apte, and mete wordes, but also take heed of placinge, and settinge them in order."[60]

Hartlib is working with the same concept of literacy as writers of the Bible concordances examined previously: namely, that words gain their meaning from placement, as opposed to a-priori meanings. In his brief discussion of grammar Hartlib suggests comparing the Latin word order to the English via a numerical system which retains the original Latin while comparing it to English word order, as in the following example:

    4   1   5   5   7 6   3   3   8

Pharisaos Christus Pastores malos, se vero multis argumentis bonum

    2   8
comprobat Pastorem.

To paraphrase, Christ makes the "bad" or corrupted arguments of the Pharisees into "good" lessons. Besides suggesting a way of teaching Latin grammar via a comparison with English grammar, Hartlib is summarizing Christian exegetical method, which itself makes the exotic and historic "Old" Testament more natural and understandable, and therefore more edifying, by comparison to the "New" Testament.

This exegetical method is illustrated graphically by the fact that the "old" word order of Latin can be appropriated to the "new" word order of English, and that the meaning of the sentence is reliant upon the new English word order.

Although Hartlib seldom discusses Latin beyond the development of a vocabulary through visual analogies to known objects, his method is continued in Joseph Webbe's *Pueriles Confabulatiunculae, or Children's Talke* (1627), an attempt at teaching Latin syntax (although again Webbe sees his method as useful for learning any language, thus technically not making this a Latin treatise).

I pray you				W. 71		hunc		
	seeke to mend this man				quaso		ne	propter improbitatem
		lest I begin to hate him					odisse incipiam	
			for his naughtinesse			emen dare stude		

Figure 6 Joseph Webbe, *Pueriles Confabulatiunculae*, 1627. Reproduced by permission of the Folger Shakespeare Library.

Webbe is attempting to teach difficult Latin clauses by an elaborate and ingenious system of lines and graphs which simultaneously remind readers of both Latin syntax and its relation to English grammar. Webbe creates these grids to illustrate the spatial relationship between clauses in his dialogues.

"In the middle or the first space you have the marke of the clause, w. 71, and on the one side thereof you have the Latine of your Author; and on the other side you have our English divided on either side by foure spaces, into foure clauses. Whereof the first on the one side, answers the first of the other, as, *I pray you*: *quaso*." The syntactical meaning of the words, however, comes not from their English word order (which would result in "Quaso hunc emendare stude, ne odisse incipiam propter improbitatem") but by placing them "more proper to the Latines" ("hunc quaso ne propter improbitatem odisse incipitam, emendare stude"). Students are able to translate the sentences, however, by utilizing the English word order. Like Hartlib, Webbe emphasizes that it is important to please the eye as well as the ear: "For though in the former we heard the daunce and the keeping of time thereof: yet we wanted one thing which we have here. For here we doe not onlye heare the daunce and time thereof as every blind man that hath eares may doe; but we also see the footing thereof; to our great advantage in the imitation of the choyest Authors, if we well consider it." Like many of these treatises, Webbe attempts to foreground Latin in the student's "natural" senses, to make the learning of it parallel to the student's understanding of their "natural" vernacular grammar. In keeping with his original pronouncements against Lily's grammar, Webbe discounts the importance of grammar as a prescriptive and foundational object of study; his method of teaching Latin suggests the "descriptive" nature of grammar which he believes resided with the ancients.

The Dictionaries

The Reformation re-examination of Latin as a useful language paralleled the rise of Renaissance philology, but while the Latin textbooks and treatises emphasized how Latin was similar to the vernacular, the dictionaries of the time focused on Latin as a fixed and stable referent. In fact, one of the ways this new fascination with language manifested itself was in the number of dictionaries and compendiums published after the sixteenth century. As Judith Anderson writes, "the dictionary is a characteristic Renaissance publication that bears significantly on changing and developing attitudes toward the classical and vernacular languages. It bears as well on the fixing and reifying of words." Anderson acknowledges that "specialized word lists, glossaries of manuscripts, topical vocabularies, and even comprehensive Latin and bilingual manuscript dictionaries" existed in the Middle Ages, but the "dictionary as a normative publication and a fixture in schoolrooms and private libraries is essentially a Renaissance phenomenon."[61] Their rise in importance can also be seen as a result of the printing press and changing conceptions of text and literacy as much as changing linguistic perception. Anderson rightly points out that the Renaissance was beginning to develop a concept of stability and normalcy which dictionaries were able to provide.[62] In addition to providing necessary stability, these dictionaries reflected a *commodification* of Latin, a concept that Latin was a marketable, value-specific language which could be measured against both vernaculars and other foreign tongues.[63] Dictionaries allowed for this materialization of language by emphasizing words as fixed, individual and exchangeable, i.e. as translatable but consistent and permanent units of meaning.

A representative early Latin dictionary is the *[H]ortus vocabulorum* (1500), which contained the following advertisement on its title page:

> Not unworthily called "the garden of words," for just as in gardens are found abundance of flowers, of herbs, and of fruits with which our bodies are strengthened and our spirits refreshed, so in this work are diverse words accommodated to beginners desirous of the pleasures of learning. With these words they may furnish the mind, adorn their speech, and finally, if the fates permit, grow into very learned men ... A work useful and profitable to all desirous of a knowledge of arts and sciences; and on account of the exposition of English speech, especially necessary to all the realm of England.[64]

Words are clearly commodities: they are "abundant," they "furnish," "adorn" and for these reasons are "useful" and "profitable." Although Latin was necessary to the well-being of the country, the reliance upon "fate" in becoming fully educated suggests that the writers of this text had realistic aspirations for their textbook. More revealing is the equation of Latin words with objects of nourishment, as well as the important role of Latin to "all the realm of England." Latin was commodified not only as a means to personal betterment, but as a necessary aspect of social and cultural well-being, necessary for "a knowledge of arts and sciences."

Some dictionaries were primarily to be used for reading classical writers and seemed to focus on humanistic aims. Even these dictionaries reflected a practicality typical of Reformation philology. One of the most popular examples of the trend to see Latin as a tool for reading classical writers was Thomas Cooper's dictionary, a corrected and expanded version of Elyot's Latin-English *Dictionary*, published in 1538. Like the exegetical guides examined in chapter three, this text was a compendium of classical references, alphabetized and translated with complete citations, re-emphasizing the grammatical nature of literal understanding. "Caeteras artes et scientias alig? fuo tempore promeuebunt, ego pro virili ..." Elyot calls his text a "Vernaculam interpretationem." The most "practical" aspect of the text was an appendix which included "poyses [weights], coines and measures" in Hebrew, Greek, and Latin, as well as augmented alphabetized entries expanding upon those included in the main text.[65]

After Elyot's death in 1546, the original publisher of *Bibliotheca Eliotae* called upon Thomas Cooper to take over the editing of the text. This revised and augmented edition of the *Bibliotheca Eliotae* was published in 1548, and was "enriched" twice in the four years which followed.[66] By the time of the publication of *Thesaurus Linguae Romanae & Britannicae*[67] in 1565, Cooper was master of Magdalen College School. After its publication, and later editions in 1873, 1578, 1584, and 1587, Cooper had become bishop of Winchester.[68] This elevation and subsequent publications suggested the esteem in which Cooper was held as a lexicographer.

Cooper's *Thesaurus* was the standard Latin–English dictionary from about 1565 to 1595.[69] However, with the publication of Thomas Thomas' *Dictionarium linguae Latinae et Anglicanae* in 1587 the esteem of Cooper's *Thesaurus* began to wain. The standardization of dictionaries, unlike primers, seems a matter of supply and demand, as well as quality, with each new text building upon the scholarship of those which came before it. Thomas' *Dictionarium*, for example, was based largely upon those of Cooper and Calepine. Based on the large number of reprints, 14, this was the most complete and popular of all dictionaries. Despite its popularity, there was very little which was unique or philologically important about this dictionary. Thomas relied on Cooper to the extent that in many cases he used the same classical references and sources for his definitions.[70]

Perhaps the most interesting dictionary of the sixteenth century was John Rider's *Bibliotheca scholastica*, published in 1589. The title page, written by the publisher Joseph Barnes, illustrates the usefulness of the text:

> Bibliotheca Scholastica. A Double Dictionarie, Penned for all those that would haue in short space the use of the Latin tongue, either to speak or

> write. Verie profitable and necessarie for Scholers, Courtiers, Lawyers and their Clerkes ...[71]

Rider's is primarily an *English to Latin* dictionary with a Latin index.[72] By Barnes' own admission it is not really a Latin dictionary useful to readers of classical text. Rather, in following Lily's pedagogy, Rider is interested in "the *use* of the Latin tongue, either to speak or write" (emphasis mine). Although an extremely important language, Latin is not to be seen as an a-priori language. Rather, it is a companion to English, and this is one of its selling points. According to Rider's own preface "To the Reader," *Riders Dictionarie* gave the English first: "no one dictionary, as yet extant, put the English before the Latin."[73] Rather than viewing Latin as a product of an earlier, less barbarous age, this dictionary treats Latin as a living and changing language, one which grows to include new words (mainly from the field of law, as the full title of the 1640 edition suggests) partly as a result of its contact with English. There is still a distinction made between authentic Latin and "barbarous" Latin, however: "The Barbarous Words which were many hundreds are expunged, to the help of young Scholars, which before they used instead of good words." The use of "good words" as opposed to bad reflects the dichotomy of Renaissance humanism— Latin gets its unique place in the education system because of its utility, but its utility is in turn based upon custom (the custom that what was good for Rome is good for England) and historical continuity. Like *Elyot's* dictionary, this text adds to its everyday usefulness by including tables of weights and measures, valuation of ancient and modern coins, and a table of Hebrew, Greek and Latin measures. The end result was a radical conglomeration of pure humanistic studies and mercantilism.[74]

John Vernon's *Dictionariolum puerom, tribus linquis*, first published in 1552, is unique in being an English, Latin, and French dictionary. Attached to a 1575 edition is the following statement addressed "To the Reader:"

> How profitable the skill of any forreine tongue is these daies to such as seeke knowledge and desire conference with *strange nations*, ... that eyther desire to be entred into other *bordering tongues* or to serch the depth of any Science, or the assurance of our salvation through the true understanding of holy scripture, is so commonly known, as so generally agreed on, that happier seems he that may attain thereto, or procure and leave it to his child as a sufficient heritage.[75] (Emphasis mine)

In addition to the obvious advantages of Latin, such as knowledge of science and "strange nations," is the "assurance of our salvation." For the first time, perhaps, the obvious is stated: those who cannot read, write, and to some extent speak Latin are likely to be left behind both economically and spiritually. Like the earlier vulgaria, these texts reminded young readers that their social (and spiritual) status was greatly defined by their language abilities. Further, Latin study was becoming nationalistic; rather than linguistic boundaries being obscured by the study of foreign tongues, the acquisition of them was seen as advantageous to the mother tongue, reinforcing preexisting linguistic and political borders.

Conclusion

The reasons for learning Latin were as varied as the methods used to teach it: the need for participation in educated society, the ability to read classical writers, and the opportunity to learn more about the "mother tongue." Ultimately, however, the need to learn Latin was reflected in the similarities found in all the pedagogical methods: it improved upon the vernacular while existing as a companion, as opposed to being prior, to it. And, of course, there was the spiritual reason for learning it: essential to good, literal interpretation was the need for accessing the true ("original") Word of God through the original languages of Latin, Greek, or Hebrew. In addition, after the Reformation it was important to study Latin, Greek, and Hebrew in order to avoid theology being limited to minute *questiones* about which "the schoolmen and their followers disputed in their barbarous idiom."[76] These "questiones" were the basis for many of the heresies followers of the Catholic Church were guilty of (or, due to their indecipherability, not guilty of), according to Richard Hooker.

Luther, in "Letter to the Mayors and Aldermen of all Cities of Germany in Behalf of Christian Schools," notes all of these elements when he writes: "But, you say again, if we shall and must have schools, what is the use to teach Latin, Greek, Hebrew, and the other liberal arts? Is it not enough to teach the Scriptures, which are necessary to salvation, in the mother tongue?"[77] Luther's response is, surprisingly, no; these foreign tongues are necessary for the right understanding of scripture as well as for civil government. Luther then goes on to exemplify both the very practical and everyday importance of these languages by comparing them to material consumer goods, and the spiritual importance of scripture. Luther, who was himself responsible for bringing the word into the German vernacular, is here arguing for Germany's renewed interest in the original biblical languages.

Furthermore, the need to learn those languages is a nationalistic one; Luther writes: "Are we not rightly called German dunces and brutes?" With access to classical languages comes both clerical power and redemptive authority. Luther equates redemption with power when he writes that "[t]he languages are the scabbard in which the Word of God is sheathed."[78]

As Ernst Cassirer has pointed out, reading and translating from another language leads to new found paradigms: "By virtue of this identity of meaning—transcending the multiplicity and diversity of momentary impressions—there emerges, gradually and by stages, a determinate 'stability,' a 'common cosmos.'" The normalization of education brought about with the Reformation is a reflection of just this "stability." However, Reformation philological theories limited the "stability" of Latin as an a-priori language; ironically, Latin gained whatever "stability" Reformation society allowed for it via its "vernacularization." For these reasons, classical languages were at once stable/historical and dynamic/contemporary. In one sense, basing contemporary biblical exegesis on classical philology was a way of making "new knowledge" couched as "old" knowledge.

Notes

1. Jaroslav Pelikan, *The Reformation of the Bible, The Bible of the Reformation* (New Haven: Yale University Press, 1996), 14.

2. *Ibid.*, 98. In the encyclical, Pius claimed the Vulgate had "juridical authority" but not "critical authority." Pius also urged that vernacular translations be derived "specially from the original texts of the sacred books" rather than from the Vulgate or the Septuagint (15).

3. *Ibid.*, 96.

4. Quoted in Pelikan, 96.

5. See Richard Marius, *Martin Luther: The Christian Between God and Death* (Cambridge: Harvard University Press, 1999), 446.

6. Debora Kuller Shuger, *The Renaissance Bible: Scholarship, Sacrifice, and Subjectivity* (Berkeley: University of California Press, 1994), 33.

7. Joan Simon, *Education and Society in Tudor England* (Cambridge: Cambridge University Press, 1967), 396.

8. This text was originally printed in Latin in Paris in 1567. This translation is the beginning of Hebrew studies in England. Udall's was the first to be available in English, although it was printed at Leyden, because of the unavailability of Hebrew type in England. Oxford press acquired matrices in 1651, although Hebrew type remained rare. Edited R.C. Alston.

9. Frederick Eby, *Early Protestant Educators: The Educational Writings of Martin Luther, John Calvin, and Other Leaders of Protestant Thought* (New York: McGraw-Hill Company, 1931), 166.

10. Edited by David C. Steinmetz (Durham, NC: Duke University Press, 1990), 83.

11. A similar argument is made by Luther in his "Letter to the Mayors and Aldermen of all Cities of Germany in Behalf of Christian Schools." "How often is St. Augustine in error in the Psalms and in other expositions, as well as Hilary, and indeed all those who have undertaken to explain the Scriptures without an acquaintance with the original tongues?" (62).

12. Richard Waswo, *Language and Meaning in the Renaissance* (Princeton, Princeton University Press, 1987), 195.

13. Quoted in Simon, 5.

14. David Armitage, "Literature and Empire," in *The Origins of Empire*. The Oxford History of the British Empire, Vol. 1. (Oxford: Oxford University Press, 1998), 100.

15. Waswo, 159.

16. Prior to the vulgaria the primary method of teaching Latin had been the very practical "Donat," elementary grammars focused on prayers and psalms and which relied primarily on memorization and repetition, not on composition or humanistic pursuits.

17. Simon, 89.

18. Folger: LA 631.3 F6. Edited by William Nelson (Oxford: Clarendon Press, 1959).

19. Nelson, viii.

20. *Ibid.*, 90.

21. Simon, 90. Magdalene College school itself probably adopted Lily's grammar, since the Stanbridge version was no longer used after 1515.

22. *Ibid.*, xxxi.

23. Translation from *The Latin Writings of John Skelton*. Edited by David R. Carlson, *Studies in Philology*, 88 (1991), 97-8.

24. *Hendecasyllabi in Scheltonum ejus carmina calumniantem*, quoted in Beatrice White, *The Vulgaria of John Stanbridge and the Vulgaria of Robert Whittinton*. Edited with intro. by Beatrice White (London: English Text Society, 1932), xxxi.

25. Translation found in White, xxxi.

26. The full tile of one of the two copies in the British Museum, according to Flynn, is, *Rudimenta Grammatices et Docendi Methodus, Non Tam Scholae Gypsuichianae per Reuerendissimum. D. Thomam Cardinalem Eboraconsem. Feliciter Institutae, quam Omnibus Aliis Totius Anglie Scholis Prescripta.*

27. *Ibid.*, 191.

28. *Ibid.*, 191.

29. This is based upon Colet's letter of dedication to Lily, dated alternately 1509 and 1510 in various editions, including copies in the British Museum. For more details about the manuscript history of Lily's various grammars, see Flynn.

30. Vincent Joseph Flynn, "The Grammatical Writings of William Lily, ?1468-?1522." *Bibliographical Society of America* 37 (1943), 3.

31. *Ibid.*, 29.

32. *Ibid.*, 29.

33. T.W. Baldwin, *Shakespeare's Small Latine and Lesse Greek* (Urbana: University of Illinois Press), 96.

34. *Ibid.*, 568.

35. Flynn, 4.

36. *Ibid.*, 15.

37. A decade after Wolsey's disgrace, Henry issued his own text based, at least partially, on Wolsey's, stating in the preface that it be used throughout England. It is clear that this preface was an attempt at asserting control over books used in a public manner, such as textbooks and, in 1549, the authorized Book of Common Prayer, which included a preface which, like Henry's grammar, gave reasons for its compilation.

38. *Ibid.*, 194.

39. Quoted in Flynn, 22.

40. Flynn, 8.

41. *Ibid.*, 106. Vives recommends Theodore Gaza's grammar, although he noted that his rules were "very unsuitable for teaching" (Simon, 112). He also suggested primary students focus on Aesop.

42. Quoted in Simon, 107.

43. Joseph Webbe, *An Appeale to Truth.* (1622) The Scolar Press Limited, 1967. Selected and edited by R.C. Alston. no. 42.

44. *Ibid.*, A2.

45. Simon, 79.

46. Christopher Syms. Printed in Dublin by the Society of Stationers, 1634 (Folger Man. VA 283).

47. Hallan, *Literature of Europe*, 1854, i. 148, quoted in the *Dictionary of National Biography*, XIV, 811.

48. *Ibid.*, 324.

49. *Ibid.*, 325.

50. Folger manuscript STC 25867.

51. Scolar Press Limited, Menston, England, 1970. Selected and Edited by R.C. Alston. No. 259.

52. Scolar Press Limited, Menston, England, 1976. No. 235.

53. Hartlib, 2.

54. *Ibid.*, 2.

55. *Ibid.*, 8.

56. *Ibid.*, 14.

57. *Ibid.*, 19.

58. *Ibid.*, 20.

59. Patricia Parker, *Shakespeare from the Margins: Language, Culture, Context* (Chicago: University of Chicago Press, 1996), 89.

60. *Ibid.*, 89.

61. *Words that Matter* (Stanford: Stanford University Press, 1996), 53.

62. Anderson provides many interesting examples of many of the dictionaries I discuss and includes a fine discussion of the graphic and spatial attributes of those dictionaries which illustrate the changing nature of text.

63. Juliet Fleming makes much the same observation about vernacular dictionaries, which she notes, attempted to replace the random variation of the vernacular with a "hierarchically organized" system which produced a "standard language" (Fleming, *Enclosure Acts: Sexuality, Property, and Culture in Early Modern England.* Ed. Richard Burt and John Michael Archer (Ithaca: Cornell University Press, 1994), 296). As she notes, "the middle of the sixteenth century then witnessed an extraordinary period of elaboration, at the end of which the lexicon [of English] had been nearly doubled through the addition of words borrowed, coined and revived" (297).

64. Quoted in Dewitt Starnes, *The English Dictionary from Cawdrey to Johnson, 1604-1755* (Amsterdam: J. Benjamins, 1991), 31.

65. Starnes, 48.

66. *Ibid.*, 68.

67. The full title is *Thesaurus Linque Romanae & Britannicae ... vel Latine complectatur amplissimus Stephani Thesaurus, vel Anglice, toties Eliotae Bibliotheca.*

68. *Ibid.*, 86.

69. *Ibid.*, 114.

70. *Ibid.*, 138.

71. *Ibid.*, 218.

72. Another example of this type of text was the *Riders Dictionarie* published in 1640 with the complete title: *Riders Dictionarie Corrected and Annotated with the addition of many hundred Words both out of the Law, and out of the Latine, French, and other languages, Such as were with us in common use, but never printed till now, to the perfecting of the worke.*

73. This claim is not entirely accurate. *A Dictionarie in English and Latine, devised for the capacity of children, and joung beginners* (London: 1616) includes a long section of English to Latin, as did Baret's *Alvearie* (1573).

74. The middle of the sixteenth century brought a profusion of Latin dictionaries inspired by Elyot-Cooper. What is interesting to note about this group of texts is the audience for which they are written. This trend toward seeing Latin as a living language began early in the century. *Promptorium parvulorum* (c. 1440) was the first dictionary in English dedicated to the needs of young students (Starnes, 3). It exists in at least seven editions. The dictionary was quite simple and generally free of revision throughout its published life. Attached to an edition of 1510 is a brief English to Latin index, provided in order to allow the student "to fynde a laten after ony manner of worde in englysshe for them that wyl lerne to wryte or speke latyn" (*Ibid.*, 5). The needs of the advanced student would be better satisfied around 1550, when dictionaries began to focus on younger readers, probably the same readers who were being taught from Lily's grammar in its various forms.

75. Quoted in Starnes, 141.

76. *Ibid.*, 85.

77. Eby, 57.

78. *Ibid.*, 60.

Chapter 5

The Grammar of Embodiment and Biblical Interpretation

> And as they did eat, Jesus toke the bread: and when he had given thankes, he brake it, and gave it to the disciples, and said, Take, eat: this is my bodie.
>
> (Matthew 26.26 Geneva Bible)
>
> That is, a true signe and testimonie that my bodie is made yours, and by me your soules are nourished.
>
> (Gloss to Matthew 26.26)

Grammatical understanding, previously equated with philological examination, translation and typological exegesis, is also closely related to questions of allegory, figuration and embodiment for two reasons: first, it represents a law regulating homogeneity in language use both at a basic metonymic sentence level and in a more general social manner, dictating correct vs. incorrect use of language. Second, since it functions metonymically and is concerned with placement, it serves as a reminder of the material facet of language. For these reasons it holds an important position in Post-Reformation culture because it simultaneously regulates language use and understanding. The grammatical understanding of language also depends upon a-priori understanding and allegorical ontological structures. The emphasis on grammatical constructs in a-priori understanding is also true of one of the central religious debates of the Reformation: the Eucharistic debate. As we shall see, the language regarding the manifestation of Christ in the Eucharist is highly suggestive of the more general theoretical issue regarding the manifestation of meaning in language for two reasons: first, both issues center around the need to find a way of explaining how something extrinsic can be ontologically intrinsic; in the case of vernacular languages, for example, meaning is both intrinsic and extrinsic to the signifier. In the case of the Eucharist, Christ's body is both external and, in a Thomistic sense, internal, to the Eucharistic wafer. Second, and more generally, both questions serve as reminders of the limits of human understanding in matters of faith. The grammatical model of Eucharistic presence shares with the earlier examples of literacy many of the same rhetorical strategies which characterize the debates surrounding biblical translation and the need for cultural homogeneity.

Realism, Grammar and the Eucharist

In 1976 Barbara Lewalski published *Protestant Poetics*, one of the seminal works of seventeenth-century criticism. In that book Lewalski argued for a renewed appreciation of the Protestant notion of a "radically" poetic biblical tradition. What made the tradition poetic was the renewed appreciation of how figurative language represented spiritual truths. Lewalski cited Malcolm M. Ross who 25 years previously wrote that in the seventeenth century poetry became more Protestant and "aesthetically the worse for it" because it flattened symbol into metaphor or simile—seemingly in response to the new way of viewing the Eucharist as the metaphoric Word of God. In Ross' paradigm to "flatten" symbol into metaphor or simile would seem to suggest that an unfortunate literalness results from self-conscious figuration. I agree with Lewalski that such an understanding is unfortunate and not accurate in terms of how figurative language-use truly works.

I take Lewalski's critical suppositions as representative of a much wider critical assumption which seems to operate unreflectively. Literary critics have tended to use terms such as "Protestant," "Anglican" and "Catholic" in a manner which says less about sincere religious doctrine and more about opportunistic and rhetorically effective labeling. For example, there has been a longstanding critical assumption, based on generalized notions of the Eucharist, that the development of a strong Anglican aesthetic brought about a distrust of figurative language, and in turn a distrust of figurative or allegorical interpretation. John Donne's "My God ... [is a] figurative, a metaphorical God"[1] sums up one view of Reformation biblical interpretation, interpretation which, according to Barbara Lewalski, "brought in its wake both a greater emphasis upon, and a more systematic analysis of, the tropes and schemes that made biblical language radically poetic."[2] Where, according to seventeenth-century paradigms, does the distrust of figurative language end and the utilization of it begin?

Additionally, the Protestant figurative emphasis was based largely on the theories of St Augustine, but, Lewalski warns: "We should, however, approach Augustinian aesthetics not in medieval but in Reformation terms, taking account of the important new factor introduced by the Reformation—an overwhelming emphasis on the written word as the embodiment of divine truth."[3] In addition, the unadorned or literal written word was seen as adequate to embody the Word of God. To suggest that divine truth is "embodied" in the written word is to suggest something profoundly spiritual about the nature of language. I will explore this notion of embodiment in some detail in order to better understand how religious doctrine is reflected in language and in turn how language itself is seen in the light of religious doctrine, with a particular eye toward exploring some of the epistemological issues which are implicit in the move from Medieval Catholicism to the Reformation, and from the Continental Reformation to the Anglican. Such an analysis questions the essentialistic pronouncements about "Protestant" and "Catholic" modes of discourse which are so central to some current understandings of seventeenth-century poetry, but it also brings to light some real and profound differences which reflect developments in ontological and Christological paradigms, and which in turn affect the pedagogical and political attempts at normalizing education and exegesis. It is important to consider carefully some possible connotations of "embodiment": what exactly does it mean to embody spiritual understanding in language?

As we saw in chapter three, the scriptural passages concerning the transubstantiation of Christ in the Eucharist were a favored subject for Renaissance exegetes who wanted to use a literal reading of applicable passages to support whatever version of presence or transubstantiation with which they aligned themselves. Despite the attempt to create a new ontology, separate from medieval Catholic doctrine, the roots of this Reformation argument can be found in medieval scholasticism. For example, Lafranc's *De Corpore et Sanquine Domini* (c. 1063-1068) was an attempt to define the "orthodox position at a high philosophical level" written "within a tradition of commentaries laid down by the fathers."[4] The search for specific solutions to very precise doctrinal and textual arguments concerning Christ's presence was developed in the context of Aristotelian metaphysics. The works of Augustine, Gregory the Great and other Church authorities were also fodder for these debates. Fundamentally, the debate focused on "realism." Lafranc's contention was that a reality exists in things no matter what words are used to describe them. Lafranc submitted that "names" are only useful in describing realities; he does not see any a-priori value in these interpretive terms.[5] Appearances and names are the same thing: that which was before consecration. Lafranc aligns himself with Augustine in the belief that spiritualiter is synonymous with invisibiliter. Logical terms such as "species," "similitude," and "figura" are used to describe real entities. ("Species, similitudo, and figura refer to realities that have disappeared; signum, mysterium and sacramentum, to Christ's actual suffering on the cross."[6]) In Lafranc's paradigm, hermeneutics are questionable because they attempt to arrive at truth through the material, i.e. language and verba. In the end, they are only useful as indicators or signs of a deeper, invisible truth. Such an argument ultimately places the debate about manifestation and ontology in faith. This view forms the basis of one of the central paradoxes of the Eucharistic debate: material signs only indicate, but do not participate in, higher truths, but at the same time, the material manifestation of the Eucharist demands an ontology which allows for material manifestation of spiritual truth. The manner in which this paradox is worked out is central to the various doctrines and belief systems which mark the later Reformation.

Berengar, one of Lafranc's adversaries and perhaps the first philologists to make a connection between many of these ontological issues and literacy, claimed that "the realists merely pandered to popular taste and to illiteracy."[7] Berengar believed that the truth of the issue was to be found in deep theological issues, not in the sort of simple questions put forth and answered by Lafranc. Berengar saw simple questions about positivistic aspects of real presence as leading to ridiculous claims, such as "Either the bread and wine are only what appears on the altar, or they are only flesh and blood, that is, what they evidently appear not to be."[8] Berengar arrives at the meaning of a linguistic statement like "this is my body" by examining logically what the words mean by basing his interpretation on that "from which inner reality can perhaps be inferred."[9]

One of Lafranc's followers and pupils, Guitmund of Aversa, supported his master in his *De Corporis et Sanquini Christi Veritas in Eucharistia*. In doing so, he developed even more clearly the analogy between words and the mysteries conveyed by them:

> For we know through "everyday experience" that our understanding, that is, "the word or our inner being," when clothed with sound, allows what was known to us alone and hidden in our hearts to be made manifest to others through the voice and at the same time to remain wholly within the mind. If a thousand men hear the sounds, the same paradox is observed: they hear the words all at once, yet each one keeps his thoughts for himself.[10]

The end result of this understanding was to render man's interpretive duty to "coordinate idea and exemplar through reading and meditation."[11] Thus interpretation bridges the natural, material world and the spiritus mundi. The tradition of literacy which corresponds to this transference sees language not as a simple grammatical construct, but as a transference of redeeming significance. This debate between what is "external" as opposed to "internal" to a text is at the heart of the later Reformation. In fact, many of the key issues of the Reformation have their roots in earlier medieval scholasticism. The evolution from Catholic medievalism to Reformation humanism would be accomplished at least partially as the result of a careful questioning of how meaning is manifested and how signs can function as relayers of truth. Furthermore, the underlying metaphor of internal/external reflects a material conception of language, i.e. one which sees meaning as constitutional and positively a part of the letter, and which defines later Protestant ontology and exegesis.

The nature of material embodiment is central to both the understanding of language and the Eucharist. Substantial presence is another way to think of literal embodiment. When Beza spoke of the substantial presence of Christ, he meant that Christ is present "personally, fully really. But Beza would not allow substantial to take on the meaning of physically, materially present."[12] In 1547 The Council of Trent sought to condemn the notion that the Eucharist functioned as a sign or manifestation; rather, in condemnation of Zwingli, it argued that the blood of Christ is actually present. In 1551 the Council of Trent again condemned any notion of the Eucharist which did not concede that the Eucharist became the body of Christ; the primary target was Luther's contention that the bread was the locus of Christ's presence while remaining bread. What was being debated at the Council of Trent, (and which is still being debated today) is the very nature of symbol and sacrament, and the debate centers around many of the same questions as my present discussion. To what extent is our language and terminology unsuitable for describing ontological truths? In the debate about transubstantiation, to what extent should modern cosmology be favored over Christology?[13] In terms of literacy, the question becomes the extent to which figurative language could be trusted to reflect spiritual understanding. At the same time that Donne was developing his metaphoric understanding of God, the use of images in the Catholic (and Anglican) Church was a point of controversy. Some images and practices of the Catholic Church were suspect primarily because the ceremonies seemingly relied upon "images" used in an allegorical manner. In Sermon 8:331, Donne wrote that the Anglican Church existed between the Lutheran and Calvinist churches on the question of the use of images, "That Church, which they call

Lutheran, hath retained more of these Ceremonies, then ours hath done: And ours more then that which they call Calvinists." But both the Lutheran, and Anglican, are "diligent to preach to the people the right use of these indifferent things." The proper use of images is to "deliver people out of that ignorance, which possesses people in the Roman captivity." In other words, images are useful only when they are actually employed, not when they are speculated on. Donne called images "indifferent" to distinguish something which is essentially a useful object, not the object of enjoyment in and of itself, to use Augustine's distinction. Such a distinction, however, does not clarify how images manifest Truth, or why speculation is such a dangerous thing.

Additionally, because of the importance of earthly religious institutions and catechisms, the truths of religious doctrine must be translated into words and symbols. Concepts such as Catholic, Lutheran, Calvinist, and Anglican find their meanings in a complex set of texts and interpretive strategies with sometimes vague demarcations. For example, Donne often rhetorically distances himself from Catholicism by characterizing it as a political and authoritarian movement; in other words, he highlights the Catholic Church's persuasive aims as characteristic of the Church in order to defend his own Anglicanism. However, beneath the public pronouncements concerning the aims of the two Churches lie important similarities, similarities which reveal common conceptions of figurative language use.

Pierre Du Moulin and the Grammar of Embodiment

One of the most prominent distinctions between Anglo-Protestants and Catholics during the seventeenth century was the extent to which spiritual truths were available to humankind. Clearly, both Catholics and Anglican Protestants believed that final spiritual truth lay beyond mere human comprehension; however, the extent to which it was possible to participate with the supra-sensible and method for participating were matters of great concern. Examining the Eucharist in light of these various positions reveals what the Eucharist implies about language and communication and the essentialistic nature of language used to communicate spiritual ideals, and the pressure put upon such representations at a time when differences between beliefs (real or imagined) are as much a subject of debate as the actual beliefs of each religion.

An example of this debate can be found in the writing of the French Protestant Pierre Du Moulin, whose treatise entitled *An Apology for the Holy Supper* was translated into English by Edward Skipwith in 1612.[14] This treatise is interesting not only for the approach Du Moulin takes, but for the translation: Edward Skipwith, Esquire, states in the preface that he has taken the liberty of translating the treatise to illustrate that laymen have a voice in the Protestant Church.

The treatise reads primarily as an argument against real presence. Du Moulin believes that the speculation on how images function is a dangerous undertaking which leads Catholics to reliance upon academics and the Pope. Note the primacy granted to scripture by Du Moulin in the following example:

> But our adversaries, which in other controversies relie upon tradition, hiding themselves in the obscurity of the unwritten word, here do change their

> manner of fight ... they would seeme desirous to stick to the words of Gospel.

From his standpoint, both written and unwritten traditions are obscured when utilized by Catholics. However, Du Moulin takes on the challenge of answering Catholic doctrine, primarily in the form of Thomas Aquinas, as seen in his use of Thomistic/Aristotelian paradigms:

> They say, that the accidents are without subject, and in their Latin, that "accidentia non accident": which is as much, as if I should say, "albentia non albent," or, those who eat, do not eat, or those who live do not live.[15]

By questioning Aquinas' use of "accidentia" Du Moulin is pointing to the impossibility of language (at least "objective" and positivistic scientific language) to describe the spiritual manifestation of Christ's presence. Even the usually deceptive "their Latin" cannot adequately describe the condition of the bread. Due to the inadequacy of language, Du Moulin consistently turns to common sense questions (did Christ eat himself at the last supper?) in order to dismiss the dialectical assertions of Aquinas and Catholic fathers.

Before returning to Du Moulin's treatise and examining it in more detail, it is important to explore the more general background of Anglican notions of spiritual manifestation. For example, the outward form of sacraments perform much like the outward meaning of literal understanding. Clothing is meant to act on the sense, and the inner "true" spiritual meaning is unintelligible. Language, John Donne writes, is an "outward thing" which "apparels" God,[16] and as such, all language points to "final things." The unique role God plays in Anglo-Protestant sign theory can best be summarized in the words of Louis Martz in writing of the "Second Anniversary:" "God is both the object of knowledge and the means of knowing; though this full knowledge and joy can never be achieved on earth."[17] We can, "come closest to it by striving to restore the Divine Likeness, as did she [Elizabeth Drury]." As Lewalski suggests, the roots of this understanding are Augustinian; Augustine's sermon on John (1 John 1:1-4) makes explicit the role the Word as sign of God plays in the world: "In the beginning was the Word, and the Word was made flesh." Augustine writes that "'The Word became flesh,' which we could see, to heal our hearts, which could see the Word."[18] The Word of Christ becomes the healing power which leads to understanding.

The Elizabethan policy was that one comes to God through language and faith. The complication arises in the extent to which language, literal or otherwise, can mirror celestial truth. In other words, for Protestants and Catholics alike, there is no such thing as a truly literal level of understanding; the real question is where and/or when embodiment happens. One of the central ironies of spiritual understanding is that the word can never fully reflect Truth, yet for many Protestants it is the only safe path to understanding. God's will is incarnated in the word, yet is more than the sum of language and human intellect. As a result, the ambiguities seen in Protestant and Catholic doctrines alike reflects a limitation of language to reflect these truths.

Richard Hooker in *Ecclesiastical Polity* believed that contemplation of real presence was in many ways beyond the realm of mere material language. Because modern cosmology could not be aligned with Christology in terms of the real presence, contemplation on the inner working of the sacraments was misguided and, if the wrong conclusions were arrived at, possibly heretical. The clearest path to redemptive sacrificial use of images was one which relied upon the obvious and outer "reality:"

> Variety of judgement and opinions argueth obscurity in those things whereabout they differ. But that which all parts receive for truth, that which every one having sifted is by no one denied or doubted of, must need be matter of infallible certainty.[19]

Here Hooker is suggesting that theologically sound, "and infallible," opinion can be found in popular opinion. Hooker is reflecting the most democratic impulse of the Reformation, but he is quick to note that this agreement lies in the careful understanding of scripture:

> Whereas therefore there are but three expositions made of 'this is my body,' the first 'this is in itself before participation really and truly the natural substance of my body by reason of the coexistence which my omnipotent body hath with the sanctified element of bread.'

Hooker notes that this is the Lutheran interpretation of Matthew 26; his use of "really," "truly," and most importantly "natural" serve as reminders that Hooker is interested in defining real presence according to faithful participation with the Eucharist; his second explication is of the "popish construction:"

> this is itself and before participation the very true and natural substance of my body, by force of that Deity which with the words of consecration abolished the substance of bread and substituteth in the place thereof my Body.

Finally, Hooker finds that the most "realistic" and universal way of understanding Christ's words are found in his English Church:

> the last, 'this hallowed food, through concurrence of divine power, is in verity and truth, unto faithful receivers, instrumentally a cause of that mystical participation, whereby as I make myself wholly theirs, so I give them in hand an actual possession of all such saving grace as my sacrificed body can yield, and as their souls do presently need, this is to them in them my body:' of these three rehearsed interpretations the last has in it nothing but what the rest do all approve and acknowledge to be most true, nothing but that which the words of Christ are on all sides confessed to enforce, nothing but that which the Church of God hath always thought necessary, nothing but that which alone is sufficient for every Christian man to believe

108 *Religion, Allegory, and Literacy in Early Modern England, 1560–1640*

>concerning the use and force of this sacrament, finally nothing but that wherewith the writing of all antiquity are consonant and all Christian confessions agreeable.

To have "nothing" which is disagreeable is the surest way to true and accurate understanding of God's will. The fact that each of the above paraphrases of "this is my body" is in itself a literal translation of the words is problematic to Hooker—he settles for the avoidance of allegorical interpretation (ala the Catholics) which renders the outer dress of the sacrifice reliant upon external interpretation and doctrine.

At the same time, however, that inner meaning is equated with external interpretation, there is an attempt to emphasize the existence of some internal spiritual manifestation of meaning. This dichotomy complicates critical assumptions of poetic meaning, such as those outlined earlier that suggest a clear demarcation between literal and figurative or between types of embodiment.[20]

If we consider each of the theories Hooker refers to in terms of linguistic manifestation, then the Lutheran's "coexistence" implies that material words are both words and that which they refer to, a position called ludicrous by some Catholic theologians who point to a Thomastic premise that something cannot be essentially two different things. The second position, the "popish" construction, suggest that the thing referred to takes precedent over the signifier, that the material word becomes irrelevant to the meaning. Hooker notes that both these situations occur before "participation," before the use is put to the bread/word. The final scenario, which Hooker aligns himself with, is the most "modern" sounding: meanings manifest themselves in words in the hearer's mind, and the union of the two is what is most mystical.

For both Hooker and Donne, no matter how meaning is manifested, metaphoric language will always be a form of mimesis, not a reality in and of itself. Note, for example, Donne's discussion of 1 John 5:8:

>That Christ was a person composed of those two Natures, divine, and humane, whereby he was a fit, and a full satisfaction for all our sinnes, and by death could be our life: for when the Apostle writ this Epistle, it seemes there had been a schisme, not about the Mysticall body of Christ, the Church, but even about the Naturall; that is to say, in the person of Christ, there had been a schisme, a separation of his two natures ... That spirit which receives not Jesus intirely, which dissolves Jesus and breakes him in pieces, that spirit is not of God. All this then is the subject of this testimony.[21]

Two things whose natures are different are the signs of two other things whose nature is one. Sacraments become metaphors for realities but are themselves not real. Like language, their mode of meaning stands apart from their usefulness. The separation of modes of meanings from the utilitarian aspect of the sign is an important distinction in developing a truly encompassing Protestant theory of representation. The true spatial representation between the various Protestant and Catholic models of manifestation and embodiment may be diagrammed as follows:

substantial

figurative   **literal**

mimetic

The separation suggests that there is an important difference in how "realism" is understood as it relates to language: for Catholics, realism manifests itself in material/substantial change, in a transformation which is both material (in terms of being "real") and figurative (in the sense of invisible and supra sensible). For many Protestants, however, "realism" is equated almost completely with metaphor: the "real" material aspect of the sign is not of final significance. It follows that material change is subordinated to figurative understanding received through faith: manifestations may never be completely material. For example, Donne noted that resemblances are "signs or images of realities, what they are in themselves is one thing and what they mean is another." Signs are both things and signs, and both things and signs must operate together in order for meaning to occur.

Richard Hooker continually downplays the importance of various aspects of Catholic doctrine not by answering them, but by noting their lack of importance compared to the sacramental power of the Eucharist, which all religions agree upon. He writes in Ecclesiastical Polity:

> But seeing that by opening the several opinions which have been held, they are grown for aught I can see on all sides at the length to a general agreement concerning that which alone is material, namely the real participation of Christ and of life in his body and blood by means of this sacrifice; wherefore should the world continue still distracted and rent with so manifold contentions, when there remaineth now no controversy saving only about the subject where Christ is.[22]

Despite the inability to agree on the where, all parties agree that there is one, and as such all parties agree that the Eucharist is a physical embodiment of Truth. The only controversy is a result of Catholic speculation; all other sides of the debate are in clear agreement. Hooker's reliance upon "common sense" functions as a tool against the Catholics whose doctrine is seen as "dark conveyances" (I.VII.5)—the literal Word of God is the guide to how God's will can be maintained.

In the following, Du Moulin writes that Catholic transubstantiation is nothing more than an opportunistic attempt to appear powerful and to control interpretation. Du Moulin uses his treatise on the Eucharist to critique papist power. He cites the Books of Holy Concernes, where, in Book 2, chapt. 14, we learn:

that the Pope will say Mass himself in person after he hathe attired himself in his chamber, like a Popinjay ... Whilst he start afore the altar singing Mass himself, they come to worship him ... During the whole action of the Mass, men do ten times more reverence to the Pope, then the Pope doth to God.

Du Moulin is citing two common Catholic stereotypes: first, the spectacle (i.e. enjoyment) of the Mass (as opposed to any real use) and importance of robes to the ritual and, second, the authority given to the Pope in place of God. Both of these stereotypes bias opinions regarding not only the Mass but the Eucharist as well. Both the outer contrivances and the reliance upon the authority of the Pope suggest that the Catholic Mass lacks inner integrity and sincerity.

One thing central to the Catholic celebration of the Eucharist is real presence. Throughout his treatise Du Moulin is suspicious of pronouncements of real presence and its centrality to the Catholic ritual. Avoiding essentialistic pronouncements concerning the real presence of Christ in the bread while denying the validity of the Catholic ritual is a common approach for many writers of this time. For example, Richard Hooker writes that "the real presence of Christ's most blessed body and blood is not therefore to be sought for in the sacrament, but in the worthy receiver of the sacrament" (II. LXVII. 6). This emphasis upon the faith of the recipient as a necessary qualification for the sacramental power of the Eucharist is a direct result of the inability to deny some form of spiritual presence while denying power to the priest.

Du Moulin develops an understanding of language which sees words as words, not reflective of anything outside themselves. Du Moulin uses this paradigm to dismiss Catholic interpretations of "This is my body." He writes that the mistakes Catholics make is to see the statement as a trope, or "some worke turned out of his natural significance." They see the relationship as between "the things signifying and signified, and not betweene the words."[23]

Du Moulin is in agreement with the broader Protestant argument against Catholic Eucharistic theory, that real presence is either a fiction or a dangerously obscure intellectual speculation, but the distinction between Du Moulin and Donne, as examples, is telling: for Donne signs are both things and signifiers. Real presence is avoided because the words can mean something figurative while also functioning as words. For Du Moulin, the literal level is first and final: the words function simply as words, "this" is a pronoun that gets its meaning from the noun closest to it, in this case "bread." To read another level of signification beyond the literal and grammatical into it is to open the door to such "fictions" as real presence. Interpretation is safe as long as words are left as things which function to point to other things:

> [W]e say, then, that this word (this) signifies this bread, for that Christ by this word (this) meant that which he held: but our adversaries grant us, that as yet he held bread. Secondly, by this word (this) we cannot conceive anything but what he gave his Apostles. Thirdly, to conclude, little children that have but learned the elements of grammar, know that this pronoun (this) is set for a noun, which noun is drawn from the present action, or the words going before, if any do go before.[24]

Du Moulin turns the debate into a grammatical one, illustrating how the debate about the nature of the Eucharist is a textual debate.

Protestant Poetics?

The two aspects of this textual understanding are both deeply rooted in the Protestant tradition. It was Calvin who popularized the notion that Catholics were overly literal in their understanding of "This is my Body." It should be read as a figurative statement, a "metonymy conforming to the common scriptural usage of such figures."[25] It is not, for Calvin, a metaphor; a metaphor, Calvin believed, should be understood as a sign of some other truth. Even Calvin's notion of metaphor is grounded in a literal understanding of the structure of metaphor.

Another example of this understanding of the metonymic and figurative nature of the Eucharist can be seen in the following from Calvin:

> I say this expression is a metonymy, a figure of speech commonly used in Scripture when mysteries are under discussion ... For though the symbol differs in essence from the thing signified (in that the latter is spiritual and heavenly, while the former is physical and visible), still, because it not only symbolizes the thing [res] that it has been consecrated to represent as a bare and empty token, but also truly exhibits it, why may it not rightly belong to the thing [res]?[26]

In other words, the invisible, spiritual truth is offered and revealed through the symbol of the bread. Our souls are fed by the flesh and blood of Christ in the same way that bread and wine keep and sustain physical life. The spiritual benefits of the Eucharist come about because of the interaction and participation of the faithful with the symbols; by the receiving in faith of the symbol, the redemptive act is done. The Eucharist works as a tool of salvation because of its spiritual representation, not because of any inherent physical or material properties.

With this statement, Calvin illustrates the problem confronting Eucharistic theories that are based on grammatical referents: Calvin must temper his definition of metonymy to include "metaphoric" aspects such as a spiritual infusion into the material res. The problem which arises with embodiment is, how can a metonymy have a spiritual component when the structure of metonymy is dependent upon an extrinsic material relationship? This same problem confronts those who attempt to translate the Word of God or who attempt strictly literal interpretations of the Bible. Attempts at using grammatical models to explain spiritual embodiment often fail at such problems, and problematize definitions such as Protestant and theories of poetic language based on such definitions.

A closer examination of the fine distinction between metaphor and metonymy is illustrated in the following from Du Moulin:

> Among the adjuncts, which follow their subjects, the manner of speech by which we discourse of this sacrament, are the most notable; the bread is the body of Christ, and the wine is the blood of Christ in the supper. Both are true, and agreeable in the intention, and the words of Jesus Christ. In these the subject remains true bread, and true wine, the attributes true body and blood; and this one substance taketh the name of another, by reason of the strait analogy, relative union, and habitude of similarity, which is betweene the one and the other, the words there retaining without trope, their native signification and the things signified there remaining in their true being. (36-37)

Du Moulin's understanding of grammar in this passage is worthy of close attention. Words are able to signify while "remaining in their true being," a suggestion that words signify things by being things. Meaning, even sacred meaning, arises out of common usage. Du Moulin's "realism" here is suggestive of an understanding of language as strictly utilitarian, as material res with a common agreed-upon relation to Truth. Such an understanding is literal and literary since the basis for the agreement is scripture: "Both are true, and agreeable in the intention, and the words of Jesus Christ." Du Moulin avoids the inevitable pitfalls of arguing for the metaphoric nature of the Eucharist by suggesting that even literary language is in some way not metaphoric.

Whether conscious of it or not, Du Moulin is taking part in a common Renaissance debate concerning the nature of language. Richard Waswo, in *Language and Meaning in the Renaissance*, suggests that when language is talked about in the Renaissance, it is "consciously regarded as the clothing of preexisting meanings," however, when it is actually employed to "reflect on its various functions," for example to teach rhetoric and grammar or to teach a proper method of interpreting Scripture or to compose literature, it is "implicitly regarded as constitutive of meaning."[27] For Du Moulin, language gains this meaning from placement: i.e. the proximity of words to each other and the mixture of agreed-upon meanings. Language means by the nature of its usage, and meaning can be arrived at by careful consideration of grammar. Because of this interest in grammar, Du Moulin is theorizing on language as much as on the Eucharist; in this way theological language becomes a meta-language and "constitutive of meaning."

As Waswo notes, however, such a distinction is prone to contradiction depending on the aspect of language referred to. Renaissance language theory is clearly Augustinian, but Reformation understanding of meaning complicates the relationship between word and idea even more than the late medieval realism/nominalism debate. Words, as things, represent only themselves; their meaning relies upon their usage in invented language. Scripture, like the Eucharist, can truly embody God's truth only because and when it operates within the faithful participant. According to this conception of participation, Catholics are wrong to rely upon an external interloper; for in doing so they avoid the necessary construction of meaning which can only occur when language comes to meaning in common usage.

The debate between "Protestants" and "Catholics" concerning the real presence of Christ in the Eucharist could be seen as a debate between "realism" and "allegory" or "fiction," as it came to be understood in the course of the debate. But to simply divide the issue into "fiction" vs. "reality" would be to oversimplify the debate. As the earlier diagram suggested, "fiction" (mimesis) and "reality" (substantive) only have meaning in relation to "literal" and "figurative." To further complicate the model, figurative and literal are themselves dependent on Cosmological and ontological considerations and Christological spiritual matters.

In fact, as the following quote from Du Moulin suggests, the search for the "reality" of real presence relies upon the utilization of Aristotelian (filtered through Aquinas) logic:

> As touching the significance of these words (This is my body) the Doctors of the Church of Rome are at warre: (After Aquinas) who saith 'this is my body' is a species of my body; So the word 'this' signifies under this, and shows indeterminately this substance which is under the accident. And this pronoun demonstrative thus indefinite, is called by our Masters, an indimiduum vagum, that is, a thing that wanders by itself, which not withstanding, is soon after confined and arrested by the word 'is.'

It is possible that Du Moulin misunderstands Aquinas on the issue of accidents and presence, or, more likely, he is putting his own spin on the notion of accidents. Aquinas is very clear that accidents have no essence without substances. On the other hand, substances can be known partly by their accidents: quoting Aristotle, *De anima*, I, 1 "the accidents contribute a good deal to the knowing of that which is."[28] Aquinas quotes John 6:64, "The words that I have spoken to you are spirit and life," possibly indicating to some that they should be understood spiritually, not literally.[29] Aquinas suggests, however, that the literal understanding of "This is my body" is necessary to explain how the accident of the bread remains along with the body. Aquinas suggests that had Christ meant that body and bread intermixed, he would have changed "this" to "Here is my body," "For by 'here' one points to the substance which is seen."[30]

Du Moulin seems to be influenced by Aquinas' attempt to put a grammatical understanding to spiritual matters of real presence, even if he did not necessarily fully understand them. The Aristotelian logic of Aquinas creates a "prescriptive grammar" in an attempt to show empirically how supra-natural occurrences are "real," and Du Moulin's modification of this scientific method comes up against the same barrier Aquinas ultimately faces in Book Four of *Summa Contra Gentile*: God does not operate according to material "rules:" at best those terms and ideas of science can help us glimpse how God operates, but God is free to change the rules and create afresh.

Nonetheless, Du Moulin wants to explain the difference in signification, and (after Aquinas) he focuses primarily on the signification of the pronoun "this." A "pronoun demonstrative thus indefinite," is called by Church Fathers, "an indimiduum vagum." Catholics who understand the Eucharist as actually Christ's body are viewing the Eucharist as a literal and substantial metonymy (because the text says it is Christ's body) and not, according to the likes of Du Moulin, as it should be seen, as a figure of speech which relies upon grammatical placement for its signification.

Du Moulin (following Calvin) insisted that Catholics accused Protestants of being overly literal in their refusal to see the bread as Christ's body; for Catholics (and

Lutherans), there is not enough distinction made between metaphor and reality. "Reality" for Du Moulin manifests itself in analogy, but in analogy understood to be between words and other words or names (what some earlier exegetes and language theorists would have referred to as "natural" typology). While tropes change their beings as things, spiritual analogies do not. This strange turn in the spiritual/material dichotomy as commonly understood suggests that language was, for Du Moulin, a manifestation of received and communal understanding, that the Word of Christ could be interpreted and understood, but it remained an accurate interpretation as long as the most literal and accessible (i.e. common) interpretation was utilized.

While claiming that the spiritual properties of the Eucharist are inherent in the Eucharist as analogy and exist solely in the power of God to make them work for the benefit of the recipient, Protestants such as Du Moulin are disembodying the Eucharist. At the same time, Catholics admit to a disembodied infusion into the bread, but support this understanding with a literal understanding of the biblical text (Christ made this metaphor, so it must suggest a real relationship/meaning).

One of the "origins" of this search for scientific and grammatical/literal certainty was the development of empirical understanding, an outgrowth of medieval nominalism and the belief that "reality" only existed in particulars, not universals. Such an attempt at explaining the world at the expense of universals led to many of the problems already outlined in the search for a usable definition and/or conceptualization of the Eucharist. Language use reflected the same dichotomy—its theoretical operational nature was spiritual and non-material, but its everyday usefulness (i.e. its existence as language) was material. Gerald Bonner writes in "The Church and the Eucharist in the Theology of St. Augustine" that we must understand Augustine's conception of the Eucharist not from a twentieth- century perspective, but from the standpoint of a fifth-century Bishop of Hippo.[31] Augustine would not be aware of a strict contradiction between the Eucharistic concepts of *figura* and *signum corporis*: the Eucharist held special, miraculous powers, yet the worshiper had not begun to look for authentic, i.e. ontologically real, presence (although Augustine certainly believed in a true presence).

It is important to remember that all of this debate is occurring in a very specific rhetorical context. Gerald Bonner puts Augustine's conception of the Eucharist into a very specific theological debate:

> In formulation of his theology of the Church and the Eucharist Augustine had, as I have said, to take account of the Donatist ideal of the pure Church, without spot or wrinkle, and its reconciliation with the all too obvious fact that neither his own congregation at Hippo nor he himself had arrived at that state of purity which was to be reached, he held, only after death. He had also to take account of the African view of the Eucharist as a sacrifice, and maintain this against the pagans, and especially the Neoplatonists ...[32]

Augustine managed to balance all of his rhetorical needs by emphasizing the notion of sacrament. On the one hand, Augustine celebrates the spiritual aspect of the sacrificial cult of the Old Testament; the acknowledgment that we "offer to Him, on the altar of the heart, the sacrifices of humility and praise, and the flame on the altar is the burning fire of charity"[33] is both an appropriation of an earlier Hebraic sacrificial cult and an acknowledgment that Christ's sacrifice is spiritual as well as physical. However, since God has no need for sacrifices (see for example Ps. 15(16)),[34] the sacrifice is not an external act, "rather the external sacrificial act is the visible sacrament of an invisible sacrifice, a sacred sign (sacrificum ergo visibile invisibilis sacrificii sacramentum, id est sacrum signum est)."[35]

The conception of the Eucharist as a sacrament, and therefore a sign or mediation, illustrates, on the one hand, what makes Catholic and most Protestant notions of sign theory so different: is the Eucharist a special sacrament, one which acts not only as a sign but also involves physical transformation, or does it function as the primary sacrament, but one which operates, like the other sacraments, merely as a sign? Or, rather, is the Eucharist a special kind of sign that is what it signifies, as in Roman Catholic doctrine? This conception also illustrates the most striking and complementary similarity: the symbolic reality of mediation which allows for signs to function in the first place.

In 1947 a group of Anglo-Catholic theologians presented a report to the Archbishop of Canterbury declaring that mistaken presuppositions about the Eucharist and real presence on both sides in the sixteenth century led to "battles in a fog."[36] The confusion could easily be blamed on a lack of complete understanding and contemplation of various terms and their connotations, as well as a general inability of positivistic discourse to make sense of spiritual matters. However, at the beginning of this discussion I suggested that Donne rhetorically distanced himself from the Catholic Church by characterizing it as a political and authoritarian movement; non-literal figurative language was denounced as a manipulative tool of this political and authoritarian movement. The differences, very real and important, are in many ways beyond the ability of language to describe, and therefore their public articulation is often confused and contradictory. Du Moulin's attempts at grammatical understanding might seem a radically literal method of approaching the question of manifestation. In fact, what they reveal is a rich understanding of how seemingly figurative language and seemingly literal language actually share a common structure in relation to spiritual truths.

Notes

1. John Donne, *Devotions upon Emergent Occasions*, ed. Anthony Raspa (Montreal and London, 1977), 99.

2. Barbara Lewalski, *Protestant Poetics and the Seventeenth-Century Religious Lyric* (Princeton, NJ: Princeton University Press, 1976), 72.

3. *Ibid.*, 6.

4. Brian Stock, *The Implications of Literacy* (Princeton: Princeton UP, 1983), 295.

5. *Ibid.*, 300.

6. *Ibid.*, 300.

7. *Ibid.*, 296.

8. *Ibid.*, 298.

9. *Ibid.*, 300.

10. *Ibid.*, 312-13.

11. *Ibid.*, 325.

12. Jill Raitt, "Roman Catholic New Wine in Reformed Old Bottles?: The Conversion of the Elements in the Eucharistic Doctrines of Theodore Beza and Edward Schillebeeckx," *Journal of Ecumenical Studies* 8 (1971): 581-604. 583.

13. See, for an example of this debate, Edward Schillebeeckx, O.P., *The Eucharist*, New York: Sheed and Ward, 1968.

14. The full title of the treatise reveals a great deal about not only its intended rhetorical purpose, but the wider debate: *An Apology of the Holy Supper of the Lord Against the Corporeal Presence, Transubstantiation, Masses Without Communicants, The Communion Under One Kind, Together with Certayn Analytical and Orthodox Propositions upon the Lord's Supper.*

15. *Ibid.*, 74.

16. See, for example, sermons 5:103-4; 4:119.

17. Louis Martz, *The Poetry of Meditation: A Study of English Religious Literature of the Seventeenth Century* (New Haven: Yale University Press, 1954), 245.

18. Augustine, *Love One Another, My Friends: Saint Augustine's Homilies on the First Letter of John*, an abridged English version ed. by John Leineweber (San Francisco: Harper and Row, 1989).

19. Hooker, "A Learned Discourse of Justification," in *Of the Laws of Eccleseastical Polity*, intro. By Christopher Morris, 2 vols. (New York: Everyman Library, 1969), L, 2:329.

20. An example of the poetic questioning of God's presence can be seen in George Herbert's "The H. Communion." Herbert questions whether the Lord is present in the bread and wine due to his usual omnipresence, or whether He is present through transubstantiation. Herbert, in a revealing discussion, relies upon his empirical senses for his answer:

> O Gratious Lord how shall I know
> Whether in these gifts thou bee so

> As thou art every-where;
> Or rather so, as thou alone
> Tak'st all the Lodging, leaving none
> > For thy poore creature there.
>
> First I am sure, whether bread stay
> Or whether Bread doe fly away
> > Concerneth bread not mee.
> But that both thou, and all thy traine
> Bee there, to thy truth, & my gaine
> > Concernth mee & Thee.

Herbert believes that Christ is present in the Eucharist, but he also believes that the argument as to what happens to the bread is not an urgent question. Later in the poem Herbert writes that:

> Then of this also I am sure
> That thou didst all those pains endure
> > To abolish Sinn, not Wheat.
> Creatures are good, & have their place;
> Sinn onely, which did all deface
> > Thou drivest from his seat.

Herbert is suggesting that arguments over the mode of Christ's presence are senseless, but given the argument, he prefers to leave the bread as bread. Since the presence of Christ is what makes the communion a sacrament, it is the spiritual presence of Christ which penetrates the soul. Herbert illustrates this point in the following poem, also entitled "H. Communion," from *The Temple*:

> Yet can these not get over to my soul,
> Leaping the wall that parts
> > Our souls and fleshly hearts;
> But as th' outworks, they may controll
> My rebel-flesh, and carrying thy name,
> > Affright both sinne and shame.
>
> Onely thy grace, which with these elements comes,
> Knoweth thy ready way,
> > And hath the privie key,
> Op'ning the souls most subtile rooms;
> While those to spirits refin'd, at doore attend
> > Dispatches from their friend.

The true debate for Herbert was not the role or gift of the sacrament, it was the *way* that grace was given by God. The debate should not be *how* the spirit manifests itself spiritually, but how the inner spiritual nature of the recipient is affected. For Herbert, the Eucharist functions as a symbolic exchange, the power of which lies in its ability to unite Christ and the soul, and to penetrate the soul and drive out sin.

21. Donne's sermons, 5:133-4.

22. II, LXVII.2.

23. Du Moulin, 36.

24. *Ibid.*, 99.

25. Lewalski, 77.

26. *Institutes*, IV. xvii.20-21. Quoted in Lewalski, 78.

27. Richard Waswo, *Language and Meaning in the Renaissance* (Princeton, Princeton UP, 1987), 80.

28. Quoted in *Summa Contra Gentiles*, Book III, vol. 1, page 189 in Bourke.

29. *Summa Contra Gentile*, 4,62,2. (254).

30. *Ibid.*, 4,63,5 (258).

31. Gerald Bonner, "The Church and the Eucharist in the Theology of St. Augustine," in *God's Decree and Man's Destiny: Studies on the Thought of Augustine of Hippo* (London: Variorum Reprints, 1987), 448-61.

32. *Ibid.*, 453.

33. St Augustine, *The City of God*, trans. by Henry Bettenson (London: Penguin Books, 1972), 375.

34. *Ibid.*, 377.

35. *Ibid.*

36. Darrell Stone, *Eucharistic Sacrifice and the Reformation* Ed. by Francis Clark, S.J. (Newman Press, Westminster NA. 1960), 9.

Chapter 6

John Donne's Metaphoric God

> There are not so eloquent books in the world, as the Scriptures: Accept those names of Tropes and Figures, which the Grammarians and Rhetoricians put upon us, and we may be bold to say, that in all their Authors, Greek and Latin, we cannot finde so high, and so lively examples, of those Tropes, and those Figures, as we may find in the Scriptures: whatsoever hath justly delighted any man in any mans writing, is exceeded in the Scriptures.
>
> (John Donne, Sermon 2:169-71[1])

The English Protestant church in the middle of the sixteenth century was a dynamic entity—it was the product of reform, debate and protest aimed at the medieval church. In this sense it resembled the Catholic Church of Augustine's fourth and fifth centuries, which found itself battling North African and Eastern sects as well as Neoplatonic and Manichean philosophies. Likewise, due to its political affinities and central role in setting social and cultural standards, both Churches had to adapt to meet the needs of the ever evolving society. Like the medieval Catholic Church, the Reformation Church was, therefore, simultaneously a stabilizing and revolutionary force. As a result, many of the churchs' practices and standards were rhetorical in nature, that is, were adopted both to respond to given controversies and to persuade and regulate beliefs and behavior. Donne's public pronouncements against the medieval church's rhetorical practices were likewise rhetorical in nature—while emphasizing differences between churches, they actually served to mask important similarities. As noted earlier, Donne wrote:

> That Church, which they call Lutheran, hath retained more of these Ceremonies, then ours hath done: And ours more then that which they call Calvinists: But both the Lutheran, and ours, without danger, because, in both places, we are diligent to preach to the people the *right use of these indifferent things*. For this is a true way of shutting out superstition, not always to abolish the thing it self, *because in the right use the spiritual profit*, and edification may exceed the danger, but by preaching, and all convenient wayes of instruction, to deliver people out of that ignorance, which possesses people in the Roman captivity. (8:331; Emphasis mine)

By emphasizing the use of "right things," Donne is affirming that ceremonies are sometimes metaphoric and true meaning is often situational and materially embodied.

Given this implication, Donne's language is revealing—erroneous religious belief "possesses" people, renders them in "captivity," while corrected practices lead to "spiritual profit," but this profit can only arise from the "right use of these indifferent things." The "use" of "indifferent things" is rhetorical—in fact, the goal of "right use" is analogous to grammar, and this analogy is not a false one since throughout his sermons Donne often turned to analogies with grammar; this emphasis on the prescriptive, versus descriptive, property of grammar is a direct result of the translation of scripture into vernaculars and the emphasis on the Word as the primary source of God's Truth. Once the Word took "concrete and artistic shape," it demanded "special refinement so that it [could] be widely apprehended." As a result of this need for dissemination, "The laws governing human discourse must therefore be understood as a divine grammar, where no feature of arrangement or form is too small for contemplation or analysis."[2]

Donne's sermons remind us that scripture is rhetorical, and therefore sharing, but also surpassing, certain ontological features of literary texts, in the right use of tropes and figures. No less an authority than Petrarch wrote, "Is it not enough that I affirm theology to be poetry concerning God? To speak of Christ as a lion, as a lamb, or as a worm (Ps. 21. 7)—what is this if not poetry?"[3] Elsewhere, Petrarch defends poetry against St Thomas Aquinas by quoting Augustine and St Gregory, and adds:

> If these things are said truly concerning those writings which are set before all readers, how much more truly may they be said of writings intended for a few! Among poets ... a majesty and dignity of style are maintained, not so that those who are worthy may be prevented from understanding, but so that, a sweet labor having been presented to them, they may be benefitted at once in memory and delight; for those things which we seek with difficulty are dearer to us and more carefully heeded. And for those who are unworthy it is provided that, lest they exhaust themselves in vain on the surfaces of these things, if they are wise, they are discouraged from approaching them.[4]

For Donne, and the other literary figures examined in the following pages, Petrarch's appropriation of a medieval Christian exegetical standard served to secularize sacred epistemologies. It follows, therefore, that Petrarch makes the distinction between those who are able to understand and those unable to understand parallel the distinction between those worthy and those unworthy. Similarly for Donne, what delights most in scripture is its eloquence, which is not, ultimately, what makes scripture worthwhile; its ultimate worth is to be found in its message or truth. Pleasing and delightful style are accidents of the Truth of scripture for Donne (and Petrarch), and as accidents are to be used, not enjoyed, by readers. As we shall note, this Augustinian distinction, is important to understanding Donne's uniquely rhetorical approach to scripture.

Crime and Punishment

The theme of the rhetorical efficiency of interpretation and right use of spiritual things, and the corresponding spatial and narrative metaphors, run throughout Donne's sermons. For example, Deborah Shuger notes this aspect of Donne's sermons when she writes, "To undertake to interpret implies the prior acknowledgment that one dwells within a master narrative; all events are pedagogic signs, for if there were no narrative, there would be nothing to interpret."[5] God's power is manifested in the fact that He ascribes meanings and plots to didactic narratives of crime and punishment. As a result, all of us are part of a larger, master narrative and are a constituent part of a higher Truth as well as part of a coherent and "metonymic" social structure. Correspondingly, sin is often the result of a refusal to interpret, to admit that a given event or action is a sign whose fixed meaning is a part of the master narrative. Textual ambiguities, therefore, are often the source of anxiety in Donne's sermons since salvation is dependent upon their right interpretation, which in turn defines who we are as readers and Christians and what our proper place in the narrative really is. Often, the "right use" cited above is defined against the practices of Calvinists and Lutherans. By situating the Anglican Church on a continuum with the Lutheran, Calvinist and Catholic Churches, Donne illustrates why exegesis must be rhetorical (as well as conservative)—it must move people along a doctrinal line they, as Christians, are already tethered to. Even conversion is not so much a radical change but a movement away from certain practices toward more acceptable and tempered ones.

Despite their metaphoric language and rhetorical sophistication, Donne's sermons always remain centered on the literal level of interpretation. However, literal understanding is, necessarily, of the world and as such, the world must be brought into alignment with scripture. As a result, Donne describes the nature of the scripture read in Church and the homilies preached to interpret that scripture in terms of the disruption of received understandings and inherited verbal constructs.[6] For Donne, the biblical text "de-signes" the world. The preacher "*pierces* us," he writes: "Solomon (in Ecclesiastes) shakes the world to pieces, he *dissects* it, and cuts it up before thee."[7] Donne's metaphor emphasizes the materiality of the spiritual Word. Further, the materiality is wordly in its ability to "de-signe" the world. Clearly for Donne exegetical sermons have serious social implications; the world is in need of "de-signing" due not only to faltering morality but also to dangerous conflicting doctrines. However, this statement should not be taken to mean that interpreters have the same liberties that Solomon did; exegetes have a duty to remain true to the doctrinal lessons of Christianity (in this case the Church of England variety) as made clear in the literal Word of God. Also, as Donne states, "no scripture is of private interpretation. I see not this mystery by the eye of Nature, of Learning, of state, of mine own private sense ..."[8] Donne resists any temptation to see interpretation as answering only to individual conscience; for example, in sermon 1:235, he writes that we are "not to rest in Nature without God, nor in God without Christ, nor in Christ without the Scriptures, nor in our private interpretation of Scripture, without the Church." "To rest" is to prematurely stop the chain of signification so central to

Donne's interpretation; this chain ultimately includes not only spiritual truths, but secular as well—immediately after this passage, Donne notes that earthly government is a "Type and Representation of the Kingdom of heaven" and therefore he prays for no changes "in Government, or in Religion." In this passage we see most clearly the hierarchy of interpretive authority; the individual is at all points subordinate to the Church, Scriptures, Christ and God, and by typological extension, government.[9]

Power, both secular and religious, has a privileged place in Donne's sermons. Deborah Shuger has written of the sermons: "They produce anxieties in order to disclose the power of the priest and to create a dependency on that power." The ability to decide meaning and to persuade, like rhetoric, is itself a form of power,[10] and as a result correct interpretation becomes a matter of punishment versus redemption. On the other hand, Donne's sermons do not so much decide meaning, since all scriptural meaning is always already interpreted, but for his audience they propagate a conception of language use which helps support his status quo Anglican beliefs. As such, his sermons represent the imperative role pedagogy and exegesis play in setting discourse standards and why interpretation is inherently challenging—Donne must make his listeners see the sign in both its theological context and in its narrative context as a part of the complete Word of God. For him, the sign always points to something else, but something in a larger, preordained and governing narrative. To this end, Donne often foregrounds language *qua* language in his sermons and treats scripture as language and as grammar, or language about language.

Among Donne's primary goals throughout his sermons is the development of a rhetorical language which would allow for the discussion of God, a conception of language (or a logology) which took into consideration God's creative power and "ineffability." Kenneth Burke, at the beginning of his *Rhetoric of Religion: Studies in Logology*, defines "logology" as the study of "words about words."[11] Since humans are symbol-using animals, Burke writes, it is not surprising that our "thoughts on the nature of the Divine embody the principles of verbalization."[12] Therefore, by studying how we verbalize understanding about God, we are studying our conception of language.

Donne also saw the study of the divine as in some way a study of language. For example, Donne wrote that the Bible "has this in common with all other books, that words signifie things; but has this particular, that all the things signifie other things."[13] In other words, the Bible can never be taken totally at face value, and for this reason Donne's notion of "literal" is more complex than the mere unambiguous equation of sign to signifier, and it allows Donne to understand scripture as simultaneously literal and symbolic. Words are, after all, meant to communicate to our enfeebled imagination.

However, merely equating things with other things is not enough. Paul's words in the First Epistle to the Corinthians ("we see through a glass, darkly") complicates Donne's concept of literal language use in the Bible. Like Augustine before him, Donne is aware that literal language is limited in its ability to represent spiritual things. Since it leaves us with the question as to *how* language can be used to discuss things spiritual, this acknowledgment of the limitations of literal understanding would seem to contradict the parallel distrust of figurative language represented by Anglican hermeneutics. Is there some explanation of literal language and understanding which does not presuppose a reliance upon metaphorical understanding? The most important considerations about figurative language for both Protestants and Catholics alike rely upon questions of how words function as signs for the purpose of mediation; words, like the Eucharist, must have a material, literal level which precedes the metaphoric in order for the sacramental nature of the sign to function.

For all these reasons, biblical interpretation is a public act; like Augustine before him, for Donne understanding and teaching the true intention of the Bible have urgent social and cultural implications. But since Donne refuses to separate scripture completely from literature, he was not averse to highly metaphoric interpretative methods, yet, given the public nature of scripture, he rarely used them in an unconscious way and when he did use them, which was often, he did so to illuminate the nature of theological language and to explicate literal lessons found *elsewhere* in the Bible. In other words, Donne's metaphoric exegetical style was performative, meant to embellish his lesson, not to render it more obscure.

"The Manna of the Church"

Basic to Donne's performative interpretation of scriptural language is his personification of the Word of God as an active, persuasive orator. This metaphor is illustrated with a unique understanding of Psalm 63; Donne writes:

> The Psalmes are the Manna of the Church. As Manna tasted to every man like that that he liked best, so doe the Psalmes minister Instruction, and satisfaction, to every man, in every emergency and occasion ... *David* was not onely a cleare Prophet of Christ himself, but a Prophet of every particular Christian; He foretels what I, what any shall doe, and suffer and say. And as the whole booke of Psalms is *Oleum effusum*, (as the Spouse speaks of the name of Christ) an Oyntment powred out upon all sorts of sores, A Searcloth that souples all bruises, A Balme that searches all wounds; so are there some certaine Psalmes, that are Imperiall Psalmes, that command over all affections, and spread themselves over all occasions, Catholique, universall Psalmes, that apply themselves to all necessities ... Now as the spirit and soule of the whole booke of Psalmes is contracted into this psalme, so is the spirit and soule of this whole psalm contracted into this verse. [Psal. 63.7][14]

The Psalms are, first, a material entity, Manna, but a material entity which can actively "minister Instruction" and "command" and "spread themselves" to all mankind. Likewise, Donne sees the Eucharist as the primary example of the divine Word, a Word otherwise delivered textually. As Barbara Lewalski suggests, the roots of this understanding are Augustinian; Augustine's sermon on John (1 John 1:1-4) makes explicit the role the Word as sign of God plays in the world: "In the beginning was the Word, and the Word was made flesh." Augustine writes that "'the Word became flesh,' which we could see, to heal our hearts, which could see the Word."[15] The Word of Christ becomes the healing power which leads to understanding.

For Donne, both the Word of God and the Eucharist play an important ministerial role, and the ontological similarity between the Eucharist and the text of the bible is obvious—both positively affect participants when used and understood *rightly*. At the same time, however, all of the Psalms are "contracted" in one psalm; as we saw in chapter three, the reduction and distillation of the total Word of God into more manageable and easily comprehended units was a widespread exegetical method, one which simultaneously emphasized the unity and continuity of the scriptures. The image Donne uses suggests that he understood the relationship between truth and language to be one of unity and continuity: scriptural language suggests higher Truths while at the same time participating in those truths. It is the combination of suggesting and participation which defines much Protestant theology, and Donne in essence performs scripture in his sermons, illustrating for his hearers the primary requirement for true scriptural understanding.

Language nourishes us in terms of logology—it orientates us in a textual relationship: our relationship with God is based on a relationship between the Word and the promise of its relationship with Truth. Christ is the performative Word of God—for Donne this suggests a real and a metaphoric relationship, one reflected in language and simultaneously beyond the material ontological relationship of word to object. The two testaments of the Bible, the text in its entirety, are the basis for understanding, as long as they are read as a *sentence*, with all the constituent parts adding to and collectively engendering meaning. However, when Donne writes of the book of Revelation, he defines literal in a way which suggests that it is not simply grammatical or of the letter:

> for the literal sense is not alwayes that, which the very Letter and Grammar of the place presents, as where it is literally said *That Christ is a Vine*, and literally, *That his flesh is bread* ... But the literal sense of every place, is the principall intention of the Holy Ghost, in that place: And his principall intention in many places, is to express things by allegories, by figures; so that in many places of Scripture, a figurative sense is the literal sense, and more in this book [Revelation] than in any other.

Although there is nothing in this passage which cannot be traced to the exegetical theory of Augustine and other Church fathers, by emphasizing *placement*, that the meaning of scripture is found "in that place" and "many places", Donne suggests that it is both the order and perfect "grammar" of the Bible as well as spiritual manifestation which is foremost in importance and which dictates what the text means, or, what its literal interpretation should be.

The true Word of God comes from the Father; understanding of this true Word is reflected in the opening words of John ("In the beginning was that Word, and that Word was with God, and that Word was God"[16]). Ultimately, Donne puts faith in the existence of God's truth through the literal letter of the text; "to *see* God, is but to *know*, that there is a God." Donne's faith is a sensual faith, and as a result is capable of being recreated. This sensual faith, more than convoluted allegorical explanation, leads to understanding. Another way of appreciating the relationship between this worldly sensory experience and the supra-natural is seen in sermon 3:288, where

Donne notes that the things of this life are "not a Parenthesis, a Parenthesis that belongs not to the sense, a Parenthesis that might be left out, as well as put in. More depends upon this life then so." Likewise, rhetoric is of this world and belongs to the sense; it, too, may not be left out or treated as parenthetical. Often, Donne turns to grammar to explain how the world fits as part of a larger Truth; it is an essential part, a grammatical constitutive component of the complete Truth. In this way earthly life is similar to the Old Testament, without which the New Testament could not fulfill its promise. Similarly, the senses are necessary components for the fulfillment of scriptural Truth.

In sermon 10:196, Donne "performs" an elaborate metaphor out of the relationship between sensory understanding and extra-sensory meaning; in so doing he again highlights the distinction between use and enjoyment: "the death of Christ is given to use, as a *Hand-writing*;" Donne has here taken Rom. 7:21, and used the concept of law as spirit as a metaphor, albeit a scripturally grounded one, for the graphic nature of God's message. It is the existence of God's Word/law as *written* language which provides for spiritual salvation, but only when it is viewed as an active agent, as a living testament to the law as opposed to a static reminder or promise of a law. He goes on to make it clear that despite the material and sensory nature of the message, however, there is an eternal nature to it: "for, when Christ naild that *Chirographum*, that first hand-writing, ... he did not leave us out of debt ... His death is delivered to us, as a writing, but not a writing onely in the nature of a piece of Evidence, to plead our inheritance by, but a writing in the nature of a Copy;" it is its nature as a copy which is pedagogical: "It is not onely given us to reade, but to write over, and practice." In this context, "evidence" is equitable with final interpretation, which for Donne implies a lack of the creative energy necessary for interpretation. As the opening of the Book of John makes clear, the first, and foremost, creative act is the Word. Only by continuing to copy that Word, and thus the original creative act, can scripture be redemptive.

In his study of Renaissance literacy, David Cressy quotes Richard Baxter on the importance of developing a "discriminating religious literacy;" the passage is worth quoting in its entirety for what it suggests about the relationship between reading and the sensual:

> The writing of divines are nothing else but a preaching the gospel to the eye as the voice preacheth it to the ear. Vocal preaching hath the pre-eminence in moving the affections, and being diversified according to the state of the congregations which attend it. This way the milk cometh warmest from the breast. But books have the advantage in many other respects. You may be able to read an able preacher when you have but a mean one to hear. Every congregation cannot hear the most judicious or powerful preacher, but every single person may read the books of the most powerful and judicious. Preachers may be silenced or banished, when books may be at hand. Books may be kept at a smaller charger than preachers ... If sermons be forgotten they are gone, but a book we may read over and over till we remember it, and if we forget it may again peruse it at our pleasure or our leisure. So that good books are a very great mercy to the world ... Books are, if well chosen,

> domestic, present, constant, judicious, pertinent, yea and powerful sermons, and always of very great use to your salvation.[17]

For Baxter, the sensual and material nature of text are what allow for its repetition and infinite rehearsal. Although vocal preaching is the warmest milk, it is not necessarily the most sound path to salvation; that is reserved to texts and sensations which may be "read over and over," each time replaying the original sermonic message. Such rehearsal creates a textual relationship with scripture and Church doctrine; such interaction, in the words of Cressy, "allowed one to interact with the holy word, nor merely to absorb it."[18]

Despite this textual relationship with scripture, Donne is clear, after Augustine, that employing Christ's written language as evidence is to mistakenly *enjoy* it, to see it as an end; to continue to learn from it by reading and writing about it is to *use* it as it was intended to be used. Again, we must remember that life is not a parenthesis, but it is, in Donne's own words above, like interpretation, limited to use and not to enjoyment. Donne's conception of scriptural language is closely based on Augustine's. This influence is clearly shown in the following excerpt from a later sermon:

> All the evils and mischiefes that light upon us in this world, come (for the most part) from this, *Quia fruimur utendis*, because we thinke to enjoy those things which God hath given to us onely to *use*. God hath given us a *use* of things, and we set our hearts upon them ... The *fruition*, the enjoying of the death of Christ, is reserved for the next life; To this life belongs the *use* of it. (10:196)

"Fruitition" and final understanding are reserved for the afterlife; with the afterlife comes finality of thought and meaning. For Donne, as for Augustine, the premature enjoyment of language and signs leads to a misunderstanding which inevitably results in the disruption of signification. Therefore, obscurity and ambiguity are necessary, and temporary, results of the correct *use* of language in the understanding of God: "And then we shall see how there is a twofold sight of God, and a twofold knowledge of God proposed to us here." As long as we are merely reading God's words solely in a material and naturalistic manner (or, are trapped by final and essentialistic Papist readings) we are bound to obscurity and partial understanding; but we avoid pure material literalism by interpreting:

> a sight, and a knowledge here in this life, and another manner of sight, and another manner of knowledge in the life to come: For, here we see God *In speculo, in a glasse*, that is by reflection, And here we know God *In aenigmate*, sayes our Text, *Darkly*, (so we translate it) that is, by obscure representations, and therefore it is called a *Knowledge but in part*; But in heaven, our sight is *face to face*, And our knowledge is *to know, as we are knowne*. (8:219-20)

Since the text is by nature a reflection and obscure, employing Christ's written language as evidence is to mistakenly *use* it; to continue to learn from it is to *enjoy* it. Like the two testaments of scripture, our understanding is not ultimately fulfilled until a later (i.e. spiritual) ontological revelation. For Donne, all written language is obscure; allegory, which for Augustine was a method of *uncovering* the hidden strengths of language's representative power, is, for Donne, a further obscuring of the literal (and therefore, ironically, more of this earth). One of Donne's favorite analogies for understanding spiritual expression is sight, whether in the sense of seeing beyond the material text, or in the sense of "face to face" sight of God, where the hindrances of language are no longer a factor; the senses are a primary component of spiritual understanding, with Christ serving as the mediator of divine knowledge, allowing our enfeebled senses to grasp the truth. For Donne it is a great mistake to confuse the *oculus corporeus* and the *oculus interior*;[19] the *oculus corporeus* is limited in its ability to reveal the will and intent of God, while the *oculus interior* leads to it but is dependent on faith for understanding, and thus, the inner eye, is transcendent and supra-material.

Donne's highly literary and often obscure exegesis is a way of negotiating with the obscurity of spiritual meaning. In a sermon on 1 Cor. 13:12, Donne makes the distinction between seeing "now" and "then ("nunc" and "tunc") analogous with the completion of God's promise: "(Now, in this Ministery of his Gospell, *we see in a glasse, we know in part*) And then the *Then*, the time of *seeing face to face,* and *knowing as we are knowne,* ... So that this day, this whole Scripture is fulfilled in your eares; for now, (Now in this Preaching) you have some sight." Although now we "see through a glass," eventually our sight will be perfect.

In Donne's "Second Anniversary" we again can see a clear distinction between earthly and heavenly sensory knowledge:

> When wilt thou shake off this pedantery,
> Of being taught by sense, and fantasie?
> > Thou look'st through spectacles; small things seem great
> > Below; but unto the watch-towre get,
> > And see all things despoyl'd of fallacies:
> Thou shalt not peepe through lattices of eyes,
> Nor heare through Labyrinths of ears, nor learne
> By circuit, or collections to discerne.
> > In heaven thou straight know'st all, concerning it.
> > And what concernes it not, shalt straight forget. (291-300)

As is always the case with Donne, there is a distinction between earthly and heavenly knowledge: "Sense" and "Fantasie" are pedantic; truth stripped of pedantry reveals things as they are (or, at least, "despoyl'd of fallacies"). It is interesting to note that Donne is not necessarily stating that the "watch-towre" lends a perfect understanding; it is enough that true understanding does not reveal "by circuit" ("In heaven thou straight know'st all"). Only in heaven is true, unadorned, and unobscured understanding possible. The reliance upon literal, unadorned (i.e. visual) understanding is based on the belief that ultimate truth is unavailable to earthly, purely material understanding. Donne is illustrating a traditionally Protestant paradigm which equated revelation "by circuit" with Catholic allegory, based as it was on an obscure and intellectually abstract interpretation controlled by the Pope and certain Church fathers, most notably St Augustine. Catholic interpretations are not available by reading. However, as Donne's sermons illustrate, certain types of "pedantry," most explicitly allegory and figurative language, are occasionally necessary in order to fully understand and participate in the creative lessons of the Bible. Unlike Luther, Donne does not limit allegory and figurative exegesis to interpretation, but sees it as a fundamental aspect of spiritual understanding and God's divine Word, and therefore as a fundamental aspect of teaching and disseminating the Word. Since the meaning of scripture always points outside the text to faith and doctrine, the text itself can only come to meaning in relation to such doctrine, which is itself tied to thorough understanding of the whole text of the Bible, both the New Testament and the Old Testament. However, how does a prejudice against allegory allow for Donne's metaphorical understanding of God? According to this aesthetic, how is metaphor, or Donne's "metaphoric God," different from allegory in terms of representational power? If we are going to see the Renaissance as developing a world view based more and more on the written word as revealing divine knowledge, then these questions problematize how reading and understanding are themselves understood.

Typology and Power

As we noted earlier, typology, according to Erich Auerbach, was a "mode of signification in which both type and anti-type are historical, real entities with independent meaning and validity, forming patterns of prefiguration, recapitulation, and fulfillment by reason of God's preordained control of history."[20] As such, typology conveniently differed from allegory and allowed exegetes to emphasize the continuity, literalness, and obscurity of the Bible. At the same time, however, the close relationship between allegory and typology is appreciated by Donne in his attempt to find a correspondence between sign and signified. According to Winifred Schleiner, "Donne ... can use the word 'type' figuratively: the transfiguration of Christ is a 'type' of the transfiguration that will occur in the general resurrection (3:120, 4:224)."[21] For example, Donne sees an analogy between the feast that Matthew, leaving his worldly job as a tax collector, gave for Christ and the feast Abraham gave for his son on the day the son was weaned. Donne also sees Matthew's feast as a "feast that was a Type of a Type, a prevision of a vision, of that vision which Saint Peter had after, of a sheet, with all kinds of meats clean and unclean in it ..." (7:148, 5:251). In short, typology is a literal metaphor, and as such Donne uses it to collapse the distinction between allegory and literal interpretation by seeing "types" as universals, moving from material/historical comparisons to more universal ones. One of the reasons Donne's sermons are rhetorically challenging for modern readers is because of this shift in ontological perspectives.

But what is most revealing is the manner in which Donne's interpretations constantly serve to remind readers that all interpretation reinforces hierarchical structures. Twenty-two years after the death of Queen Elizabeth, John Donne would illustrate clearly the divine typology which would allow a sovereign to take on the role of a pure and consistently holy figure. God, Donne believed, was not the sole author of goodness; that role could be played by mortals to other mortals. He writes:

> So the Priests and the Elders come to *Judith*, and they say to her, Thou art the exaltation of Jerusalem, thou art the great glory of Israel, thou art the rejoicing of our Nation, thou hast done all these things by thy hand;[22] And all this was true of *Judith*, and due to *Judith*; and such recognitions, and such acclamations God requires of such people, as have received such benefits by such instruments:

Judith was a beautiful and pious widow who helped secure a key battle for the Jews, and, as Robin Hedlam Wells points out, she was one of the personae for Elizabeth in Elizabeth's middle years. She makes a fitting symbol for the unique role a *mortal* ruler has in God's charity—blasphemy against a ruler mirrors the blasphemy against a God.[23] Therefore, interpretative blasphemy is a form of treason:

> For as there is Treason, and petty-treason, so there is Sacrilege, and petty-sacrilege; and petty sacrilege is to rob Princes and great persons of their just praise. But then, as we must confer this upon them, so must they, and we, and all transfer all upon God: for so *Judith* proceeds there, with her Priests and Elders, Begin unto my God ... So likewise *Elizabeth* magnifies the blessed Virgin *Mary, Blessed art thou amongst women*: And this was true of her [the Virgin Mary], and due to her [Virgin Mary]. (6:230-31)

The corroboration of succeeding events which makes typology such a suitable trope for Donne also provides an opportunity to lend praise to historical and political leaders. As we shall see in the next chapter, Edmund Spenser searched for the same corroboration within the framework of his allegory, finding instead that allegory mystified the historical connections. However, for both writers, the act of interpretation was an act of capitulation and conformity. The combination of these two writers is telling—two writers not often considered together due to their drastically different aesthetics share an important conviction about interpretation and its relationship to power. For example, Donne turned to typology to praise King Charles in a sermon on Isaiah 32.8 delivered to King Charles at Whitehall. Donne wrote that the commentators dispute "whether this prophecy of *Essay*, in this chapter, beginning thus, *Behold, a King shall reigne in righteousness, and Princes shall rule in judgement*" should be understood to be of an *Hezekias* or a *Iosias*, or any other good King, which was to succeed, and to induce vertuous times in the temporal State" (8:238-39). In the same sermon Donne notes that Hezekiah is "a type of Christ, but yet a Type of Christ." The repetition and "but" are important components in understanding seventeenth-century Protestant figurative theory, for analogies, Protestants believed, are always only shadows of higher truths. Like allegory, typology is also limited in its ability to represent higher truths; in this respect allegory and typology share very important ontological similarities while maintaining distinct relationships with history and philological manifestation. Donne shared with the writers of allegory the desire to question the limitations of language and its ability to reveal God's Truth.

Notes

1. Sermon text and numbering based on John Donne, *The Sermons of John Donne*, ed. and intro. Evelyn M. Simpson and George R. Potter, 10 vols (Berkeley: University of California Press 1962).

2. P.G. Stanwood and Heather Ross Asals, eds. *John Donne and the Theology of Language* (Columbia, Mo.: University of Missouri Press, 1986).

3. D.W. Robertson, *A Preface to Chaucer: Studies in Medieval Perspectives* (Princeton: Princeton University Press, 1962).

4. Quoted in D.W. Robertson, trans. with intro., *On Christian Doctrine* (New York: Macmillan Publishing Company, 1958), xvi.

5. Deborah Kuller Shuger. *The Renaissance Bible: Scholarship, Sacrifice, and Subjectivity* (Berkeley: University of California Press, 1994), 201.

6. John Wall, *Transformations of the Word : Spenser, Herbert, Vaughan* (Athens: University of Georgia Press, 1988), 40.

7. Simpson and Potter, III, 48.

8. *Ibid.*, III, 210.

9. In sermon 6:282-83, Donne gives an even more elaborate explanation for this hierarchy: "That which the *Scripture* says, *God* sayes, (says St. Augustine) for the Scripture is his word; and that which the *Church* says, the Scriptures say, for she is their word, they speak *in her*; they authorize her, and she explicates them; The Spirit of God *inanimates* the Scriptures, and makes them *his* Scriptures, the *Church actuates* the Scriptures, and makes them *our Scriptures* ... Then still to submit a mans owne particular reason, to the authority of the Church expressed in the Scriptures ... It is not because the Church doth truly take *too much* power, but because they would be under *none*; it is an ambition, to have all government in their own hands, and to be absolute Emperors of themselves, that makes them refractory."

10. *Ibid.*, 217.

11. Kenneth Burke, *The Rhetoric of Religion: Studies in Logology* (Berkeley: University of California Press, 1970), 1.

12. *Ibid.*, 1.

13. Winifred Schleiner, *The Imagery of John Donne's Sermons* (Providence: Brown University Press, 1970), 130.

14. Simpson and Potter, VII:51-2.

15. Augustine, *Love One Another, My Friends: Saint Augustine's Homilies on the First Letter of John*, an abridged English version ed. by John Leineweber (San Francisco: Harper and Row, 1989).

16. *Geneva Bible* (1602), Pilgrim Press, 1989.

17. Quoted in David Cressy, *Literacy and Social Order* (Cambridge: Cambridge University Press, 1980), 5. Baxter, *A Christian Directory* (1673), 60.

18. Cressy, 6.

19. *Ibid.*, 139.

20. Wall, 111.

21. Schleiner, 190.

22. Judith 15:8.

23. Robin Headlam Wells, *Spenser's 'Faerie Queene' and the Cult of Elizabeth* (Beckenham, Kent: Croom Helm Ltd., 1983), 19.

Chapter 7

Educating Gentlemen: Allegory, Literacy and Spenser's *Faerie Queene*

> Scripture condescends to your intelligence, and attributes both hands and feet to God, whilst meaning something else.
>
> (Dante, *Paradiso*, iv. 43-5)

One of the primary goals of English Renaissance education was the strengthening of aristocratic values, and in order to meet that goal, humanistic values needed to be aligned with the values of the aristocracy. Specifically, it needed to create a new kind of gentlemen who could carry out the wishes of the Church *and* State. Edmund Spenser's "Letter to Raleigh" reveals much about the mutual goals of education and literary creation at a time when, as David Lee Miller notes, "the Reformation in England had hastened the long-term process through which the national state assumed the role of preeminent corporate entity in political live." *The Faerie Queene* could "only have been formulated *after*" that time and "before the Restoration separated the state from the person of the monarch."[1] This historical moment not only makes possible a particular collapsing of the distinctions between state and monarch, but also the English Reformation's collapsing of distinctions between political monarch and head of the Church. Further, this historic moment highlights the cordia/discordia inherent in the monarchical/Protestant figure of the Queene. The dissimilarities are compounded by the announced, but exaggerated, distinctions between Protestant and Catholic, and the necessity of maintaining that separation despite the sometimes seemingly wavering sympathies of Elizabeth.[2]

But this historic moment also owed a debt to the medieval allegorical and exegetical theory outlined earlier. During the Renaissance, allegory was primarily an instrument for education, and this fact is often overlooked in discussions of allegory which favor strictly grammatical or thematic discussions. The same could be said of literacy: it is all too simple to see literacy as a simple and stable aptitude with no dependence on social or cultural constraints. The changing concepts of literacy outlined throughout this book are as much defined by religious and spiritual issues as economic or political issues (although those forces are undoubtedly important); the same can also be said for the allegory of *The Faerie Queene*, which must be read according to culturally defined representational norms and customs. Just as literacy became equated with morality in the fourth and fifth centuries of Augustine, Spenser's poem relies upon allegory to create a moral, normalizing poetic representation of Queen Elizabeth.

In short, the goal of education was to educate gentlemen for the better management of government. As Stephen Greenblatt has noted of the *The Faerie Queene*, "It is to a culture so engaged in the shaping of identity, in dissimulation and the preserving of moral idealism, that Spenser addresses himself in defining 'the general intention and meaning' of his poem."[3] The goals of the "educative discipline"[4] reflected in *The Faerie Queene* mirror those of Renaissance exegetes and pedagogues; literacy was the primary conduit for the dissemination of religious and social orthodoxy. At the same time, however, the demands for more practical and universalized literacy required the English education system to meet highly utilitarian aims while also lending support and rationalization to the official church; practical religious, mercantile and nationalistic needs influenced educational trends throughout England and the continent.

As Joan Simon notes, "Ideas about English education are endlessly reiterated but seldom examined in the light of the social forces which have shaped them and the century after the Reformation particularly invites historical investigation in this sense."[5] Like the debate concerning the Eucharist, isolating spiritual issues which are central to *political* and *societal* movements (i.e. the Reformation) from the very components which make up and promote those movements, i.e. educational treatises and educational tracts, distorts them. Similarly, the rhetorical means used to debate these topics also distort the real structure and content of spiritual belief while at the same time defining those beliefs within the public sphere. The real presence of the Eucharist, the use of images, and finally, the subject of this chapter, the courtly use of allegory and its role in the education of a nation as well as a gentleman, all illustrate the complex manner in which beliefs rooted in christological paradigms also reflect new philological beliefs and paradigms.

Fashioning a Gentleman: Spenser's "Letter to Raleigh"

As Joan Simon points out, "Gentlemen who came within the system of taxation numbered less than a thousand; in 1579 Burghley listed only a hundred names among the inner core of county notables, peers and gentlemen."[6] Spenser's audience was probably supplemented by those who, like himself, aspired to be gentlemen, despite their middle class upbringing. In this sense *The Faerie Queene* functioned like the popular courtesy books of the time which, although purportedly written for an aristocratic audience, in fact appealed more to those who wished to appear aristocratic by normalizing their behavior to what appeared to be the standard. Although Spenser's poem was by no means a treatise on behavior, as we shall note, it served to normalize reading habits and general moral lessons in alignment with societal and cultural standards.

Spenser's "Letter to Raleigh" provided his audience with a guide to understanding how to properly read; further, the letter reflected the humanistic/pedagogical tradition: it is, in essence, modeled on a medieval scholarly tradition of adding learned prologues to significant works. In the words of A.J. Minnis, the tradition of writing scholarly introductions began as lessons in a particular discipline with the reading of a particular text as an example; the opening lecture on a given text usually consisted of a close consideration of a text.[7] Eventually these lectures were written down and, in many cases, included as the preface to a given manuscript of a text. In his thorough discussion of the tradition in *Medieval Theory of Authorship*, Minnis outlines the various types of prologues, or *accessus*, which were popular in the later Middle Ages and into the Renaissance. Although there were several types of prologues in use well into the Renaissance, the type which has the most direct relevance to Spenser's Letter would be the "Aristotelian," and the earlier "type C" prologue from which it developed.[8]

In general these prologues were used to lend authority or legitimacy to a work of literature, sometimes secular but often spiritual. As a rule, the prologues were written for ancient literary works or for Scriptural texts, but later developments in the genre allowed for *accessus* which lent authority to living writers, namely by suggesting that their work was of spiritual importance or, at least, not contrary to Christian ideals. This tradition had started with commentators of Horace and Virgil, who set out to use allegorical readings of them to suggest that their lessons were always moral and in line with Christian beliefs, and it was appropriated by Spenser to likewise suggest that his poem was in line with both Christian beliefs and courtly decorum.

In these prologues, the commentators situated the work in a "hierarchy of ultimate goals and goods," to use Minnis' description, by examining the various Aristotelian causes for a given *autores*, or literary work. Spenser follows this model in his letter so as to make his intentions clear and to avoid "jealous opinions;" in short, in order to negotiate between and with both courtly and Christian rhetorical norms. In order to make the intention clear, the writers of the prologues examined the "cause efficient," or the person who wrote the work, the "cause material," the specific literary materials (or, for our purposes, genres) used as sources for the writer, the "cause formal," or method of treatment or organization of the work," and finally the "cause final," the ultimate justification for the existence of the work.[9] The four causes, the formal, material, the efficient, and the final, can be best understood according to Aquinas' example of a statue in which the formal cause is its shape or proportions and organization of its various parts, its material cause is the bronze from which it is made, its efficient cause is the artist or craftsman, and its final cause is the artist's reason for making it.

Even a quick glance at Spenser's "Letter to Raleigh" suggests how relevant the *accessus* were to him and his goal in the letter. For example, the letter's opening reference to the poem's title and its definition as a "continued Allegory, or darke conceit" notes the poem's material cause and Spenser's desire "to discover unto you the general intention and meaning ... without expressing of any particular purposes or by-accidents therin occasioned" reflects a general Aristotelian logical breakdown and analysis of the topic.[10] Specifically, Spenser's organization, outlined so thoroughly in his "Letter to Raleigh," reveals the structural importance of Aristotelian logical division and the appropriateness of the Aristotelian prologue in describing it. Spenser mentions Aristotle twice in his letter, both times in reference to how he has divided his poem according to the display of virtues. As A. Leigh DeNeef writes, "Aristotle" is Spenser's "way of referring to a tradition of ethical exegesis that from antiquity through the Renaissance analyzed the qualities and characteristics of any one virtue" by means of classification and division.[11]

The letter has long served as a point of contention among Spenser scholars who question its relationship to the poem. As DeNeef notes in an entry on the letter in the *Spenser Encyclopedia*, many critics have traditionally seen the letter as offering "only generalizations, inaccuracies, and inconsistencies"[12] in its attempt to explain the poem. DeNeef notes that many critics are bothered by the letter's seeming focus on "narrative" and "structural machinery" rather than the poem's "moral or allegorical methods."[13] I would suggest, however, that by viewing the letter in the context of the medieval prologue tradition we can see that the intent of the letter is *not* to provide accurate details, rather to provide an Aristotelian analysis of intentions useful to the reader concerned with reading the text in a doctrinally sound manner. Specifically, these prologues were, traditionally, examinations of literary works according to how the narrative and structural elements were constituent parts of the work's allegorical machinery, and that focus is in accord with Spenser's intention in both the letter and the poem.

The most important connection between this medieval exegetical tradition and Spenser's intentions in the "Letter to Raleigh" is their function as public declarations of literary intention. In noting how German literary works of the sixteenth and seventeenth centuries were often augmented with prefaces, dedications, and epilogues, Walter Benjamin makes an illuminating point of the public nature of such materials, which provided "an elaborate surrounding framework to the larger editions and the collected works. For it was only rarely that the eye was able to find satisfaction in the object itself."[14] The final "absorption" of a work of literature is not private but public in the sense that it is brought into line with orthodoxy and the aims of "educative discipline." In its publicness, Spenser's "Letter to Raleigh" reminds us of an important aspect of the Renaissance aesthetic: literature, allegories especially, are a form of public spectacle. As A. Bartlett Giamatti notes in his discussion of Spenser's allegory, "To consider pageantry as a public language signifying private concerns is to approach an idea of allegory. For allegory is a way of talking about substances by way of surfaces, a means of focusing on the private, inner, and hidden through the public, available, and open. Such an approach to allegory (or to pageantry) means we must always absorb the surface, the literal level, in order to penetrate to the substance."[15] As a form of pageantry, allegory serves as a master trope for understanding the aims and methods of Renaissance literacy.

Elizabeth's reign was filled with allegorical gestures aimed at solidifying her image while strongly and overtly intimating an all important textual relationship with truth. For example, at her accession, Elizabeth was symbolically handed an English Bible by a child representing Truth, and "She kissed it; and afterwards applied it to her breast ... promising to be a diligent reader thereof."[16] Shortly after her accession, Elizabeth refereed to herself as "God's creature ... but one body, naturally considered ... by His permission a body politic, to govern."[17] These anecdotes illustrate Elizabeth's propensity to turn to allegory to endear herself to the masses (while also dramatizing her position as monarch) and to signify the importance of subordinating secular, mortal rule to spiritual guidance and suprasensible Truth; in so doing, Elizabeth shows herself to be spiritual messenger and conduit for God's will.

Spenser's letter makes it clear that he found himself in the position of writing an epic poem for a reigning monarch whose public self-fashioning called for a very specific aesthetic. Spenser notes at the beginning of his letter that allegory as a general species is somewhat suspect:

> Sir knowing how doubtfully all Allegories may be construed, and this book of mine, which I have entituled the Faery Queene, being a continued Allegory, or darke conceit, I have thought good aswell for avoyding of gealous opinions and misconstructions, as also for your better light in reading therof (being so by you commanded), to discover unto you the general intention and meaning ... without expressing of any particular purposes or by-accidents therein occasioned.

Clearly, Spenser's desire is to write a didactic poem, one which creates a common doctrinal understanding for his audience. Throughout the "Letter to Raleigh" Spenser makes it clear that he desires that all readings of the poem be normalized with accepted and traditional courtly rhetoric. This warning to readers serves the purpose not only of praising the Queen but also of suggesting that the meaning of the poem could involve a process of normalization between spiritual Truths and poetic (and therefore, for Spenser, courtly and political) truths, Truths which in his specific case necessitate allegory. But Spenser is clear in his desire to have his allegory read, first, for its general meaning *and* intention, which is singular and prior to the figuration of the poem, and to leave particular interpretations to the realm of the accidental and, seemingly, the unintentional. To this end Spenser would have found a model for describing and defending his intention in the medieval *accessus*. In order to fulfill his complex rhetorical aspirations, Spenser looked for a rhetorical framework which would allow him to maneuver safely between the secular (the court) and the transcendent (the perfect nature of the Queen) and create a work with the expressed desire to "fashion a gentleman or noble person in virtuous and gentle discipline," and his "Letter to Raleigh" serves to reflect that desire.

The letter also serves to remind us of the difficulty and potential danger of reading allegory. In addition to the spiritual reasons already discussed, one of the reasons for this difficulty is that commonly held concepts of rhetoric which rely on clarity and consistency (grammatical and "literal" consistency, that is) are ill-suited for the task of understanding how a writer in Spenser's social and economic situation could create a work of art both suitable to himself as a poet and to Elizabeth the monarch and patron. Spenser spends a good part of the letter not only describing his materials and sources, but defending them. Spenser's materials are, of course, also literary, and the letter outlines and defends his specific literary choices. The most important thing the letter emphasizes is that the poem is a hybrid; it is not only an historical fiction, but it is also a romance; the material for it comes from the romances of Arthur and Ariosto. It is important to Spenser's humanistic intentions to situate his poem in a carefully defined tradition; he writes: "I chose the historye of king Arthure, as most fitte for the excellency of his person being made famous by many mens former works." Spenser carefully places his poem in a long tradition of such poems which used famous persons, namely Arthur, as paradigms of virtuous behavior. He writes that:

> I haue followed all the antique Poets historicall, first Homere, who in the Persons of Agamemnon and Vlysses hath ensampled a good gouernour and a vertuous man, the one in his Ilias, the other in his Odysseis: then Virgil, whose like *intention* was to doe in the person of Aeneas: after him Ariosto comprised them both in his Orlando: and lately Tasso disseuered them againe, and formed both parts in two persons, namely that part which they in Philosophy call Ethice, or vertues of a priuate man, coloured in his Rinaldo.

The letter affords Spenser the opportunity to note how one particularly important structural component of his poem, the division of virtues into public and private, is related both to the traditional materials which he utilizes and the breakdown of philosophy into ethics and natural philosophy. This is another role of the *accessus*—to place the work into a formally defined disciplinary context, one which defines its practical purpose and intent. The same distinction between private and public characterizes the distinction Spenser makes later in the letter between the public and private representations of Elizabeth: "For considering she beareth two persons, the one of a most royall Queene or Empresse, the other of a most vertuous and beautifull Lady, this latter part in some places I doe expresse in Belphoebe."

More importantly, the primary material of the poem is allegory, which Spenser makes clear at the begining of his letter: "entituled the Faery Queene, being a continued Allegory, or darke conceit." Spenser joins a long tradition of prologue writers who use the *accessus* to explain the importance and necessity of allegory as a literary method: Spenser writes, "To some I know this Methode will seeme displeasaunt, which had rather haue good discipline deliuered plainly in way of precepts, or sermoned at large, as they vse, then thus clowdily enrapped in Allegoricall deuises." This sentence has long been cited by critics as an important statement of Spenser's concept of allegory for it reflects the ambiguity and anxiety which rightly characterized allegorical discourse for Spenser's readers. If we follow Spenser's lead, however, and consider allegory as the material of the poem, as opposed to a static genre with specific/accidental episodes, then the letter no longer must make sense of every episode and event in the poem, and it makes it clear that allegory is a *rhetorical* strategy, one which exists alongside "plainly delivered" moral lessons. When considering allegory as an active *cause* of the poem rather than a stagnant genre, the essentialistic pronouncements about the poem's specific and local meanings and allegorical representations, which some critics find missing from the letter, become less important, and the work's

Augustinian "use" and "enjoyment" become more relevant to Spenser's overall artistic and rhetorical intentions. In this sense, the brief letter can, therefore, serve as a *moral* guide to the poem as a whole.

The Aristotelian language of the letter reminds us of the importance of understanding the causes of the poem, especially in a courtly setting. The *final cause* is "the ultimate justification for the existence of a work, the end or objective (*finis*) aimed at by the writer."[18] Given this definition, Spenser points to two final causes, both of them defined by the court and courtly rhetoric. He writes first, "The general end therefore of all the booke is to fashion a gentleman or noble person in vertuous and gentle discipline."

Later Spenser makes it clear that the true final cause is Queen Elizabeth: "In that Faery Queene I meane glory in my general intention, but in my particular I conceiue the most excellent and glorious person of our soueraine the Queene, and her kingdome in Faery land. And yet in some places els I do otherwise shadow her." It is here, in considering the final cause of the *F.Q.*, that we can see the true significance of the *accessus* model; it is important to remember that the purpose of an *accessus* was to make it clear that nothing in the text was contrary to Christian faith; in the case of the *F.Q.*, the purpose behind the "Letter to Raleigh" is to make it clear that nothing, not even the poem's structure and material, is contrary to the public praise of Queen Elizabeth, and that all aspects of the poem are subordinate to her, including the "bi-accidents" of characterization.

The "Courtly Figure"

As the prologues made clear, the use of allegory sometimes needed defending. Richard Puttenham in his *The Art of English Poesie*, defines allegory as a "duplicitie of meaning or dissimulation under covert and darke intendments."[19] Later, when discussing allegory in detail, Puttenham calls it "the Courtly figure:"[20]

> The use of this figure is so large, and his vertue of so great efficacie as it is supposed no man can pleasantly utter and persuade without it, but in effect is sure never or very seldome to thrive and prosper in the world, that cannot skillfully put in use, in so much as not onlie every common Courtier, but also the gravest Counsellour, yea and the most noble and wisest Prince of them all are many times enforced to use it.[21]

Notice the language of this passage; allegory is not solely a trope of the "poetic" imagination, rather it is a fundamental aspect of courtly literacy. Also of note is the use of "pleasantly utter" and "persuade," two terms which, although never mutually exclusive, take on a new connotation when put into the context of Puttenham's courtly rhetoric. To use allegory to please is also to "speake other wise than we thinke, in ernest aswell as in sport, under covert and darke termes." The ever-present Queen Elizabeth and her specific aesthetic preferences made the need to walk a fine line between political patronage and artistic freedom the overriding artistic impulse; the "Letter to Raleigh" illustrates how that could be done within the humanistic, courtly tradition.

Whereas allegory served the upper class in this specific manner, it had similar yet more wide-ranging uses for the culture at large. Richard Sherry, in *A Treatise of Schemes and Tropes*, writes that allegory is the "seconde parte of Trope," and irony and proverb were its subspecies.[22] Irony and proverb are interesting subspecies for they suggest the sort of culturally-grounded understanding which is important to true allegorical understanding. Allegory and irony both require shared cultural knowledge in order to be rhetorically effective. All three of these tropes, irony, proverb and allegory, are edifying only when they are properly understood to have a *non-literal* relationship to truth. What Michael Murrin writes of allegory could also be said of proverb and irony: "Allegory is intimately associated with the society in which the poet writes; it demands human participation and must be explicable in social terms."[23]

But not just any "social terms." Turning back to the *F.Q.* as the eminent example of allegory for the sixteenth century, we are reminded that allegory must be read against the backdrop of the society which made it possible. In 1961 A.C. Hamilton sarcastically asked why the Red Cross Knight could not stand for modern Russian Communism:

> The Red Cross Knight stands for the working class armed with the Marxist faith: naturally his colour is red, and his cross refers to the *crossed* hammer and sickle. Una is clearly the spirit of Communism. The opening battle against Error refers to the Revolution. That monster's books and papers which she spews at the knight refer to the flood of the Trotskyite writings, and her death marks the first triumph of the oppressed peasant class.[24]

In his hypothetical example, Hamilton emphasizes that the poem cannot be abandoned totally to the "moral level" for to do so blurs the uniqueness of the poem's individual and distinctive episodes. However, the real reason the Red Cross Knight cannot represent communism is because to isolate the figure from the purpose it was to serve in its "original context," i.e. its original audience or rhetorical setting, is to utilize it for propaganda. Ironically, this is exactly the argument used by some Protestants against allegorical interpretation.

What Hamilton is suggesting is that modern readers are limited in how they can, or should, read literature. We, as modern readers, must, to the extent possible, attempt to read *F.Q.* as Elizabethan readers. To this end, the *F.Q.* must be read according to and against two distinct matrixes, the religious and the secular. Doing so necessitates reading allegorically, for, in the words of Walter Benjamin, one must be able to "grasp the synthesis which is reached in allegorical writing as a result of the conflict between theological and artistic intentions, as synthesis not so much in the sense of a peace as a *treuga dei* between the conflicting opinions."[25] Accordingly, in this conception of allegory, reading "allegorically" means not simply translating the literal words from one set of referents to another, but constantly moralizing our reading. When Spenser writes in the proem to Book I that he wishes to "moralize my song" he is affirming that his text is in need of normalization by the subject of the song, Queen Elizabeth. To "moralize" is to bring into alignment with a system of understanding higher than and prior to that of the secular song which Spenser has written. We see this tension in the various proems to the various books of the poem; for example, note Spenser's equation of Elizabeth with divine Truth in the following example from the proem to Book IV:

> To such therefore I do not sing at all,
> But to that sacred Saint my soueraigne Queene,
> In whose chast breast all bountie naturall,
> And treasures of true loue enlocked beene,
> Boue all her sexe that euer yet was seene;
> To her I sing of loue, that loueth best,
> And best is lou'd of all aliue I weene:
> To her this song most fitly is addrest,
> The Queene of loue, and Prince of peace from heauen blest.
>
> Which that she may the better deigne to heare,
> Do thou dred infant, Venus dearling doue,
> From her high spirit chase imperious feare,
> And vse of awfull Maiestie remoue:
> In sted thereof with drops of melting loue,
> Deawd with ambrosiall kisses, by thee gotten
> From thy sweete smyling mother from aboue,
> Sprinckle her heart, and haughtie courage soften,
> That she may hearke to loue, and read this lesson often.

These two stanzas clearly illustrate the tension between the secular and the transcendent. The references to "The Queene of loue, and Prince of peace from heauen blest" and "sacred Saint ... In whose chast breast all bountie naturall" suggests that Queene Elizabeth is one embodiment of Truth on earth, and in the following stanza the lines, "From thy sweete smyling mother from aboue,/ Sprinckle her heart, and haughtie courage soften,/That she may hearke to loue, and reade this lesson often" suggest that even Elizabeth is in need of *some* form of guidance and effort to read out the correct understanding of the poem. Spenser is reminding his readers that *both* the subject of the poem and the Truth of the poem (and conversely the Truth of Elizabeth) are heavenly sent. In short, the poem *The Faerie Queene* is an earthly and rhetorical manifestation of divine knowledge, and as such it serves two dual purposes; one, to praise Elizabeth and two, to serve as a humanist treatise on good, moral reading habits. In doing so, the poem demonstrates the secular and spiritual ends of Reformation education.

Whereas Hamilton's comment reflects his own cultural anxieties, the prologue to Book 2 suggests that for Spenser the standard by which his allegory was to be read began and ended with Elizabeth:

> And thou, O fairest Princesse under sky,
> In this faire mirrhour maist behold thy face,
> And thine owne realmes in lond of Faery,
> And in this antique Image thy great auncestry.[26]

Clearly, Elizabeth is the spiritual and material/historical standard (or "cause") to which the allegory points. Joel Fineman explains that allegory is a "courtly figure" for Puttenham and Spenser because "in deferring to structure it insinuates the power of structure, giving off what we can call the structural effect."[27] What Fineman calls the "structural effect" I call, in the context of Christian ontology, grammar. By deferring its meaning to an a-priori system, courtly allegory resembles Christian allegory, in fact relies upon its authority in order to function. Fineman goes on to note that Philo of Alexander, the first to employ allegorical interpretation extensively, was "also the first to introduce the terms of negative theology into theological discourse."[28] Allegory must be asked to do the impossible: to make sense of supra-material truths while doing so in material signs and signifiers.

In the three stanzas which precede the two cited above from Book IV, Spenser criticized the writing of love poems which are read by their audience in order to "haue their fancies fed." True praise and understanding of love can only come from "them that love, and do not liue amiss."[29] True understanding can come only to those who are inherently prone to appreciate it, those who have already shown a propensity for love, and of those worthy readers, Elizabeth is the best example. The two stanzas cited illustrate, first, that Elizabeth is the source of all truth, love, and peace, and second, that the "lesson" (i.e. the poem) should be read *carefully* and *often* in order to be fully, and correctly, understood.

As we have already noted, the sources for this exegetical strategy are late classical and medieval. In addition to the influence of the Aristotelian tradition, Augustine's thematic influence on Spenser is widely documented. Sean Kane, in his book *Spenser's Moral Allegory*, for example, traces many of the philosophical debts Spenser owes to Augustine. He writes: "The Church Fathers and particularly Saint Augustine (who, we shall see, is an informing presence on Spenser) regarded the code of rational improvement and moral self-sufficiency as a dangerous form of pride."[30] Kane sees Spenser's challenge as the need to negotiate between two commonly held yet often contradictory strands of humanism, one which strove for perfection on earth, the other which strove for a perfection outside of earthly desires. Kane's discussion relies primarily on thematic interpretations of the various books of *The Faerie Queene* and the various knights and virtues of those books; I hope to make sense of these topical allusions by asserting that not only is Augustine a thematic influence, but the concept of allegory which allows these themes to function in developing the goal of the poem "to fashion a gentleman" are likewise influenced by the particular courtly aesthetic values, values which in turn are products of the Protestant Reformation.

Sean Kane notes that the Renaissance courtly dichotomy of earthly versus spiritual fulfillment led to a form of "norming;" he writes that the tendency to view allegorical structures as "diametrically opposed poles" serves to de-emphasize the

Educating Gentlemen: Allegory, Literacy and Spenser's Faerie Queene 143

hierarchical, Neoplatonic axis of allegorical discourses, and instead focuses on personal experience:

> The spacious hierarchical metaphor of Christian Platonism offered sufficient room for classical ethics. Following the Augustinian hierarchy of faith over reason, Aristotelian ethics was accommodated to Christian doctrine by Thomas Aquinas in the Middle Ages. Yet the priority given to an aggressive practical ethics in the Renaissance, along with the corresponding tendency to define matters of faith strictly in relation to individual conscience, began to return experience to concrete and literal formulations.[31]

Spenser's allegory, Kane goes on to explain, is an attempt to break through the barriers imposed by this opposition. In short, in the same way that Augustine's conception of allegory as a "master code" allowed for the norming of two distinct texts (the Old and the New Testaments), so too does allegory allow for the norming of two opposing ethics (classical and Christian).

As already noted, Augustine's rhetoric is a suitable model for Elizabethan courtly poets for two reasons—one, it allows for (in fact makes necessary) a conception of allegory as a dark and dense writing and interpretive strategy which must be *read*, and read carefully, to be understood, and secondly, Augustine's rhetorical structure allowed for a given text to include an a-priori interpretation (Spenser's 'general intention'), one which in Spenser's case, was aimed at furthering the poetic image the Queen favored. As the "Letter to Raleigh" also illustrates, this reading strategy is carefully formulated to allow Spenser the opportunity to dissimulate his text, while at the same time preventing a chaotic descent into indeterminacy through the reference to a "master code" analogous to Augustine's rule of faith.

Spenser's early critic Kenelm Digby seems to understand a crucial aspect of Spenser's allegory so often missed by modern readers; he writes (c. 1628):

> Spenser in what he saith hath a way of expression peculiar to himself; he bringeth down the highest and deepest mysteries that are contained in human learning to an easy and gentle form of delivery—which showeth he is master of what he treateth of, he can wield it as he pleaseth. And he hath done this so cunningly that if one heed *him not with great attention*, rare and wonderful conceptions will unperceived slide by him that readeth his works, and he will think he hath met with nothing but familiar and easy discourses; but let one dwell awhile upon them and he shall feel a strange fulness and roundness in all he saith. The most generous wines tickle the palet least, but they are no sooner in the stomach but their warmth and strength there, they discover what they are; and those streams that steal away with least noise are usually deepest and most dangerous to pass over.[32] (Emphasis mine)

Digby's language is revealing for two reasons—one, the method of reading which Digby is describing is clearly one which favors obscurity and ambiguity over simplicity. Second, Digby notes that the "simple" level of the poem is the most pleasing, yet contained in that level are matters of "fulness and roundness" which could slip by the inattentive reader. Digby is privileging the literal, more sensual level of interpretation while acknowledging the necessity of the allegorical. However, Digby is also careful to acknowledge that the only proper reading of Spenser is one which is attentive to *both* levels, a lesson that ought to be well heeded by modern readers.[33]

Digby goes on to note examples in the text where there is some room for subjective interpretive choices, but those choices are limited by the a-priori truths to which the text points. We can return to Augustine here in order to understand the role subjectivity has in interpreting transcendent Truth.

Augustine's interpretive paradigm introduced, for better or worse, morality into hermeneutics: a correct reading is in agreement with correct understanding and behavior. Likewise, the Elizabethan moral aesthetic so beautifully displayed in *F.Q.* relies upon an equation of right understanding with moral uprightness and the avoidance of damning error. However, various episodes in *The Faerie Queene* raise questions about the connection between moral readings and moral behavior. For example, the adventure of Guyon in the Bower of Bliss seems to call for less than temperate and puritanical thoughts on the part of the reader, and such readings suggest that Spenser has allowed his poetic imagery to dismiss his moral lesson. However, the lesson always prevalent to the careful ("worthy") reader of Spenser is that rationality, something which should always take precedent over the senses alone, is in danger of being overcome by the senses; this normalizing lesson in reading is a fine example of the "collective experience that transcends [the work of art] and completes it"[34] which Stephen Greenblatt traces in his classic study of the episode. This episode is another example of the need for both readers of the poem and the heroes of the poem to *read carefully*, and with fore-knowledge of the intended truth ("general intention") in order to understand the true moral aim of the poem.

Rather than claiming that Spenser's moral intention is subdued by his sensual imagery we should read the Bower of Bliss episode as an example of how easy it is to misread and to be seduced by the senses alone. Only a virtuous, attentive and educated reader can avoid this trap. In the words of one critic, the "Bower is lovely in a way that it should not be to a man who is intent on living the temperate, Christian life."[35] The true lesson for a temperate hero (and reader) is that art is only beautiful when it reveals a higher, moral truth; the Bower does not do this, rather, the Bower exists for the senses alone; the opening of canto vi clearly states that:

> A harder lesson, to learne Continence
> In joyous pleasure, then in grievous paine:
> For sweetnesse doth allure the weaker sence
> So strongly, that uneathes it can refraine
> From that, which feeble nature covets faine. (II.vi.1-5)

Taken as a whole, *The Faerie Queene's* allegory exists to contradict "art for arts sake." It is ironic that one of the most controversial passages in the poem, one often cited as an example of Spenser's collapse into sensual poetics, is one of the passages which best illustrates Spenser's intended reading strategy outlined throughout the poem and "Letter to Raleigh."

Another early critic of Spenser's poem, the anonymous author of *Spenserus Redivivus* (1687), makes a clear connection between the courtly poetics of Spenser's poem and "holy Writ," writing that:

> Some there are that would so far unsoul Poesy, as to allow nothing represented by it other than what familiarly resembles the ordinary Results of our Actions and Converse, and this they term likening of Truth; not considering that there is a similitude allowable for Contemplation and Opinions receiv'd by Men ... By which means incorporeal Apparitions have been conceded to appear: and he that denies their Credibility, must likewise disallow the Revelations of holy Writ, which gives authority, more than enough, to Poesy to take that for Truth which is there affirmed to be such.[36]

The author is primarily concerned with the fantastical or supra-natural aspect of Spenser's poem (which it shares with "holy Writ"), but his reasoning for allowing "miracles" into discourse reveals a poetic understanding clearly similar to Digby's. Poetry can speak with the "authority" of "holy Writ" because understanding functions in similar ways with both types of texts.

"Mayd full of divinitie"

All allegories acquire their meaning from above, not from below. Queen Elizabeth is consistently referred to as "higher" than the author or even the various allegorical events. "In mirrours more then one her self to see,/But either *Glorianna* let her chuse,/Or in *Belphoebe* fashioned to bee." The "truths" represented by allegory are spiritual (or quasi spiritual, in the case of Elizabeth) or cultural, i.e. they represent a notion of the world which is far more general than either the poet, reader, or poem. Golding, for example, reads Ovid as a Christian allegory, as a typology of Christian belief, following the order of Genesis. The textual evidence for such a reading is vague at best, and presupposes a mythic understanding of the literal words of Ovid. One *starts* with a Christian understanding and works backwards to the text, imposing an analogical pattern where possible and ignoring those details which do not reflect the analogy. As Michael Murrin writes, "an allegorist can find meanings in a text for which there is absolutely no verbal basis, and he may even reverse his original meanings."[37] The proper model for understanding allegory, according to Murrin, is myth: "A myth, like a metaphor or an extended allegory, is by definition open-ended: it invites interpretation."[38] To mythologize means to return to *origins*, to write stories which explain the lineage and heritage of the world in its present state.³⁹ The *Faerie Queene* justifies Elizabethan culture through a retelling of its history, and does so by allegorizing its very human source, Queen Elizabeth.

Spenser makes his poem, and more importantly its correct meaning, an inextricable product of his society. The difference between those able to correctly understand the poem and those not able to is the difference between those who will have access to *secular* redemption and those who will not. As *The Faerie Queene* makes so clear, the basic allegorical paradigm for reading the poem resided with the State; but the State, in the form of Queen Elizabeth, is also a material signifier necessitating literal interpretation, which as we have seen, is often equated by Protestants with historical continuity. For example, in addition to being a self-fashioned arbiter of Truth, Elizabeth also existed as a member of a Royal Family, and therefore existed historically as part of lineage, a lineage which often put contemporary chronologers in an awkward position. Given the history of Elizabeth's birth and the controversies surrounding her mother and her own birth, Elizabeth's own *body* is of the utmost importance, and Spenser is careful to portray her in an historically flattering light. Elizabeth's employment of her mother's motto, "Semper Edem," suggests both her refusal to turn her back on her mother and her desire to be seen as a paradigm of foundational values. *The Faerie Queene* is, among other things, an attempt at normalizing Elizabeth's history and lineage, utilizing Elizabeth herself as the normalizing trope, as a metaphoric "New Testament."

In his "Letter to Raleigh," Spenser mentions Belphoebe as one of the figurations for Elizabeth in the poem: "For considering she beareth two persons, the one of a most royall Queene or Empresse, the other of a most vertuous and beautifull Lady, this latter part in some places I doe expresse in Belphoebe." Upon seeing Belphoebe for the first time, Timias, whose wounds she is kind enough to heal, falls in love, but immediately realizes the unethical and immoral nature of the lust: "But foolish boy, what bootes thy service bace/To her, to whom the heavens do serve and sew?/Thou a meane Squire, of meeke and lowly place,/She heavenly borne, and of celestriall hue" (IV.iiii.47). Here Spenser is allegorically representing the proper monarch/courtier servant relationship, but it is the "latter part" of Elizabeth's historically defined body which is the source for it: Belphoebe will be described in the very same Christian analogies available to Elizabeth through her own subjugated court poets. Belphoebe, like Britomart, is a chaste virgin, and is described in v.34 as a "Mayd full of divinitie." As such she is a figuration of Christian spirituality *and* earthly lust.

Throughout Book III it is essentially Spenser's aim to "commend ... by their genealogies or pedigrees, their marriages and alliances, their notable exploits in the world for the behoose of mankind." Spenser is clearly moving between two realms, the spiritual and the classical, and by doing so mirrors the complicated aims of Elizabethan pedagogical reforms which often emphasize the need to moralize earlier, classical traditions.

Angus Fletcher writes that "to say that a given work is allegorical is therefore not to say anything about its value, since allegory is only a mode of symbolizing."⁴⁰ Fletcher, however, does point out that allegory's reliance on a limited audience is a hindrance, one which subordinates allegory to "normal" aesthetic judgements. "Obscurity seems to be a price necessarily paid for the lack of a universal, common doctrinal background."[41] I would tend to reverse Fletcher's model and see obscurity as the *result* of a common doctrinal background since the poet is relying upon careful readers to eventually, with effort, lift the veil of allegory; it is just this common background which makes the meaning of allegory comprehensible to those willing to struggle and understand. Common, universal doctrinal understanding is available to all readers through struggle, effort, and prayer/meditation on the universal order, order which for Augustine comes from God's charity, and for Spenser from Elizabeth's infallible persona.

What effect, then, does this undermining of communication have on a poem such as *The Faerie Queene*, a poem which sets out to educate the audience? How can a poem which sets out to educate also set out to deceive? The answer is clear for the Renaissance audience, an audience which accepts complex allegories and veiled truths not only as one means of communication but as the preferred way. Rebuilding the perfect audience for Spenser's allegory—one which understands ambiguity and the need for edification—is certainly an impossibility; but Augustine's model allows us to see how Spenser's communication is, in the end, even if out of our reach, "meaningful," as well as to reaffirm obscurity as a rhetorical tool useful in understanding Spenser's Protestant allegory. Finally, Augustine's deliberate obscurity and ambiguity can be ways of justifying what Coleridge called the "mental space of faerie."[42] Spenser often relies upon misdirection to justify the portrayal of the various heroes of his books, heroes who must exist not only as romantic heroes of a poem, but as real life representations of courtly politics and morals. At the same time, however, he makes it clear what his intention is and how to avoid mistaken or "jealous" reading and textual misdirection. Coleridge seems aware of Spenser's talent for misdirection when he writes of reading Spenser, "The poet has placed you in a dream, a charmed sleep, and you neither wish, nor have the power, to inquire where you are, or how you got there ... Ambiguity is, of course, the very language of dream. And dream is nourishing because it allows the mind to escape from the categories of everyday consciousness."[43]

Elizabeth Bieman writes that "[w]e learn from those critics who 'refuse ... to identify the force of literature with any concept of embodied meaning' as they set themselves against 'logocentric or incarnational perspectives.'"[44] Here Bieman is quoting Geoffrey Hartman's warnings against essentialistic interpretation, and by doing so illustrates the parameters of my discussion. Bieman goes on: "From a more historical perspective, I find it highly improbable that a professedly Christian poet of the Renaissance was involved in exercises denying the bases of his faith." What Bieman means is that at one time a rhetoric was available which allowed for obscure or ambiguous meanings while still reflecting a decipherable meaning. Such an understanding helps to unite the more conservative and formalistic strains of criticism which have been foundational to Spenserian studies with some of the poststructural agendas which concern themselves with the poem's seeming indecipherability, but grounds them both in the pedagogical goal of Reformation England.

The motto found over the door in the house of Busyrane, "Be bold, be bold ... [but] be not too bold" (III.xi.54), is not just a warning against rashness in matters of love but could easily serve as a reminder to all readers of allegory to be careful in assuming either finality or relying too much on subjectivity in their interpretation. What Augustinian rhetoric provided for Spenser was a model of Christian justification and a system for situational self-censorship, while at the same time allowing Spenser to meet his stated goal of educating "a gentleman or noble person in virtuous and gentle discipline."

Notes

1. Miller, *The Poems Two Bodies* (Princeton: Princeton University Press, 1988), 17.

2. See my "Pierre Du Moulin on the Eucharist: Protestant Sign Theory and the Grammar of Embodiement," in *ELH* (65), 1988.

3. Stephen Greenblatt, *Renaissance Self-Fashioning: From More to Shakespeare* (Chicago: University of Chicago Press, 1980), 169.

4. *Ibid.*, 170.

5. Joan Simon, *Education and Society in Tudor England* (Cambridge: Cambridge University Press, 1967), ix.

6. *Ibid.*, 296.

7. A.J. Minnis, *Medieval Theory of Authorship*. 2nd Edition (Philadelphia: University of Pennsylvania Press, 1988), 14.

8. *Ibid.*, 28.

9. *Ibid.*, 29.

10. On the distinct connotation of "material" in this Aristotelian sense, the following from Jonathan Gil Harris' "Shakespeare's Hair: Staging the Object of Material Culture," (*Shakespeare Quarterly* 52.4 (2001), 483-84), is illustrative:

> A long tradition of materialist philosophy has insisted on the diachronic dimension of matter. In *De Anima*, Aristotle drew a critical distinction between 'form' and 'matter,' according to which 'form is actuality' and 'matter is potentiality [dynameos]' (Aristotle, *De Anima* in *The Basic Works of Aristotle*, trans. Richard McKeon, 2 vols. New York: Random House, 1941, 2:555). In other words, Aristotle understood matter as a synonym not for physical presence but for dynamic process; matter, in his writing, is always worked upon. Marx attributed the same meaning to matter in his 'Theses on Feuerbach,' in which he criticized Feuerbach for conceiving matter 'only in the form of the object' (Karl Marx, *Writings of the Young Karl Marx on Philosophy and Society*, trans. Lloyd D.

Easton and Kurt H. Guddat, New York: Doubleday, 1967, 400). Marx understood the materiality of objects to belong to the domain of labor and praxis, and thus to entail diachronic temporality; as Judith Butler has trenchantly observed, Marx conceived of matter 'as a principle of transformation, presuming and inducing a future' (Judith Butler, *Bodies That Matter: On the Discursive Limits of Sex.* New York and London: Routledge, 1993, 31).

11. A. Leigh DeNeef, "Allegory," in *Spenser Encyclopedia*. Ed. A.C. Hamilton (London: Routledge, 1990), 582.

12. *Ibid.* 581.

13. *Ibid.* 581.

14. Walter Benjamin, *The Origin of German Tragic Drama*. Trans. John Osborne (Frankfurt: Suhrkamp Verlag, 1963), 181.

15. A. Bartlett Giamatti. *Play of Double Senses: Spenser's Faerie Queene* (Englewood Cliffs, NJ: Prentice-Hall, Inc., 1975), 83.

16. Quoted in Anne Somerset, *Elizabeth I* (New York: St. Martin's Press, 1991), 71.

17. *Ibid.*, 59

18. Minnis, 29.

19. Richard Puttenham, *The Art of English Poesie*, intro. by Baxter Hathaway (Kent State University Press, 1970), 166.

20. *Ibid.*, 196.

21. Of this same passage Angus Fletcher writes: "While one can justify the Puttenham aesthetic on the Augustinian basis that whatever is acquired with difficulty is more highly valued, and one can invoke the standard Renaissance belief in this view, that is not Puttenham's view." Rather, Fletcher believes, Puttenham is writing for the courtier who must carefully hide his message: "One can politically justify the 'figure of false sembluant' when the status quo is being maintained by censorship from above, since at such time the model would allow the writer to attack" (*Allegory: The Theory of a Symbolic Mode* (Ithaca: Cornell University Press, 1964), 331).

22. Facsimile edition, 1961, 45.

23. Michael Murrin, *The Veil of Allegory: Some Notes Toward a Theory of Allegorical Rhetoric in the English Renaissance* (Chicago: University of Chicago Press, 1969), 74.

24. A.C. Hamilton, *The Structure of Allegory in The Faerie Queene* (Oxford: Clarendon Press, 1961), 9.

25. Benjamin, 177.

26. All quotes and references to the poem are to *The Faerie Queene*, edited by A.C. Hamilton (New York: Longman Press, 1977).

27. Joel Fineman, "The Structure of Allegorical Desire." In *Allegory and Representation: Selected Papers from the English Institute, 1979-80*. Edited, with a Preface, by Stephen J. Greenblatt (Baltimore: Johns Hopkins Press, 1981), 33.

28. *Ibid.*, 29.

29. In the dedication to the 1596 edition of the poem Spenser claims that the poem will "liue with the eternitie of her [Elizabeth's] fame," thus affirming that the truth of the poem is divine and supra-natural.

30. Sean Kane, *Spenser's Moral Allegory* (Toronto: Toronto University Press, 1989), 5.

31. Kane, 18.

32. Quoted in Isabel Rivers, *Classical and Christian Idea in English Renaissance Poetry* (London: George Allen and Unwin, 1979), 178. Originally found in BM MS. Harleian 4153 (Cummings, *Critical Heritage*, 147).

33. The Folger library contains a second edition French printing of St Augustine's *The Confessions* which contains a preface addressed "To the Reader" which John F. Fulton (in *Kenelm Digby*, 67) attributes to Kenelm Digby. If this assertion is correct then we have even stronger textual evidence for Digby's attempt to impose an Augustinian interpretive order on *The Faerie Queene*.

34. Greenblatt, 179.

35. Okerlund, 67. In another article concerned with the artifice of the Bower of Bliss episode, Hans Guth writes that "He [Spenser] does not impose over-all symbolic correspondences, such as modern criticism encourages us to look for in literary works. In short, his method is allegory rather than symbolism" ("Allegorical Implications of Artifice in Spenser's *Faerie Queene*," by Hans P. Guth, *PMLA* lxxvi (1961): 474-9). Guth's contention that part of the problem with reading this episode in a way consistent with the poem as a whole is that at times it seems that Spenser is contradicting himself; for example, throughout the poem Spenser praises artifice and ornamentation, so the problem with the Bower of Bliss cannot be simply that it is artificial. Guth's interpretive strategy allows him to rightfully note that a careful reader will understand where the Bower of Bliss exceeds acceptable artifice and becomes evil. An essentialistic reading of every example of artifice in the poem will inevitably lead to misunderstanding.

36. Quoted in Cummings, 219.

37. *Ibid.*, 140.

38. *Ibid.*, 99.

39. This definition of allegory stands in stark contrast to the model of allegory forwarded by Henri De Lubac, who in his classical *Medieval Exegesis*, notes that allegory in a Christian sense is different, ontologically, than allegory in a classical sense; Christian allegory is essentially true; allegory in a classical sense may be mythic and fictional. Christian allegory and the literal are not separable—quoting Stephen Langton, De Lubac notes that "History ... is the foundation of allegory" (Eerdmans: Grand Rapids, MI, vol. 2, 49). From the discussion which follows, it should be clear that Spenser is appropriating a classical and mythic understanding of allegory, but at key moments in his text he returns to a Christian model, especially in terms of how his allegory is to be read.

40. *Ibid.*, 358.

41. *Ibid.*, 359.

42. Kane, 22.

43. *Ibid.*, 187.

44. Bieman, 11.

Chapter 8

Lily, Latin Literacy and "Enfranchisement" in Shakespeare's *Love's Labour's Lost* and *Two Gentlemen of Verona*

> Remuneration! Why it is a fairer name than French crown. I will never buy and sell out of this word.
>
> (*Love's Labour's Lost*, III.i.132-138)

Ernst Cassirer notes a fundamental and practical aspect of Post-Reformation humanism: "But even the humanism of the Renaissance was no mere scholarly movement; for it, too, in such great minds as Erasmus, embodied a universal educational and cultural ideal which resolutely encountered life head on."[1] At the foundation of this pedagogical reformation was the teaching of classical languages, most specifically Latin, and the importance of Latin pedagogy is illustrated in the following from Martin Luther in a "Letter to the Mayors and Aldermen of all Cities of Germany in Behalf of Christian Schools," who compared the attitude of those who would argue that learning classical languages was a waste of time to those who would argue "to what use to us are silk, wine, spices, and other foreign articles, since we ourselves have an abundance?"[2] The logic of Luther's metaphor equates abundance with vernaculars, suggesting that classical languages are a rarity and a luxury. Correspondingly, silk, wine and spices are luxuries since they have an exchange value, at least metaphorically, based on their availability. Luther's equation relies upon an acknowledgment that language can be metaphorically reduced to a material commodity, i.e. a unit of exchange. The Lutheran Reformation "resolutely encountered life head on" because it saw that the need to learn was connected, at least partially, with the need to believe, and as a result the Reformation led to a reformation of education throughout Europe. In the course of this reformation many of the key distinctions between secular and religious motives and goals were broken down, with the result that the State sought to control not only individual belief, but all aspects of education and literacy.

Furthermore, the need to learn Latin was a nationalistic one; Luther wrote in response to his country's lack of classical literacy: "Are we not rightly called German dunces and brutes?" For Luther, the use of classical Latin justified the modern state; in order for Latin to do so, the learning of it must itself be motivated by real and pressing everyday issues, not just the desire for knowledge or access to classical texts. On the other hand, the spreading use of vernaculars emphasized the distinction between literature and life, as it allowed for a language which could be used for everyday situations and a more distant and exotic literary language.

"[F]airer name than French crown"

The importance placed upon classical training which resulted in England having an official Latin grammar ten years before an official Bible is the same emphasis which I see as an important influence on *Love's Labour's Lost* and *Two Gentlemen of Verona*, as well as throughout Shakespeare's comedies. The use of language education and acquisition was not only thematically important to Shakespeare's comic intentions, but they served as philological exemplars of a new way of conceiving of language and meaning. Shakespeare's comedies exemplify these issues because they represent some of the complications which resulted from Protestant Reformation educational reforms, complications which were reflected in the discord between power and individuality, and between upper-class homogeneity and lower-class heterogeneity. These disruptions are played out in Shakespeare's comedies. The learning and utilization of Latin was just one manifestation of these controversies, but as *Love's Labour's Lost* makes clear, it was a fundamental one for many reasons.

Love's Labour's Lost reflects two defining attributes of the Reformation: the use of vernaculars to disseminate the Word of God and the utilization of classical languages to understand the literal Word of God. Both attributes reflect the goal of universalized access to texts while simultaneously limiting and controlling their interpretation. Indeed, the separation of *dissemination* and *understanding* are themselves problematic since Reformation exegesis emphasized the importance of universal access to the Word of God through individual faith, not centralized interpretation. Widespread understanding of classical languages could solve both goals by freeing the individual conscience and by breaking the Catholic Church's monopoly on interpretation. Therefore, rather than seeing vernacular and classical languages as opposing factors, a more dynamic view of Reformation humanism suggests that it was profoundly influenced by the coexistence of both a literary/historical language and a vernacular. It is this coexistence, as we shall see, which defines many of the comic exchanges found in Shakespeare's comedies.

Luther's union of the practical and the patriotic in his reference to "silk, wine, spices, and other foreign articles" reflects the widening audience for Latin learning. Both the nationalistic and everyday uses of Latin are illustrated in the following often cited passage from *Love's Labour's Lost*:

> Now will I look to his remuneration. Remuneration! O that's the Latin word for three farthings: three farthings, remuneration. 'What's the price of this inkle?' 'One penny': 'No, I'll give you a remuneration': why, it carries it. Remuneration! why it is a fairer name than French crown. I will never buy and sell out of this word. (III.i.132-138)[3]

Much has been written about this passage. William Carroll writes that "the scene suggests the equation, already hinted at before in Costard's various errors, of sound=thing. The strange sound becomes a thing, completely apart from its connection with a coin."[4] Later Carroll notes that for Costard "remuneration" becomes a literal, and therefore useful, verbal coin. But it is important to note that Costard is aware that his transference is a verbal act since he states "O that's the Latin word for three farthings." In other words, his fascination, which as Carroll notes borders on reverence, takes the form of a conscious *metaphor*. It is also important to note that technically Costard's transference is not an error since he has not mistaken the meaning of the word so much as substituted a very specific meaning for a more general one. In short, he has made the word more useful while maintaining a reverential and spiritual relationship to it. His appropriation of the terms, I would argue, follows the pedagogical models which defined the Latin texts examined earlier: the purpose of Latin study and its primary role is as a companion to English, not as an end in itself.

In the end, Costard has taken a general term for payment and "translated" it into a very specific and useful unit of currency; in so doing he has utilized Latin for patriotic ends ("why it is a fairer name than French crown"). For Costard, access to classical languages gives him both power and authority. Costard follows the model set by Luther: classical languages are practical and material, which allows them to be utilized for nationalistic purposes, purposes reflected in Luther's equation of silks and foreign articles with classical languages. More importantly, by emphasizing the importance and practicality of Latin, Costard's speech reminds us of the centrality of pedagogy to the play. On one side are the wealthy lords and royalty who are sequestering themselves in order to create a humanistic academy, and on the other side are the laborers, and at the beginning of the play when the young lords opt to remove themselves from the material world via their academy, it is the servants who are brought in to serve as their bridge to the "outside" material world. But of course, since this is a comedy, the distinction between "inside" and "outside" is complicated (but never eliminated). The whole play takes its comic motivation from teacher/student relationships and the corresponding class distinctions; however, the play is unique in that all of the characters are isolated by their pedagogical pursuits, and only the women, who are ethically victorious in the end, are in any way grounded by the "real" world. The student/pedagogues of the play are generally quite foolish, and except for the women, no character can be said to be stable and above comic reproach. This lack of stability is reflected in the lack of a central pedagogical ethic or philological model by which the characters can be judged. Despite this lack of stability, however, *Love's Labour's Lost* is dominated by the world of pedagogy in the same way *A Midsummer Night's Dream* is dominated by the world of magic and faeries.

As Patricia Parker notes, Shakespeare often stages links between "humanist discipline and its influential links with the apparatus of civil power"; she notes, for example, that among Jack Cade's numerous complaints aimed at the power elite is that they have:

> most traitorously corrupted the youth of the realm in erecting a grammar school; and whereas, before, our forefathers had no other books but the score

and tally, thou has caused printing to be used, and contrary to the King his crown and dignity thou hast built a paper mill. It will be proved to thy face that thou hast men about thee that usually talk of a noun and a verb and such abominable words as no Christian ear can endure to hear. Thou hast appointed justices of the peace to call poor men before them about matters they were not able to answer. Moreover, thou hast put them in prison, and because they could not read thou hast hanged them, when indeed only for that cause they have been most worthy to live. (*2 Henry VI*, IV.vii.30-43)[5]

Although Cade's comically absurd accusations are politically motivated and reflect real social anxieties in the face of a changing conception of literacy, Shakespeare, in many of his early comedies, portrays hyper-concern for linguistic stability or correctness, and the resulting need for pedagogical authority, as comic: see for example, the Schoolmaster from *Two Noble Kinsmen*, Evans from *Merry Wives of Windsor*, and Holofernes from *Love's Labour's Lost*, who are all examples of pedagogues used for comic purposes. For example, in act IV, scene ii of *Love's Labour's Lost*, Holofernes corrects Nathaniel's use of Latin: "You find not the apostrophus, and so miss the accent" (l. 115-16). Later, in act V, Holofernes gives a lecture on the correct pronunciation of "debt." In the much later *Two Noble Kinsmen*, the Schoolmaster clearly summarizes the normalizing and authoritative role pedagogues play in Renaissance society: "By title pedagogus, that let fall/The birch upon the breeches of the small ones/And humble with a ferula the tall ones" (III.v.109-11). What each of these characters has in common is a notion of fixity, or correctness, in language, a fixity which is contrasted to the "malapropisms" and puns of lower-class characters and the wit (and punning) of upper-class characters.

In this sense, the lower-class characters are the comic "heroes" of many of Shakespeare's comedies since they are not imprisoned by the same notions of fixity as pedagogues and some upper-class characters. For example, in Launce's first speech in the play, opening act II, scene iii, he confuses Latinate words such as "proportion" with "portion" and "prodigious" with "prodigal," thus creating alternative but nonetheless meaningful utterances. Compared with Speed, Launce seemingly lacks education and by extension, linguistic competency and creativity. In this case, and in many others throughout the play, Launce is attempting to *sound* more educated and more literate than he really is by appropriating words which he has undoubtedly *overheard* from the upper-class characters with whom he is in contact throughout the play and with whom he has an economic relationship. The same reliance upon sound over print can be found in Costard from *Love's Labour's Lost* and, of course, Dogberry from *Much Ado about Nothing*, to cite just two examples.

Specifically, *The Two Gentlemen of Verona* reflects Shakespeare's comic reversal of pedagogical stability by emphasizing individuality (wit) and destabilization (puns), via spoken, as opposed to overtly stable written, language, and it does so while emphasizing the continued importance of literacy to all of English society. Although Latin literacy is not as prevalent a theme in *Two Gentlemen* as it is in *LLL* and *MWW*, for example, there is a clear privileging of the spontaneous spoken over the more "stable," but never effective, at least in this play, written word. The play seems to take this concept one step further: the written word is not trustworthy and reading is important only if it leads to wit and conversation.[6] This is seen between the two characters in the following exchange, where the two characters, Speed and Launce, test each other's literacy:

> Sp. Let me read them.
> La. Fie on thee, jolt-head, thou canst not read.
> Sp. Thou lyest; I can.
> La. I will try thee. Tell me this: who begot thee?
> Sp. Marry, the son of my grandfather.
> La. O illiterate loiterer! It was the son of thy Grand-mother: this proues that thou canst not read. (III.i .285-291)

This exchange begins with Launce reading a list of his love's qualities (itself a nod toward normative Petrarchan literary conceits), and it is his task to test his fellow servant Speed. For Launce, all knowledge, including knowledge of one's origins, comes from the ability to read, an ability which Speed possesses, as he goes on to prove in the exchange which follows. Launce jokes on Speed's list of his lover's attributes—the whole exchange could be seen as an opportunity for Speed to improvise his wit using printed material as his source. For example, when Speed reads that one of Launce's beloved's vices is that she is "slow in words," Launce replies, "To be slow in words is a woman's only virtue" (III.i.326-7). Obviously, among the lower-class characters, literacy is the domain of men only, as was much of the education system (see for example, Walter Ong's "Latin Language Study as a Renaissance Puberty Rite."[7] Similar examples of women excluded from literacy occur in *Love's Labour's Lost* and *Merry Wives of Windsor*.) In terms of interacting in the world and with others, it is wit (or, in the words of Lily's grammar, "conversation"), not reading, which is most beneficial and rewarding.

Granted, this is a great deal of weight to put upon the shoulders of Shakespeare's comic intentions, but it does allow for a better understanding of what makes the characters funny as characters for an Elizabethan audience and helps us to understand better the inherent theatricality of some of Shakespeare's now obscure "quibbling." The tension found within the play between Launce and Speed, and between these two characters and the more privileged upper-class characters, is appropriated by Shakespeare in the development of the theme of literacy and education. For example, these exchanges by lower-class characters stand in relief with the speech of characters such as Thurio and Valentine, who calls the former an "exchequr of words" (II.iv.29-42) who has nothing else of worth to give but his words:

> Val. I know it well, sir, you always end ere you begin.
> Sil. A fine volley of words, gentlemen, and quickly shot off.
> Val. Tis indeed, madam: we thank the giver.
> Sil. Who is that, servant?
> Val. Yourself, sweet lady, for you gave the fire. Sir Thurio borrows his wit from your ladyship's looks, and spends what he borrows kindly in your company.

Thur.   Sir, if you spend word for word with me, I shall make your wit bankrupt.
Val.   I know it well: you have an exchequer of words, and I think no other treasure to give your followers; for it appears by their bare liveries that they live by your bare words.

Both Valentine and Thurio and Speed and Launce are interested in showing that their language abilities are superior. Therefore, the important distinction between literate and ill (or "less") literate is fought out within all classes rather than between classes. More importantly, both pairings suggest that at some level language is money, and money is an important, perhaps the most important, source of social connectiveness. As a result, the "volley of words" (II.iv.33) between these two characters (and between Launce and Speed) reflects the extent to which language use must be creative and connotative in order to be truly effective in defining one's place in society. But this exchange reveals even more about the importance of literacy—there is a clear economic metaphor at work: it is possible to run out of words, to become bankrupt, or, as in the case of Thurio, to have only bare words, and nothing else. In a play in which payment to servants is seen (at least by the servants) as an act not only of goodwill but of an indication of virtue, Valentine's comments serve to undermine Thurio's character. Wit is a commodity of very real worth, and is, usually, manifested in spoken language. Often, it is manifested in the ability to creatively destabilize meaning, as it is in the following exchange between Proteus and Speed, who are quibbling over the word "noddy:"

Pro.   No, no, you shall have it for bearing the letter.
Spe.   Well, I perceive I must be fain to bear with you.
Pro.   Why, sir, how do you bear with me?
Spe.   Marry, sir, the letter very orderly, having nothing but the word noddy' for my pains.
Pro.   Beshrew me, but you have a quick wit. (I.i.115-20)

For his reward in delivering the letter (and his puns?), Speed demands that Proteus "open [his] purse, that the money and the matter may be both at once delivered." Speed is wise enough to know that the written letter is "orderly," but his significant puns, which run throughout the exchange, are anything but "orderly." Similar to Valentine's comment to Thurio above, Speed acknowledges that one cannot live on "words" alone, a speaker or deliverer must be rewarded. Again, the value of language lies in the spoken.[8]

The economic significance of language education for the upper class is revealed when, in the second line of the play, Valentine notes that "Home-keeping youth, haue euer homely wits," a pronouncement which comes true when, in act IV, scene i, the second outlaw asks Valentine, "Have you the tongues?," to which Valentine responds, "My youthful travel, therein made me happy,/Or else I often had beene often miserable" (33-5). With this affirmation, Valentine is accepted into outlaw society: "And partly seeing you are beautified/With goodly shape; and by your own report,/A linguist, and a man of such perfection,/As we do in our quality much want." The importance of "tongues" and wit extends from the ordered city to the outlaw Green World. In this sense, Valentine is truly a gentleman in the most stereotypical Renaissance manner: he is well-educated in languages. But this moment in the play also suggests an even deeper importance for language ability—his gift of "tongues" literally saves Valentine's life (assuming that one sees the Outlaws as real dangers).

The Two Gentlemen of Verona is one of only two Shakespearian comedies (along with *The Merchant of Venice*) to specify class in its title; what makes the two title characters "gentlemen" is their language ability. However, the play resists the notion that only gentlemen are eloquent and witty; instead, a great deal of comic energy is spent parodying the notion of both eloquence and pedagogy, a telling combination at the heart of Shakespeare's comic intentions. Rather than being distinguished for their language abilities, I would argue, Proteus and Valentine's linguistic abilities foreground them in a dramatic and parodic dialectic with members of the lower classes, a dialectic which suggests that Shakespeare was satirizing the pedagogical standards and norms of his time.

For example, the importance of pedagogical texts is illustrated at lines 16-20 of scene i of act II:

> Val.   Why, how know you that I am in love?
> Speed. Marry, by these special marks: first, you haue learned (like Sir
>   Proteus) to wreath your arms like a malcontent; to relish a
>   love-song, like a robin red-breast; to walk alone, like one that
>   had the pestilence, to sigh, like a schoolboy that had lost his
>   ABC.[9]

"A schoole-boy" who has lost his grammar books joins Love songs, sighing lovers, or Robin red breasts as literary images, or "markes," as shared knowledge and objects of satire for Shakespeare's audience. Throughout the play Shakespeare appropriates literary and cultural artifacts in order to parody them; for example, Shakespeare uses Marlowe's "Hero and Leander" as an ironic referent throughout the play: although Valentine makes repeated reference to Marlowe's lovers, Shakespeare makes it clear that he is anything but a tragic lover. Petrachian conceits are also appropriated (as they are in the above passage) and highlighted by Shakespeare as fashionably normative codes which, in the course of his play, become objects of satire. In this case, the normative referent is a schoolboy's ABC, or grammar lesson; for Shakespeare and his audience, there was not a more popular, and therefore normative, ABC than Lily's grammar. Many of the misunderstandings in *The Two Gentlemen of Verona* and *Love's Labour's Lost* can be traced to an assumption that the usual equation of eloquence=class is valid for all comedies. Eloquence, in a pedagogical and vernacular sense, is different from eloquence in a humanistic sense, and *Love's Labour's Lost* reflects a society defined by pedagogy. The play self-consciously reflects the pedagogical constraints which result from the clash of a vernacular ontology with a classical one.

"Vernacular" Latin

Not only did Lily's grammar privilege spoken over written discourse, its very existence as an officially sanctioned text suggests that Latin literacy and advanced language skills were not simply for the privileged "gentlemen;" in fact, in most of the instances where Shakespeare references Lily's grammar, he does so either by a lower-class character or by a foolish pedagogue, thus suggesting that its existence as a universally available text was what lent it its comic potential. Many of Shakespeare's early plays reflect a society in which verbal representation is unstable, while also central to social conformity. This "paradigm crisis" is fodder for the basic subversive, yet ultimately conformist, structure of comedy. Over and over we find characters struggling to use the right sounding word for a given situation, regardless of the word's denotative meaning (Dogberry's "Thou shall be condemned into everlasting redemption for this"[10]); young students trying to learn and utilize a new language (*Merry Wives of Windsor*, *Taming of the Shrew*, *Henry V*); and, most frequently in the comedies, characters punning on words so as to destabilize the word's denotative meaning. These various situations reflect a world in which language is simultaneously mutable and foundational.

As we noted earlier, the reformation of the English educational system focused a great deal on litteratus, the learning of Latin grammar, which created a new way of speaking and understanding shared experience, one which Marc Bloch notes "forced [those who used it] to resort to perpetual approximations in the expression of their thoughts."[11] These comedies often emphasize the ironic juxtaposition of stability and approximation. By decentralizing meaning, by suggesting that the same meaning could appear in more than one language, and that one language reflected only tentative and situational meaning, the simultaneous rise of vernaculars and classical Latin highlighted the philological challenge which was at the root of the Reformation.

It is also true that with the rise of vernaculars Latin became at least partially an historical language, and as such a "dead" language with only minor relevance to everyday life. However, as the Costard example above illustrates, what relevance it did have was based upon its "vernacularization" into English. Costard is approximating his thoughts by utilizing, in an English context, a Latin word. At the same time that Costard is utilizing the word in a very practical way, and by repeating the word, he is seemingly viewing it as magical and incantational, as if it holds some unknowable and unutterable meaning.

The juxtaposition of practical/vernacular uses and abstract/foreign uses is again seen in the following exchange between Costard and Armado:

> Moth. Wonder, master! here's a costard broken in shin.
> Arm. Some enigma, some riddle: come thy l'envoy; begin.
> Cost. No egma, no riddle, no l'envoy; no salve in the mail, sir. O, sir, plantain, a plain plantain! no l'envoy, no l'envoy: no salve, sir, but a plantain!

Although there have been a number of well-educated and argued attempts at explaining this colloquial exchange, no editor has satisfactorily glossed the references. It seems clear that Costard is assuming, from the context, that "l'envoy" is some fancy French cure for his aches, but he wants a simple (and domestic) cure, a plantain. Moth, who usually puns effortlessly between languages, also assumes that "l'envoy" must be a "salve." This misunderstanding provides fodder for the numerous puns which follow, all of which are based upon a misunderstanding of the aural, as opposed to textual, representations of words. The fact that "l'envoy" means a moral or conclusion to an exchange, provides a subtle and ironic touch—in the world of bilingual puns and constant verbal sparring as a means of exchange, the final meaning of any word is inevitably withheld and delayed. Likewise, "salve" usually serves as a greeting, and should come at the beginning of the exchange.[12] The term "l'envoy" serves as a refrain as the play continues and becomes Shakespeare's way of signaling this type of linguistic exchange. Through its use Shakespeare highlights the central comic inversion of philological meaning which defines many of the comic characters and situations of the play.

What makes Armado a comic character, in contrast, is his pretentious misuse of language against the backdrop of the witty colloquialisms and punning of Moth and Costard. Note his response to Costard's "mistake:" "By virtue, thou enforcst laughter; they silly thought my spleen; the heaving of my lungs provokes me to ridiculous smiling: O, pardon me, my stars! Doth the inconsiderate take salve for l'envoy, and the word l'envoy for a salve?" Armado's discourse is often marked by the overuse of Latinate words and sentence structure. Unlike that of Costard and Moth, his language is overly stable to the point of being dead. The whole exchange is based upon mutual criticism about the other's use of language and manner of representation. Armado's mention of "a salve" suggests that he understands Costard's confusion to lie in seeing a specific and utilitarian meaning in a term meant to be abstract and general. This is the movement that most of the confusion in the play takes, replacing general meaning with a more specific (and utilitarian) meaning.

With the simultaneous use of both vernaculars and Latin, all Latin use is to some extent utilitarian. Shakespeare's thematic use of Latin acquisition reflects this utilitarianism in that any attempt to stabilize Latin is seen as foolish and unproductive. Throughout the play "false Latin" is juxtaposed with classical Latin, yet there is no character who speaks consistent and correct classical Latin. In act V of *LLL*, Armado illustrates the unintentional pun (on Armado's part) of using Latinate words in a vernacular setting: "for I must tell thee, it will please his grace, by the world, sometime to lean upon my poor shoulder, and with his royal finger, thus, dally with my excrement, with my mustachio" (V.i.93-5). Armado is a laughable character because he thinks he makes sense, which he does, but only to the dead. His language does not show the brilliance assigned to those who are truly witty. Armado's seeming mistake is a pun only to those who also hear "excrement" as an Anglo word, i.e. the audience and the other characters. For the listening audience, Armado has made the same sort of spoken pun that characterizes the lower-class characters, but he has done so unwittingly. Shakespeare's stagecraft is effective in the scenes between these characters for it reveals to the audience both a character's comic personality and the social relationships between characters. Shakespeare's comedies especially remind us that puns are inherently theatrical because they allow the audience to empathize with the most comic and witty characters. Additionally, puns are verbal since they only work when a word is heard, as opposed to read. The "vulgar" vernacular is the source of puns and witty exchanges, and it is through the vernacular that *LLL* reflects a "vulgarizing" of classical Latin for comic effect. Many of the play's most humorous moments are a result of bilingual puns. These puns depict the changing nature of Latin: neither vernaculars nor Latin have the sole position of referent, rather, it is the translation or transformation of meaning which occurs across languages and cultures which produces useful meaning.

This creative use of punning is also seen in *The Merry Wives of Windsor* where Shakespeare again uses an exchange between pretentious teacher of Latin and naive listener. In Act 4, scene I Evans is teaching William his Latin lesson, and Mistress Quickly puns on the Latin words with their comic English equivalents:

> Evans *Nominativo, hic, haeg, hog.* Pray you mark: *genetivo, huius.* Well, what is your accusative case?
> William *Accusativo, hinc.*
> Evans I pray you have your remembrance child. *Accusativo, hung, hang, hoc.*
> Quickly 'Hang-hoc' is Latin for bacon, I warrant you. (38-44)

Here Shakespeare is taking his pedagogical example (with some liberties in pronunciation) from the Lily/Colet grammar example for pronoun declensions.[13] (It can be safely assumed that "hic, haec, hoc" was a marked characteristic of Lily's grammar, for in 1641, Thomas Farnaby in his *Systema Grammaticum*, one of the texts published in an attempt to supplant Lily, wrote that the "memories of children were perplexed and clogg'd with *hic, haec, hoc*").[14] Likewise, in *The Taming of the Shrew*, Tranio quotes Terence via Lily's grammar: "Redime te captum quam queas minimo" ("Ransom yourself from capitvity as cheaply as you can") (I.i.162). Again, in *The Two Noble Kinsmen*, it is Terence who is quoted, again in a phrase contained in Lily's grammar: "Proh Deum! Medicus Fidius!" (III.v.11). This line is especially telling since it is uttered by the Schoolmaster who is showing his frustration at the inability of the lower-class characters to understand him. After the above passage, Mistress Quickly puns on caret/root and horum/whore, in each case transferring meaning from the stable textual referent Evans has in mind to a vernacular spoken "Latin" via a pun. In her brilliant commonsensical manner, Quickly chastises Evans for teaching such words: "He teaches him to hick and to hack, which they'll do fast enough of themselves, and to call 'horum'" (60-61). Again, the wittiest characters see Latin as a vernacular language, a living language capable of puns. As Patricia Parker notes, this scene reverses the "officially prescribed sequence of following and response—the scholar's exercise of translation from Latin or the *sermo patrius*—is subverted by the vagrancy of a schoolboy called Will Page and by Mistress Quickly's unschooled vernacular."[15] The result is that "translation—literally a carrying or transporting away—is here transported beyond both father tongue and the official *Grammar's* system of control. Latin returns not to Latin ... but rather escapes into meanings that betray their original, wandering too far afield to be called back or reigned in."[16]

Although these bilingual puns are the result of a complete ignorance of Latin, they function much like the puns in *LLL* in that they are verbal and reflect enfranchisement of Latin terms. Evans, like Armado, chastises Mistress Quickly for not paying enough attention to Latin grammar: "Hast thou no understandings for thy cases, and the numbers of the genders? Thou art as foolish a Christian creature as I would desire" (63-5). For Mistress Page, who is amazed by her son's knowledge, Latin is every bit as incantational as it is for Costard.[17]

From a Reformation standpoint, the concept of Latin as a stable and "mystical" language is medieval. Reformation theology had managed to divest Latin of its stature as the language of worship, and therefore many comic episodes result from treating Latin in a "medieval" manner. The extent to which medieval English citizens were well-versed in Latin is open to debate, but as Eamon Duffy has noted, the utilization of Latin in spiritual matters did not presuppose complete competency in the language. In fact, the use of Latin in the forms of liturgical hymns and prayers reflected the kind of magical and incantational uses to which Costard puts Latin. For medieval users, Latin was a spoken language, one which had powers, even if the meaning was obscure, as a result of its production, either by a priest or by worshipers. Duffy notes that Latin primers "were books of prayers, to be recited, rather than sacred objects mediating grace or power simply by being handled or contemplated."[18] Costard likewise recites his new Latin word in order to bring out its mystical qualities. At the same time, however, it should be noted that one of the Protestant pronouncements against Catholicism was the use of obscure tongues in religious services; for example, John Donne asks: "Are the Scriptures delivered, and explicated to them? so much of the Scriptures is read to them, in their Lessons and Epistles, and Gospels, is not understood when it is read, for it is in an unknown language; so that, that way, the Holy Ghost teaches them nothing."[19] But as we shall see, the most popular Latin treatises in Reformation England emphasized the speaking of Latin while also emphasizing the otherwise practical nature of Latin as a companion to English. Costard represents a character caught between the medieval adulation of Latin and a Reformation suspicion of it, and the play reflects this dichotomy and utilizes it for comic purposes.

"Enfranchisement" and Lily's Grammar

The text most influential on Shakespeare's conception of Latin pedagogy was the Lily–Colet primer, which was itself a product of Reformation pedagogical reform. It is probable that the specific text William Shakespeare was using in *Merry Wives of Windsor* and *Love's Labour's Lost* was the 1577 printing. As we have seen, the Lily–Colet grammar was one of the most popular texts of the sixteenth and seventeenth centuries, and its influence is seen in the linguistic sparing in *Love's Labour's Lost*. T.W. Baldwin notes that the text was so commonly known that it is "[n]o wonder the Elizabethan dramatists, even Shakespeare, could quote at will more or less learned tags from Lily's Grammar—by their time the only approved one—with full expectation of being understood. He who knew not that knew nothing."[20] The play's indebtedness to this pedagogical text is one reason why it is considered to be Shakespeare's most contemporary play. The grammar reflects, as does the play, the tensions inherent in the move away from medievalism to Protestantism, and it is ironically this tension which makes the play so contemporary. The observation that *LLL* contains references to Elizabethan persons or situations is not new. My argument is that what lends some contemporaneity to the play is its utilization of classical humanistic training as its defining comic attribute. I am not interested in adding yet another layer to the already dense field of *LLL* criticism which reads the play as an allegory of contemporary society. However, *LLL* is the most contemporary of Shakespeare's early comedies precisely because it is, in its language and references, the most classical.

Costard's reverential use of Latin reflects the spiritual conception of it, while his specific utilization of it as a unit of exchange reflects more the nature of Latin. As I have already suggested, the practicality of Latin often results in a conception of language as a commodity. This is reflected in *The Elementarie* (1582) where Richard Mulcaster champions the practice of "enfranchising" foreign terms, to take foreign words and make them "becom English to serve our nede, as their peple ar to thank our tung, for returning the like help, in cases of like nede, tho their occasions to use ours be nothing so often, as ours to use theirs."[21] By "enfranchisment" Mulcaster means that the words "become bond to the rules of our writing, which I haue named before, as the stranger denisions to the lawes of our countrie."[22] Mulcaster is suggesting that foreign words are exchangeable commodities, but that English owes more of a "debt" to foreign languages than foreign languages do to English: "for returning the like help, in cases of like nede, tho their occasions to use ours be nothing so often, as ours to use theirs." Mulcaster emphasizes the utility of words to serve specific purpose, and from that use alone they gain their worth.

The movement Mulcaster is suggesting is between different vernaculars and between vernaculars and classical languages, but the result is the same, a dynamic exchange of words. "It is best for the strange words to yield to our lawes, because we are both their usuaries and fructuaries." Grammar is prior in Mulcaster's conception of foreign language acquisition, since he equates it with "lawes," with vocabulary becoming merely a source for developing the vernacular. Mulcaster's famous remark that "I love Rome, but London better, I favor Italie, but England more, I honor the Latin, but I worship the English"[23] serves as a reminder of the limits and contexts in which English classical studies existed: throughout *LLL* the characters honor Latin through their mystification and misuse of it, while they show the worship and love they have for English by enfranchising the Latin to it. Latin is a utilitarian language—it is important, but its role can safely be confined to proper situations and for certain rhetorical ends. The use of Latin became questionable when it was seen to supplant English or was used as an end ("enjoyed" as opposed to "used," to use an Augustinian paradigm). For these reasons Latin possessed a unique place in English culture: it was of the utmost practical importance, but it was also subject to corruption. Shakespeare thematically utilizes this dichotomy in order to create comic situations which remind his viewers of real pedagogical controversies, and also remind them that language is often the most telling trait in defining a person's class and socio-economic status.

For example, the notion of economic bonding is seen in Act III when Armado reminds Costard of his hold and position over him: "Sirrah Costard, I will enfranchise thee." Costard hears a different, earthier and less "latinate" word, however: "O! marry me to one Frances—I smell some l'envoy, some goose in this" (III.i.118-20). Beyond the fact that "goose" is slang for "prostitute," the real irony of this exchange is deepened with the realization that, as we noted earlier, "l'envoy" means a moral, or final word, while Costard's vernacular use of it prevents this very closure and leads to a whole new set of connotations. For both Mulcaster and Shakespeare the term "enfranchise" suggests the dynamic nature of language across linguistic borders. This movement, however, is checked by the need to put the new term into the new language. For both Mulcaster and Shakespeare, it is the practical and vernacular which takes precedence.

Latin pedagogical texts and Latin dictionaries of the time often sought to further the understanding of classical languages from two perspectives: one, as an ancient language better capable of reflecting fixed meaning, especially spiritual meaning, and second as a source for new and more useful English words. Both of these perspectives counter the notion that Latin was merely a "dead" language. What is clear is that it existed as a "living" language only to the extent to which it could be "used." And it could be used for two very different yet central purposes: first as an ontological means for understanding the Word of God, and second, as a practical end or goal of pedagogical effort. The second of these uses was dependent upon the first, yet it is clear when examining contemporary treatises that they are dependent upon Reformation ideals of interpretation and spiritual manifestation. Again we see this dichotomy reflected in Mulcaster's *Elementarie*: on the one hand, "For grammar of it self is but the bare rule, and a verie naked thing" and on the other:

> doth it not I praie you, show us Englishmen a verie great pleasure, it if help to the finding of our own English tongue, & thereby to make it to be of such account, as other tongues be, which be therefor of best account, because they be so fined? whereby we ourselves also shall seeme not to be barbarous, even by mean of our tongue, seeing fair speech is some parcell of praise, and a great argument of a well civilized people.

Like Luther before him, for Mulcaster Latin was a way of appearing more civilized and fair of speech, but only in a broad social context where language had an exchange value. Languages, like material goods, were valuable only in relation to other material goods. Likewise, languages were valuable when the best of one language could be compared with the best of another, and both languages benefit from the exchange. Foreign languages, like money, must be stable and exchangeable; capable of always reflecting one referent while also capable of being "enfranchised" by another system of referents.

Mulcaster views Latin as both a stable referent (it is the "source" of English, and from the source comes stability and civility) and as a dynamic language, capable of enfranchisement. Similarly, in seeming contrast to the stability Latin provided for ontological and purely humanistic understanding, Shakespeare's thematic use of Latin and Latin pedagogy suggests that the value and use of Latin was dependent upon its ability to change. For example in Costard's speech, remuneration is misused by Costard, but it is the misuse which makes the term useful for him and provides him with a unit of exchange. The "significant" that Armado gives to Costard and which leads to the above exchange is a letter meant to convey Armado's love, thus illustrating one of the main themes of the play, the exchange, often mistaken, of meaning. What makes comedies work as comedies is that even though mistakes occur in communication, some communication and meaning is conveyed, and that translated meaning leads to new situations and entanglements. On a more specific thematic level, *Love's Labour's Lost* gains most of its comic tone from the constant bilingual punning, both deliberate and mistaken, and more specifically from the pretentious use of Latinate English and the misuse of Latin phrases. Throughout the play new meanings are constantly being created out of the miscommunication of the characters, and new word/thing relationships are "coined."

As is typical of Shakespeare's comedies, class differences are made evident through language; however, in the play an exclusive "incorrect" vs. a "correct" use of Latin is not possible, as it is, for example, in *Much Ado About Nothing*, where Dogberry clearly misuses words in an attempt to sound erudite: "Our watch, sir, have indeed comprehended two aspicious persons, and we would have them this morning examined before your worship" (III.v.45). Dogberry is not a witty character because the exchange of meanings is a mistake, not a pun. No new meaning is the result of the exchange, as is the case with puns. It is interesting to note that Dogberry usually mistakes Latinate words, such as "comprehend" and "aspicious," and in the earlier quote Dogberry simply transposes the Latinate "redemption" for "damnation." Dogberry's relationship to enfranchised terms is completely auditory; he does not find any subtlety of meaning which renders his translations/substitutions suitable or creative. For example, Shakespeare has fun with Dogberry's relation to Latin in act III, scene v: "We will spare for no wit, I warrant you; here's that shall drive some of them to a non-come. Only get the learned writer to set down out excommunication, and meet me at the jail." Dogberry is probably mistaking "non-come" for the Latin legal phrase Anon compos mentis," and the irony is clear: Dogberry himself does not understand what he has inevitably overheard in legal circles. There is no pun created; the "change" which occurs in the translation of the phrase does not make sense in any intelligible way.

In *LLL* all the characters are in some way corrupted by language. The earlier exchange between Costard and Armado is typical: Armado, a "fantastical Spaniard," cannot clearly communicate with Costard due to their different language abilities. Likewise, Armado's signification will be miscarried, resulting in a comic failure to communicate with Jaquenetta. Furthermore, the play serves to highlight not only the comic results of class and social linguistic differences, but to highlight more general cultural paradigms of language pedagogy and acquisition.

The pedagogical and corresponding class inversion which often occurs in the play as a result of enfranchisement is seen in the lines which follow Armado's first use of the word "l'envoy." Note that Moth refuses to be taught by Armado, and he and Moth are each trying to find fitting "l'envoy":

> Arm. I will example it:
> The fox, the ape, and the humble-bee,
> Were still at odds, being but three.
> There's the moral; now the l'envoy,.
> Moth. I will add the l'envoy. Say the moral again.
> Arm. The fox, the ape, and the humble-bee,
> Were still at odds, being but three.
> Moth. Until the goose came out of door,
> And stay'd the odds by adding four.

The exchange becomes more witty as Moth and Costard gradually get the best of Armado. At Moth's request, Armado repeats the l'envoy after Moth's moral, leading to Costard's response that:

> The boy hath sold him a bargain, a goose, that's flat
> Sir, your pennyworth is good and your goose be fat.
> To sell a bargain well is as cunning as fast and loose:
> Let me see; a fat l'envoy; that's a fat goose.

Costard notes at line 107 that the exchange "ended the market," or the purchasing of witty language use. Since it is Costard, and not Armado, who ends the exchange, we again see a reversal of authority—Costard and Moth are in control of the exchange. The market place of language, where words have currency, is the domain of the lower and middle classes.

The above exchange serves to remind us that Reformation education reform sought to normalize society through universal literacy and reading practices. Shakespeare often represents the differences in class by the differences in approaches to the utilization of foreign tongues. With the particular economic demands of the early modern period, and the corresponding Reformation attempts to meet those demands, namely the demand and need for strong national identity and a developing merchant class, came necessary realignments of the goals and methods of Latin pedagogy. Within the Reformation educational paradigm proposed by Luther, the emphasis on study was not on a consistent and stable (i.e. "correct") relationship with a distant past, but on a new social conformity/hegemony. Shakespeare reflects this view of education in *LLL*. The view that Latin is superior to, due to it being prior to, the vernacular is limited to the comic pedagogues in *LLL*. "I think I smell false Latin," (V.i.72) says Holofernes to Costard, representing the view that the only good Latin is correct Latin.

The Latin used throughout the play by the rest of the characters is a vernacular Latin, a "living" and enfranchized Latin dramatically seen against the backdrop of a dead/stable Latin. While Latin may remain historically prior to vernaculars, that distance is what gives it its incantational force, not its stability. It is, essentially, a spoken Latin. Holofernes and Armado are comic, at least partially, because when they speak formal Latin, they sound like a Latin textbook. The object of much of Shakespeare's satire is classical pedagogy. Characters such as Moth and Costard, who could be seen as merely foolish, and who are often written off as such by critics, are in fact products of an educational system which emphasized Latin not as a classical language, but, following the lead of the earlier donats and vulgarias, as a vernacular language with practical application to daily life.

"honorificabilitudinitatibus"

The official status reserved for a Latin text reminds us that Latin was a practical and fundamental part of Renaissance society. Ideally, Latin pedagogy could be a source of societal homogeneity, and any attempt at homogeneity had to be at least partially economic. The defining character distinctions in *LLL*, as with most of Shakespeare's comedies, are economic. In this economic system words are equated with the value of the exchange. The whole courtship process in the play begins due to a misunderstanding regarding the exchange of land. Servants must answer to their masters and be paid for their labors. Thus Costard's "remuneration" not only exemplifies the commodification of Latin in the play, but suggests the essential economic role communication plays throughout the comedies.

On the other hand, there is at least one famous example in the play of classical Latin utilized in a completely *non*-material manner, an exception which proves the rule. When Costard says "honorificabilitudinitatibus" he is using a word, which, according to an interesting footnote in the Arden edition, has survived despite being "purely literary," i.e. not practical. The purely literary nature of the word is reflected in Moth's comment that "They have been at a great feast of languages, and stolen the scraps" (V.i.35). Moth reminds us that the word is a "scrap," that Armado and Holofernes, the figures being made fun of by Costard and Moth, are using the leftover Latin words, the ones not "digested," the ones not useful. They are not commodities, and according to the philology of the play, the word is therefore meaningless.

The use of purely "literary" terms was a matter of controversy not only for Latin pedagogy, but for rhetoric in general. Thomas Wilson, in his 1553 *Arte of Rhetorique*, warns readers against using "strange inkhorn terms, but to speake as commonly received."[24] He compares those who bring foreign words home (i.e. to England) to those who wear foreign apparel after they return from a trip abroad. "He that cometh lately out of France will talk French English, and never blush at the matter. Another chops in with Anglo-Italian." Wilson cites many other examples, finally noting that these pretentious persons will turn to Latin so "that the simple cannot but wonder at their talke, and think surely they speak from some Revelation."[25]

A similar condemnation of European tastes and fashion, in similar language, appears in Shakespeare's *Henry VIII* when the Lord Chamberlain and Sir Thomas Lovell are complaining about the ubiquitous nature of French fashion in the court:

>   Lov.   They must either
>   (For so run the conditions) leave those remnants
>   Of fool and feather that they got in France,
>   With all their honorable points of ignorance
>   Pertaining there unto, as fights and fireworks,
>   Abusing better men than they can be

Out of a foreign wisdom, renouncing clean
The faith they have in tennis and tall stockings,
Short blist'red breeches, and those types of travel,
And understand again like honest men,
Or pack to their old playfellows. (I.iii.23-33)

The new international economy and England's emerging presence as a world power brought with it more than a little tension, and national boundaries often served to emphasize differences rather than lessen them. Such differences are illustrated later in *Henry VIII* when the Spanish Queen Katherine takes exception to the Latin spoken around her: "O, good my lord, no Latin;/I am not such a truant since my coming,/As not to know the language I have liv'd in./A strange tongue makes my cause more strange, suspicous;/Pray speak in English" (II.iv. 42-6). Latin is still the international tongue in the court of Henry VIII, but the Queen's desire for English is a clear example of the patriotic tone of the play, and her desire to speak in the vernacular could be a way of making her more sympathetic to the audience.

Wilson would have Latin used only when fitting, and Latin and Greek "further our meaning in the english tongue, either for lack of some, or else because we would enrich the language."[26] Despite his distrust of Latin and other foreign tongues, Wilson came to a conclusion in alignment with Mulcaster and others, namely that Latin, although far from a better language, can benefit English. Armado and Holofernes are comic characters because they fit very neatly into Wilson's paradigmatic fashionable traveler: their Latin does not benefit English, it is merely fashionable. This comic stereotype reflects a real cultural tension about the role of the vernaculars in national identity.

For these reasons *Love's Labour's Lost* does not simplify the class distinctions along the lines of many of Shakespeare's comedies. For example, when Berowne and Costard communicate, it is likely that Costard will aid Berowne in understanding:

> Cost. Pray you, sir, how much carnation ribbon may a man buy for a remuneration?
> Ber. O what is a remuneration?
> Cost. Marry, sir, halfpenny farthing.
> Ber. O! why then, three farthing worth of silk. (III.i.140-144)

Again, the opportunity for this comic exchange and punning is economic. Costard has finally gotten an opportunity to practice (use) his new found Latin, but Berowne is unable to understand him. The upper-class Berowne, who has some familiarity with Latin, does not recognize Costard's "vernacular" use of it. However, once he is "taught" what the new word means, he can use it himself. Latin is far from a stable universal referent when the users are from different classes. The problem therefore is textual—educated users of Latin are familiar with a "textual" and stable dead Latin, while the lower-class characters are familiar with a "living" and therefore more unstable Latin. What communication does occur occurs only as a result of *translation*, an exchange of a word's denotative meaning for a connotative or a brand new denotative one. This particular episode illustrates that for these characters Latin is a mercantile language, one which must be used and exchanged before it has any real worth. "Remuneration" has a value, in this case three farthings, a purchasing power which is the same in English or Latin. What does remain stable across languages and translations is its practical economic value. Berowne is capable, as was the higher-class Armado, of providing Costard with a new coinage. In the following exchange, Berowne, like Armado before him, is asking Costard to serve as a go-between to deliver his "signification" to his secret love, in this case Rosyln:

> Ber.   ask for her,
> And to her white hand see thou do commend
> This seal'd-up counsel. There's thy guerdon:
>   go.
> Cost.   Gardon, O sweet gardon! better than remuneration; a'leven-pence farthing better. Most sweet gardon! I will do it, sir, in print. Gardon! Remuneration!   (III.i.161-167)

Linguistically, Costard has received a raise. The work is the same, but the coinage he receives is of more worth. According to the editor of the Arden edition, "print" means *exactly, most carefully*, meaning that with more money comes more exact representation. For example, at line 159 of act II, scene i, of *Two Gentlemen of Verona*, Speed states that, "All this I speak in print, for in print I found it." It should not be surprising that mistakes and malapropism are a source for comic commentary on education. In this line, Speed's speech is "printed" since he is either reading from a text or relying on his memory of one. Print obviously suggests writing, with writing in turn implying exactness or correctness. Costard's misuse does not change the word's meaning, but it does reflect different understandings or models of language use, the textual and the verbal. Such "misuse" results in new, equally useful, meanings. William Carroll quotes Coleridge who noted that "even the mere difference, or corruption, in the *pronunciation* of the same word, if it have become general, will produce a new word with a distinct signification; thus 'property' and 'propriety.'"[27] This production represents what is truly witty in the play, the production of new meaning.

On the other hand, Holofernes is funny because he speaks archaically: his conception of Latin as a dead, stable referent should, in the philology of the play, render him *speechless*. As Carroll points out, Holofernes prefers to speak in synonyms, often multi-lingual. His favorite trope is the synonym, as exemplified by his reference to "terra, the soil, the land, the earth" (IV.ii.6-7). He "simply insists that there be no deviation from the original source."[28] Synonyms are the least commodifying tropes because rather than exchanging meaning across words or languages (and thereby producing new meanings), as metaphors or puns do, listing synonyms simply refers words to other words, as opposed to seeing them connected to things, and therefore more material, as Costard does. As with many of the dictionaries of the time, Holofernes views Latin as a collection of classical, denotative words, not as a viable language. In his discourse, nothing new is created. Costard is closer to the Reformation spirit Luther cited. As a result, Holofernes seems the least "witty" of all the characters. He is also the most classical, as is evident in his etymological insights.

Holofernes' insights suggest that for him words are only denotative and only have meaning in connection to their etymology or "literal" meaning.

The comparison of Holofernes and Costard should suggest a model by which Shakespeare and his audience understood Latin learning. For Shakespeare's audience puns, and the corresponding transference of meaning from one denotation to another, liberate language. For Holofernes, who is a teacher, Latin is a dead language. Rather than patronizingly seeing the characters who make these puns as "ignorant" or "silly," and thus obscuring any real observations Shakespeare might have been making through them, we learn more about the dichotomous nature of language use and acquisition by treating their linguistic feats seriously. One way in which this is evident is in Shakespeare's own seeming distinction between high and low literacy in the form of good Latin and bad Latin, but this distinction is not simply one of high-class characters and low: rather, the distinction is made between those who are truly witty and those who are merely foolish. Since there is no such thing as pure, appropriate Latin in the play, satisfactory distinctions between true Latin literacy and partial literacy are impossible, and attempts to make such distinctions deflect from the intent of the play.

Moth, for example, can work in both realms of Latin—his puns are good, as in Act V scene 1 when he gets the best of both Armado and Holofernes, only to be dismissed by Holofernes as "an infant." Moth responds with, "Lend me your horn to make one, and I will whip about your infamy *manu cita*. A gig of a cuckold's horn!" Here Moth has turned the pedagogical horn book into a penis, which Moth threatens to use to make Holofernes a cuckold. Costard, as we can imagine, takes great delight in this exchange, and proclaims that if he "had but one penny in the world, thou should'st have it to buy gingerbread." Costard continues:

> Cost. Hold, there is the very remuneration I had of thy master, thou halfpenny purse of wit, thou pigeon-egg of discretion. O, and the heavens were so pleased that thou wert but my bastard, what a joyful father wouldst thou make me. Go to; thou hast it *ad dunghill*, at the fingers' ends, as they say.
> Hol. O, I smell false Latin: dunghill for *unguem*.
> Arm. Arts-man, preambulate; we will be singled
> from the barbarous. (V.i. 70-74)

Holofernes and Armado believe that "good," i.e. stable Latin has a redemptive force, that it will save them from barbarism. For this reason, Armado and Holofernes are singled out from the rest of the characters, not because they are more witty, but because in their eyes their Latin is more "correct" and that correctness is an end in itself. They confuse the more "proper" use of Latin, that is one which is seen as a companion to the vernacular, with an antiquated one which sees Latin as merely a dead historical language and not an aural or spoken one. As is often typical of the comedies, even the mistakes made by the lower-class and less educated characters are in alignment with the values and aims of the ruling class, as is illustrated in the official standing of Lily's text. Such confusion results in the comic reversal of "high" and "low" culture.

As T.W. Craig notes in the Arden edition of *The Merry Wives of Windsor*, when Evans is giving William his Latin lesson and asks William "what is a 'stone,' William" (IV.i.30), he is following Colet's advice to test students by their ability to "Latin" an English term. William's reply, "A pebble," undermines Evan's attempts at teaching a textual Latin. Again we see a pedagogical inversion, with the student refusing to be taught and likewise refusing to limit the word to a single etymological meaning. As the comedies show, attempts to control society inevitably break down against the forces of individuality, i.e. the personalities of those characters who are truly witty, regardless of class, dominate over those who only seem witty or who represent law or "tradition." Henry's attempts to control the dissemination of Latin treatises is an example of this attempt at homogeneity.

A very clear example of all of these linguistic attributes and how they reflect comic characterization is illustrated by Holofernes' lecture on the correct way to pronounce words:

> I adhor such fanatical phantasimes, such insociable and point-devise companions; such rackers of orthography, as to speak dout, fine, when he should say doubt; det, when he should pronounce debt, –d, e, b, t, not d, e, t; he clepeth a calf, cauf; half, hauf; neighbour *vocatur* nebour; neigh abbreviated ne. This is abhominable, which he would call abominable, it insinuateth me of insanie: *ne intelligis domine*? to make frantic, lunatic. (V.i. 17-25)

Not only is this speech representative of Holofernes's silly and misplaced application of Latin, it clearly illustrates the tension between print and orality, text and spoken language, which defines early modern pedagogy. Further, such attempts at fixing meaning are reminiscent of the role of dictionaries. For example, in the *Catholicom Anglicum*, the oldest extant English dictionary, dated 1483,[29] we find the following examples of "proper" pronunciation: "to pay dett" (the English entry) is defined as "pacare, reddere," and the proper pronunciation is noted as "dett— debitum." This example of orthography is based upon the original Latin etymological source. Another example of pronunciation found in the *Catholicom Anglicum* is "dowte" defined as "ambiquitas, dubietas, dubitacio, dubium, dubitancia, cuncta, cunctacio, heresis, hestitacio, hesitacium, hesitacula." Again, the word the English speaker might be looking for is written according to its "usual" pronunciation, while what it means, or how it should be pronounced for anyone wanting to be "classical" and "correct," is given in Latin. It is no surprise that a medieval dictionary would contain such a bias, and by extension it is no surprise that a modern man reflecting the same bias would be seen as laughable. What all of these examples suggest is that rather than presenting instability by holding one class, teachers/scholars, to one standard and "clowns" to another in terms of language use, Lily's Grammar was such a standard referent that it could serve as the basis for both ridicule and praise. In other words, it was not Lily's text which was the object of scorn, but its misuse. Like the *De recta et emendata Linguae Anglicae Scriptione*, *Lily's Grammar* fulfilled a Renaissance desire for homogeneity in education and language use. Typical of comedies, on the other hand, the practical use to which that homogeneity was put resulted in a complex and unstable world.

The privileging of tongues or spoken language exists for Shakespeare against the backdrop of the more stable and "fixed" written word. Father Walter Ong's conception of writing as a "technology" which "restructures thought," to take from a title of a recent essay, is illuminating in our present context. Ong writes, "Recalling sounded words is like recalling a bar of music, a melody, a sequence in time. A word is an event, a happening, not a thing, as letters [in written discourse] make it appear to be." This is essentially what Launce does (as do Costard and Dogberry)—they recall the sounds, but not the exact letters, of words they hear. Later, Ong notes that once written, "words are frozen and in a sense dead" (22). They are removed from the living word, which ironically results in their permanence. We find this conception of "dead" language with characters such as the various pedagogues and braggarts who people many of Shakespeare's early comedies. Shakespeare emphasizes that written language is artificial and, therefore, material. Throughout *Two Gentlemen* there is a focus on the fragility of the written word—in no other play are so many letters misdelivered, not delivered, or literally torn up, as in the following from act IV, scene iv:

> Julia: There, hold.
> I will not look vpon your master's lines:
> I know they are stuff'd with protestations,
> And full of new-found oaths, which he will break
> As easily, as I do tear his paper. (125-29)

There is an interesting equation in these lines: oaths are equated by Julia as "material," like writing, and therefore easily torn. Throughout the play, oaths are continually broken and are examples of the fragility of "fixed" language. At one point, at act I, scene ii, Julia literally tears up a letter and then attempts to reconstruct it:

> I'll kiss each several paper, for amends.
> Look, here is writ 'kind Julia': unkind Julia!
> As in revenge for thy ingratitude,
> I throw thy name against the bruising stones,
> Trampling comtemptuously on thy disdain. (109-13)

For his pains in acting out the role of the lover in writing a letter, Proteus' message is torn, trampled and left out in the cold. Although Julia attempts to restructure his message, she only finds fragments and must reconstruct his message in her mind (which is not hard to do, given the stereotypical nature of the original letter). In this way, individuality, as manifested in wit, and destabilization, as manifested in spoken puns, are opposed to overtly stable, written language. In the end, it is individuality and destabilization which prove to be successful.

In 1581, Richard Mulcaster published *Positions wherin those primitive circumstances be examined, which are necessarie for the training up of children, either for skill in their booke, or health in their bodie.* The stated aim of this book was to "help bring the generall teaching in your Maiesties dominions, to some one good and profitable uniformitie, which now in the middest of great variety doth either hinder much, or profit little, or at the least nothing so much, as it were like to do, if it were reduced to one certaine fourme."[30] We again see an attempt at *reduction* for the purpose of simplicity and uniformity. What Mulcaster assumes, along with many of the pedagogues and exegetes already studied, is that uniformity itself leads to greater "profit" for students. The ultimate aim of education is therefore not so much the well-being of the individual student, nor the foundation of sound pedagogical method, but that every student know the same things and, in addition, that they come to know them in *the same manner*. This emphasis on method and means is the result of philological issues surrounding the proper way of reading and interpreting; in short, they result from a reformation of the most basic relation between sign and thing signified.

Notes

1. Ernst Cassirer, *The Logic of the Humanities*. Trans. Clarence Smith Howe (New Haven: Cambridge University Press, 1961), 19.

2. *Early Protestant Educators: The Educational Writings of Martin Luther, John Calvin, and Other Leaders of Protestant Thought*, edited by Frederick Eby (New York: McGraw-Hill, 1931), 57.

3. All references are to the Arden Shakespeare, unless otherwise noted.

4. William Carroll, *The Great Feast of Languages in Love's Labour's Lost* (Princeton: Princeton University Press, 1976), 36.

5. Patricia Parker, *Shakespeare from the Margins: Language, Culture, Context* (Chicago: University of Chicago Press, 1996), 28-29.

6. This is also an important component of stagecraft: theatrically, plays by definition emphasize and privilege the auditory. Those characters who can pun are playing to the audience and their sympathies more than a character entrapped in a purely textual relationship with language.

7. In *Rhetoric, Romance, and Technology* (Ithaca, NY: Cornell University Press, 1971): 113-41.

8. Another example of money and its relationship to the importance of Latin literacy is seen in the following from *Love's Labour's Lost*, where Costard, a servant, has just received a "remuneration" from his master:

Now will I look to his remuneration. Remuneration! O that's the Latin word for three farthings: three farthings, remuneration. 'What's the price of this inkle?' 'One penny': 'No, I'll give you a remuneration': why, it carries it. Remuneration! why it is a fairer name than French crown. I will never buy and sell out of this word. (III.i.132-138)

9. All citations from the following Arden editions of the plays: *Two Gentlemen of Verona*, edited by Clifford Leech (Methuen, 1969); *Love's Labour's Lost*, edited by R.W. David (Methuen, 1951); *The Two Noble Kinsmen*, edited by Lois Potter (Thomas Nelson and Sons, 1997).

10. *Much Ado About Nothing*, IV, ii.55-56.

11. Marc Bloch, *Feudal Society*. Trans. L.A. Manyon. 2 vols (Chicago: University of Chicago Press, 1961), 23.

12. See Parker, 31.

13. Bedford edition, 58.

14. Thomas Farnaby, *Systema Grammaticum* (1641) (Menston, England: Scolar Press Limited, 1969), selected and Edited by R.C. Alston. No. 160.

15. Parker, 35.

16. *Ibid.*, 118.

17. Baldwin notes more examples of Shakespeare's use of Lily in *Merry Wives of Windsor*, 561-564. Baldwin also notes echos of *MWW* in Brinsley's remembrance of Lily's textbook: "when Gentlemen or others come in and examine them, or their friends try them at home, in the things which they learned a quarter or halfe a yeere before; they are ordinarily found so rawe, and to haue so forgotten, that I doe receive great reproach, as though I had taken no paines with them, or as they had profited nothing" (From *Ludus Literius* (1627), p. 90. Quoted in Baldwin, 564).

18. Eamon Duffy, *The Stripping of the Altars: Traditional Religion in England, c. 1400-c. 1580* (New Haven: Yale University Press, 1992), 217.

19. *The Sermons of John Donne*, edited with intro. by Evelyn M. Simpson and George R. Potter, 10 vols. (Berkeley: Univ. Of California Press, 1962), VII. 16. 401.

20. T. W. Baldwin, *Shakespeare's Small Latine and Lesse Greeke* (Urbana: University of Illinois Press, 1944), 136.

21. Mulcaster, 157.

22. *Ibid.*, 174.

23. *Ibid.*, 269.

24. Thomas Wilson, *Arte of Rhetorique for the use of all such as are studious of Eloquence* (1553), 183.

25. *Ibid.*, 185.

26. *Ibid.*, 186.

27. Carrole, 21.

28. *Ibid.*, 43.

29. London, Published for the Early English Text Society, mdccclxxxi.

Bibliography

Alpers, Paul. "Pastoral and the Domain of Lyric in Spenser's *Shepheardes Calendar.*" In *Representing the English Renaissance,* ed. by Stephen Greenblatt. Berkeley: University of California Press, 1988.
Anderson, Judith. *Words that Matter.* Stanford: Stanford University Press, 1996.
Armitage, David. "Literature and Empire." In *The Origins of Empire:* The *Oxford History of the British Empire, Vol. 1.* Oxford: Oxford University Press, 1998.
Articles of Faith. London: Richard Jugge and John Cawood, 1571.
Augustine, *Confessions of Augustine.* Ed. John Gibb, Cambridge Patristic Texts. Cambridge: Cambridge University Press, 1908.
——— *On Christian Doctrine.* Trans. with intro. by D.W. Robertson, Jr. New York: Macmillan, 1958.
——— *Confessions of Augustine.* Ed. Rex Warner. New York: New American Library, 1963.
——— *The City of God.* Trans. by Henry Bettenson. London: Penguin Books, 1972.
——— *Love One Another, My Friends: Saint Augustine's Homilies on the First Letter of John.* Ed. by John Leineweber. San Francisco: Harper and Row, 1989.
Baldwin, T.W. *Shakespeare's Small Latine and Lesse Greeke.* Urbana: University of Illinois Press, 1944.
Benjamin, Walter. *The Origin of German Tragic Drama.* Trans. John Osborne. Frankfurt: Suhrkamp Verlag, 1963.
Bigger, Charles Purcell III. "The Nature of Aesthetic Judgement in Augustinian Interpretation." Ph.D. diss. University of Virginia, 1951.
Bloch, Marc. *Feudal Society.* Trans. L.A. Manyon. 2 vols. Chicago: University of Chicago Press, 1961
Bloom, Harold. *The Western Canon: The Books and School of the Ages.* New York: Riverhead Books, 1995
The Book of Common Prayer 1559: The Elizabethan Prayer Book. Ed. John Booty. Charlottesville: The University Press of Virginia, 1976.
Bonner, Gerald. "The Church and the Eucharist in the Theology of St. Augustine." In *God's Decree and Man's Destiny: Studies on the Thought of Augustine of Hippo.* London: Variorum Reprints, 1987.
Bossy, John. "The Character of Elizabethan Catholicism." *Past and Present,* no. 21, April 1962.
Broke, Arthur. *Agreement of sundry places of Scripture,* Folger manuscript STC 3811, 1563.
Brown, Peter. *Augustine of Hippo: A Biography.* Berkeley: University of California Press, 1967.
———*Power and Persuasion in Late Antiquity: Towards a Christian Empire.* Madison, WI: University of Wisconsin Press, 1992.
Buick, Stephen. "'A leaden mediocrity': Competing Views of the Elizabethan Settlement of Religion in *The Stripping of the Altars* and *The Seconde Tome of Homilies.*" In *Renaissance Papers, 1996.* Camden House, Columbia, SC.

Burke, Kenneth. *The Rhetoric of Religion: Studies in Logology.* Berkeley: University of California Press, 1961.

Cardwell, E., ed. *Documentary Annals of the Reformed Church on England.* Oxford, 1844.

Carre, Myrick H. *Realists and Nominalists*. London: Oxford University Press, 1946.

Carroll, William. *The Great Feast of Languages in Love's Labour's Lost.* Princeton: Princeton University Press, 1976.

Cassirer, Ernst. *The Logic of the Humanities.* Trans. Clarence Smith Howe. New Haven: Cambridge University Press, 1961.

Colish, Marcia L. *The Mirror of Language: A Study in the Medieval Theory of Knowledge.* Lincoln, NE: University of Nebraska Press, 1968.

Collinson, Patrick. *The Religion of Protestants: The Church in English Society 1559-1625.* Oxford: Clarendon Press, 1982.

Cressy David. *Literacy and Social Order: Reading and Writing in Tudor and Stuart England.* Cambridge: Cambridge University Press, 1980.

Cummings, Robert. *Spenser: The Critical Heritage.* Critical Heritage Series; London: Routledge and Kegan Paul, 1970.

De Lubac, Henri. *Medieval Exegesis.* Vol. 1. Trans. Mark Sebanc. Grand Rapids, MI: Williams B. Eerdmans Publishing Co., 1998.

De Man, Paul. *Allegories of reading: Figural Language in Rousseau, Nietzsche, Rilke, and Proust.* New Haven: Yale University Press, 1979.

———*Blindness and Insight: Essays in the Rhetoric of Contemporary Criticism.* Minneapolis : University of Minnesota Press, 1983.

DeNeef, Leigh. "Allegory." In *Spenser Encyclopedia.* Ed. A.C. Hamilton. London: Routledge, 1990.

Dickens, A.G. and John Tonkin. *The Reformation in Historical Thought.* Oxford: Basil Blackwell, 1985.

Dillistone Frederick W. "The Anti-Donatist Writings." In *Companion to the Study of Augustine.* Ed. Roy Battenhouse. New York: Oxford University Press, 1956.

Donne, John. *The Sermons of John Donne.* Ed. with intro. by Evelyn M. Simpson and George R. Potter. 10 vols. Berkeley: University of California Press, 1962.

———*Devotions upon Emergent Occasions.* Ed. Anthony Raspa. Montreal and London, 1977.

Duffy, Eamon. *The Stripping of the Altars: Traditional Religion in England, c. 1400-c. 1580.* New Haven: Yale University Press, 1992.

Du Moulin, Pierre. *An Apology of the Holy Supper of the Lord Against the Corporeal Presence, Transubstantiation, Masses Without Communicants, The Communion Under One Kind, Together with Certayn Analytical and Orthodox Propositions upon the Lord's Supper.* Trans. Edward Skipwith. London, 1612.

Eby, Frederick. *Early Protestant Educators: The Educational Writings of Martin Luther, John Calvin, and Other Leaders of Protestant Thought.* New York: McGraw-Hill Company, 1931.

Edmundson, Henry. *Lingua Linguarum, or The Natural Language of Languages* (1655). Menston, England: Scolar Press Limited 1970. Selected and Edited by R.C. Alston. No. 259.

Edwards, Mark Jr. *Printing, Propaganda, and Martin Luther.* Berkeley: University of California Press, 1994.

Farnaby, Thomas. *Systema Grammaticum* (1641). Menston, England: Scolar Press Limited, 1969.

Fielding, Henry. *The History of Tom Jones, A Foundling.* Oxford, 1974.

Fineman, Joel. "The Structure of Allegorical Desire." In *Allegory and Representation: Selected Papers from the English Institute, 1979-80*. Ed. Stephen J. Greenblatt. Baltimore: Johns Hopkins Press, 1981.

Fleming, Juliet. "Dictionary English and the Female Tongue." In *Enclosure Acts: Sexuality, Property, and Culture in Early Modern England*. Ed. Richard Burt and John Michael Archer. Ithaca: Cornell University Press, 1994.

Fletcher, Angus. *Allegory: The Theory of a Symbolic Mode*. Ithaca: Cornell University Press, 1964.

Flynn, Vincent Joseph. "The Grammatical Writings of William Lily, ?1468-?1522." *Bibliographical Society of America* 37 (1943).

Foucault, Michel. *The Archaeology of Knowledge and The Discourse on Language*. Trans. A.M. Sheridan Smith. New York: Pantheon Books, 1972.

The Geneva Bible: A Facsimile of the 1560 edition. Intro. Lloyd E. Berry. Madison: University of Wisconsin Press, 1969.

Giamatti, A. Bartlett. *A Play of Double Senses: Spenser's Faerie Queene*. Englewood Cliffs, NJ: Prentice-Hall, Inc., 1975.

Graff, Harvey J. *The Legacies of Literacy: Continuities and Contradictions in Western Culture and Society*. Bloomington: Indiana University Press, 1987.

Greenblatt, Stephen. *Renaissance Self-Fashioning From More to Shakespeare*. Chicago: University of Chicago Press, 1980.

———— ed. *Allegory and Representation*. Baltimore: Johns Hopkins University Press, 1981.

Guillory, John. *Cultural Capital: The Problem of Literary Canon Formation*. Chicago: The University of Chicago Press, 1993.

Guth, Hans P. "Allegorical Implications of Artifice in Spenser's *Faerie Queene*." *PMLA* lxxvi (1961): 474-9.

Hamilton, A.C. *The Structure of Allegory in The Faerie Queene*. Oxford: Clarendon Press, 1961.

Harris, Jonathan Gil. "Shakespeare's Hair: Staging the Object of Material Culture." *Shakespeare Quarterly* 52.4 (2001); 483-4.

Hartlib, Samuel. *The True and Readie Way* (1614). Scolar Press Limited, Menston, England, 1976. No. 235.

Hooker, Richard. "A Learned Discourse of Justification." In *Of the Laws of Ecclesiastical Polity*. Intro. Christopher Morris, 2 vols. New York: Everyman Library, 1969.

Hirsch, E.D. Jr., *Cultural Literacy: What Every American Needs to Know*. Boston: Houghton Mifflin, 1987.

Johnston, David. *The Rhetoric of Leviathan*. Princeton University Press, 1986.

Kane, Sean. *Spenser's Moral Allegory*. Toronto: Toronto University Press, 1989.

Lakoff, George, and Mark Johnson. *Metaphors We Live By*. Chicago: University of Chicago Press, 1980.

Levine, Lawrence W. *Highbrow/lowbrow: The Emergence of Cultural Hierarchy in America*. Cambridge, Mass.: Harvard University Press, 1990.

Lewalski, Barbara. *Protestant Poetics and the Seventeenth-Century Religious Lyric*. Princeton, NJ: Princeton University Press, 1976.

Marius, Richard. *Martin Luther: The Christian Between God and Death*. Cambridge: Harvard University Press, 1999.

Martz, Louis. *The Poetry of Meditation: A Study of English Religious Literature of the Seventeenth Century*. New Haven: Yale University Press, 1954.

Meredith, Anthony. "Later Philosophy." In *The Oxford History of the Classical World*. John Boardman et al., eds. Oxford: Oxford University Press, 1986.

Miller, David L. *The Poems Two Bodies: The Poetics of the 1590 Faerie Queene*. Princeton: Princeton University Press, 1988.

Miller, J. Hillis. "'Reading' Part of a Paragraph in *Allegories of Reading*." In *Reading De Man Reading*. Ed. Lindsay Waters and Wlad Godzich. Minneapolis: University of Minnesota Press, 1989.

Minnis, A.J. *Medieval Theory of Authorship*. 2nd Edition. Philadelphia: University of Pennsylvania Press, 1988.

Mulcaster, Richard. *Positions wherin those primitive circumstances be examined, which are necessarie for the training up of children, either for skill in their booke, or health in their bodie*. (1581) London, Published for the Early English Text Society, 1881.

Murrin, Michael. *The Veil of Allegory: Some Notes Towards a Theory of Allegorical Rhetoric in the English Renaissance*. Chicago: University of Chicago Press, 1969.

Nelson, William. Ed. *A Fifteenth Century School Book*. Oxford: Clarendon Press, 1959.

Okerlund, Arlene N. "Spenser's Wanton Maidens: Reader Psychology and the Bower of Bliss." *PMLA* lxxxviii (1973): 62-8.

Ong, Walter. *Rhetoric, Romance, and Technology*. Ithaca, NY: Cornell University Press, 1971.

—— *Orality and Literacy: The Technologizing of the Word*. New York: Methuen, 1982.

—— "Writing Is a Technology that Restructures Thought." In *Literacy: A Critical Sourcebook*. Ed. Ellen Cushman et al. Boston: Bedford/St. Martin's, 2001.

Parker, Patricia. *Shakespeare from the Margins: Language, Culture, Context*. Chicago: University of Chicago Press, 1996.

Patterson, Annabel. *Censorship and Interpretation: The Conditions of Writing and Reading in Early Modern England*. Madison: University of Wisconsin Press, 1984.

Pelikan, Jaroslav. *The Reformation of the Bible, The Bible of the Reformation*. New Haven: Yale University Press, 1996.

Pendergast, John. "Spenser's 'General Intention': Christian Allegory and Courtly Poetics." *Studies in Philology* (Summer) 1996.

—— "Pierre Du Moulin on the Eucharist: Protestant Sign Theory and the Grammar of Embodiement." *ELH* (65), 1988.

Preus, James. *From Shadow to Promise: Old Testament Interpretation from Augustine to the Young Luther*. Cambridge: Belknap Press of Harvard University Press, 1969.

Preuse, Mary. *Eloquence and Ignorance in Augustine's "On the Nature and Origin of the Soul."* American Academy of Religion Series, no. 51. Atlanta: Scholars Press, 1985.

Puttenham, Richard. *The Art of English Poesie*. Intro. Baxter Hathaway. Kent, OH: Kent State University Press, 1970.

Raitt, Jill. "Roman Catholic New Wine in Reformed Old Bottles?: The Conversion of the Elements in the Eucharistic Doctrines of Theodore Beza and Edward Schillebeeckx." *Journal of Ecumenical Studies* 8 (1971): 581-604.

Rivers, Isabel. *Classical and Christian Idea in English Renaissance Poetry*. London: George Allen and Unwin, 1979.

Robertson, D.W. *A Preface to Chaucer: Studies in Medieval Perspectives*. Princeton: Princeton University Press, 1962.

Scarisbrick, J.J. *Henry VII*. Berkeley: University of California Press, 1969.

Schillebeeckx, Edward O.P. *The Eucharist*. New York: Sheed and Ward, 1968.

Schleiner, Winifred. *The Imagery of John Donne's Sermons*. Providence: Brown University Press, 1970.

Shakespeare, William. *Two Gentlemen of Verona*. Ed. Clifford Leech. Methuen, 1969.

—— *Love's Labour's Lost*. Ed. R. W. David . Methuen, 1951.

—— *The Two Noble Kinsmen*. Ed. Lois Potter. Thomas Nelson and Sons, 1997.

Sherry, Richard. *A Treatise of Schemes and Trope*. (1550) Folger Library STC 22428.

Shuger, Deborah Kuller, *The Renaissance Bible: Scholarship, Sacrifice, and Subjectivity*. Berkeley: University of California Press, 1994.

Simon, Joan. *Education and Society in Tudor England.* Cambridge: Cambridge University Press, 1967.
Skelton, John. *The Latin Writings of John Skelton.* Ed. David R. Carlson. *Studies in Philology* (88), 1991.
Somerset, Anne. *Elizabeth I.* New York: St. Martin's Press, 1991.
Spenser, Edmund. *The Faerie Queene.* Ed. A.C. Hamilton, New York: Longman Press, 1977.
Stanwood, P.G. and Heather Ross Asals, eds. *John Donne and the Theology of Language.* Columbia, Mo. University of Missouri Press, 1986.
Starnes, Dewitt. *The English Dictionary from Cawdrey to Johnson, 1604-1755.* Amsterdam: J. Benjamins, 1991.
Steinmetz, David C., Ed. *The Bible in the Sixteenth Century.* Durham, NC: Duke University Press, 1990.
Stock, Brian. *The Implications of Literacy: Written Language and Models of Interpretation in the Eleventh and Twelfth Centuries.* Princeton, NJ: Princeton University Press, 1983
———*Augustine the Reader: Meditation, Self-Knowledge, and the Ethics of Interpretation.* Cambridge: The Belknap Press of Harvard University Press, 1996.
Stone, Darrell. *Eucharistic Sacrifice and the Reformation.* Ed. by Francis Clark, S.J. Newman Press, 1960.
Syms, Christopher. Printed in Dublin by the Society of Stationers, 1634. Folger Man. VA 283.
Thomas, Keith. *Religion and the Decline of Magic.* New York: Scribner, 1971.
Wall, John. *Transformations of the Word : Spenser, Herbert, Vaughan.* Athens: University of Georgia Press, 1988.
Waswo, Richard. *Language and Meaning in the Renaissance.* Princeton: Princeton University Press, 1987.
Watson, Foster. *The English Grammar School to 1660.* London: Frank Cass and Co., 1968.
Webbe, Joseph. *An Appeale to Truth.* (1622) The Scolar Press Limited, 1967.
Wells, Joseph. *Oxford and its Colleges.* London: Methuen, 1897.
Wells, Robin Headlam. *Spenser's 'Faerie Queene' and the Cult of Elizabeth.* Beckenham, Kent: Croom Helm Ltd., 1983.
White, Beatrice, ed. *The Vulgaria of John Stanbridge and the Vulgaria of Robert Whittinton.* London: Kegan Paul, Trench, Trübner for the Early English Text Society, 1932.
Wilson, Thomas. *Arte of Rhetorique for the use of all such as are studious of Eloquence* (1553). Ed. Peter E. Medine. University Park, PA.: Pennsylvania State University Press, 1994.
Wimsatt, William K. and Cleanth Brooks. *Literary Criticism: A Short History.* New York: Knopf, 1967.
Wise, Thomas. *Animadversions upon Lillies Grammar, or Lilly scanned. An extract of Grammatical Problems. Gathered out of the Inquiries and Disputes of the most judious Grammarians* (1625). Folger manuscript STC 25867.

Index

accessus 135, 137–9
Albans, St 37, 40
allegorical interpretation 48, 49, 50, 54, 56, 57, 60, 61
allegory 7–12, 18, 21–4, 26, 32, 50, 68, 101–2, 106, 110, 124, 127–9, 133–6, 137–47
Allen, William 40
Alpers, Paul 42
ambiguity 9, 13, 23–6, 126
Anderson, Judith 92
Andrewes, Lancelot 69
Anglican Church 39, 121, 122
Anglican Church doctrine 102–3, 106–8
Aquinas, St 101, 107, 117–18, 120, 135, 142; *Summa Contra Gentile*, 118
Ariosto, Ludovico 137–8
Aristotle 117, 135
Armado 160, 161, 163, 165–71
Arte of Rhetorique 30, 32, 168
Arthur, King 60, 137–8
Articles of Religion 38, 42
auctore 49
Augustine, St 1, 2, 7, 8, 10–13, 17, 18–28, 30, 31, 45, 61, 62 102–4, 106, 108, 119, 120, 122–4, 126–8, 133, 142–4, 146, 147; *De Genesi ad litteram,* 7; *City of God,* 23; *Confessions,* 21–4, 26; *On Christian Doctrine,* 21–3, 25, 26, 30
autores 135

Baldwin, T.W. 76, 164

Barnes, Joseph 93–4
Baxter, Richard 125–6
Bellarmine, Cardinal Robert 67
Belphoebe 138, 145–6
Benjamin, Walter 9, 136, 140
Berengar of Tours 104
Berowne 169
Beza, Theodore 68
Bird, John 79–80, 88
Bloom, Harold 4, 5
Book of Common Prayer 42
Bower of Bliss 144
Britomart 146
Broke, Arthur 60–61
Brooks, Cleanth 10
Brown, Peter 20, 21, 24
Burke, Kenneth 23, 122
Busyrane, House of 37, 147

Cade, Jack 155
Calvin, John 47, 49, 5–2, 62, 68, 114–15, 118
Calvinist doctrine 106
Cambridge, University of 40, 69
Canterbury, Archbishop of 120
Carleton, Bishop George 42
Carre, Myrick 1, 2, 174
Carroll, William 155, 170
Castiglione, Baldassare 71
Catholic Church 7–9, 11, 12, 17, 19, 21–3, 25, 39, 40–43, 45–9, 54, 56, 61, 62, 67–9, 76, 78, 95, 102, 103, 105–8, 109, 110, 111–13, 119–21, 128, 133, 154
Catholicom Anglicum 172
Charles, King 61, 82–3, 129

Church of England 38, 41
Clapham, Henoch 44, 49, 50, 54, 55–8
Coleridge, Samuel Taylor 147
Colet, John 72, 74–6, 78, 80, 162–3, 172
Colish, Marcia 8
Collinson, Patrick 5, 6, 38, 43, 48
Cooper, Thomas 93
Corinthians 1, 61
Costard 155–6, 160–71, 173
Cox, Richard 74, 77
Craig, T.W. 172
Cranmer, Bishop Thomas 45–6
Cressy, David 3, 125, 126, 174
Cromwell, Thomas 74

Dante 133
De Man, Paul 8
dictionaries 70, 92–3
Digby, Kenelm 143, 145
Dogberry 156, 160, 166, 173
Donne, John 44, 45, 47–8, 82, 102, 105, 106, 108, 111, 112, 114, 119–30
Douai College 40
Drury, Elizabeth 108
Du Moulin, Pierre 62, 106–8, 112–21
Duffy, Eamon 43, 163

Ecclesiastes 121
Ecclesiastical Polity *see* Hooker, Richard
Edmundson, Henry 86–9
Elizabeth I, Queen 6, 75, 85, 108, 129, 133–4, 136–42, 145–6, 148
Elyot, Thomas 93, 94
Ephesians 44
Erasmus 43, 44, 67, 75–6, 78–9
Eucharist 25, 56, 62, 76, 101–5, 107, 109, 112, 113, 114–20, 123–4, 134
Exodus 57, 60

Faerie Queene, The 133, 134, 141–2, 144–6
Farnaby, Thomas 162
Fielding, Joseph 6
figura 7, 104, 119
figurative interpretation 7, 10
figurative language 102, 105–6, 110–12, 114, 117, 120
Fletcher, Angus 146
Flynn, Vincent Joseph 75–7
formalism 10
Foucault, Michel 17
French language 94, 107, 153–5, 161, 168

Gardiner, Stephen 41–2, 52
Genesis 22–3, 26, 57, 58, 145
Geneva Bible 58, 62, 101
Golding, William 145
Graff, Harvey 3, 174
grammar 10, 12, 20, 25, 29, 32, 46, 48, 50, 68, 70, 72–8, 80–83, 85–6, 88–92, 114, 116, 118, 120, 122, 124–5
Granger, Thomas 86, 88
Greek 46, 68–9, 71, 78–9, 81, 89, 93–5
Greenblatt, Stephen 38, 134, 138, 144
Gregory, St 103, 120
Guillory, John 1, 174
Guitmund of Aversa 104
Guyon 144

Hamilton, A.C. 140–41
Hartlib, Samuel 88–91
Hebrew 46, 51, 57, 68, 69, 71, 79, 80, 81, 89, 93, 94, 95
Henry VIII, King 38, 40, 47, 50, 54, 68, 73, 74, 76–7, 85, 89, 168–9, 172
Hero and Leander, 159
Hezekiah 129
Hirsch, E.D. 12, 17

Index

Holofernes 156, 167–72
Hooker, Richard 41–2, 61, 109–13
Hopkinson, Edward 69
Horace 135
Horman, William 72–3
humanism 5, 69, 80, 83, 85, 94, 105, 142, 153–4

Inman, Frances 45–8
Isaiah 51

Jerome, St 67–70
Judith 129

Lafranc 103, 104
Latin 7, 12, 29, 46, 51–2, 54, 67–83, 85–6, 88, 89, 90–95, 107–8, 119, 153–7, 160–72
Letter to the Ephesians 44
Levine, Lawrence 12
Leviticus 56–7
Lewalski, Barbara 49
Lily, William 70, 72–81, 83, 85, 86, 88–90, 92, 94, 153, 157, 159, 160, 162–4, 172–3
literacy 1–5, 7–9, 11–13, 17–21, 23, 24, 27–30, 32, 44, 46, 48, 54, 75, 90, 92, 101, 104–5, 125, 133–4, 136, 139, 153, 156–8, 160, 167, 171
literal 4, 6–11, 20–23, 25–7, 30– 31, 38, 43–6, 48, 50–51, 54, 56–8, 60–62, 67–9, 80, 90, 93, 95, 103, 105, 108, 110–12, 114–24, 127–128
literal interpretation 7, 10–11, 21, 23
logology 122, 124
Luther, Martin 2, 3, 29, 39, 46, 47, 62, 67–9, 71–2, 95, 105, 128, 153–5, 165, 167, 171, 174
Lutheran Church 2, 3, 39–40, 46– 7, 67, 106, 109, 110, 119, 121

malapropisms 156

Manichean 10, 18, 21, 24, 119
Marbeck, John 51–2, 54
Marlowe, Christopher 159
Martz, Louis 108
Mary, Queen 29, 37, 42, 50
Mary, Virgin 129
materia 7
material 101, 104, 105, 109, 110, 112, 115–16, 118–19
Matthew, Gospel of 101, 109
Matthew, St 51, 62
metaphor 102, 105, 112, 114–15, 118–19
metonym, 114–15, 118
Miller, David Lee 133
Miller, J. Hillis 8
Mistress Quickly 162
More, St Thomas 4, 73
Mulcaster, Richard 164–6, 169, 174
Munster, Sebastian 68
Murrin, Michael 140, 145
Mylbourne, Robert 58

Neoplatonism 20, 22, 119
New Testament 7, 11, 18, 21–2, 29, 43, 47, 49, 51, 54, 57, 61
nominalism 116, 119

Ocland, Christopher 83, 85
Old Testament 7, 13, 18, 22–3, 60, 68, 70, 120
Ong, Walter 12, 17–18, 20, 27, 28, 157, 173
Ovid 145
Oxford, University of 40

Paris, University of 67
Parker, Patricia 90, 155, 162
Patterson, Annabel 9
Paul, St 42, 51, 61, 73, 80
Petrarch, Francesco 120, 157
Philo of Alexander 22, 142
Preus, James 7
Psalmes 123–4

puns 156, 158, 161–2, 166, 171, 174
Puritans 6
Puttenham, Richard 139, 141

Raleigh, Sir Walter 133–7, 139, 143–4, 146
Ramus, Peter 86
realism 103, 112, 116–17
Red Cross Knight 140
Reformation 2, 3, 5–8, 11, 17, 28, 29, 31, 37, 39, 40, 42–4, 46–8, 50, 52, 54, 69, 70, 76, 78–9, 81, 83, 92, 93, 95, 101–3, 105, 109, 116, 119, 133–4, 141–2, 147, 15–14, 160, 163, 165, 167, 171
remuneration 154–5, 166, 168, 169–71
Restraint of Appeals Act 40
Reuchlin, Johannes 69
Revelation, Book of 57
Rider, John 93–4
Rous, Francis 88

Shakespeare, William 12, 55, 59, 76, 84, 87, 91, 153–7, 159–69, 171, 173; *Henry V*, 160; *Henry VIII*, 85; *Love's Labour's Lost*, 153–7, 159, 161–9; *The Merchant of Venice*, 159; *Merry Wives of Windsor*, 156–7, 160; *A Midsummer Night's Dream*, 155 162–3, 172; *Taming of the Shrew*, 160, 162; *Two Gentlemen of Verona*, 153–4, 156, 159, 170; *Two Noble Kinsmen*, 156, 162
Sherry, Richard 29–31, 78–9, 90, 139
Shuger, Deborah 121–2
signum, 7 104, 119–20
Simon, Joan 37, 44, 58
Sixtus V, Pope 67
Skelton, John 73
Skipwith, Edward 107

Song of Songs 49, 54, 57
Spenser, Edmund 12, 37, 48, 129, 133–47
spiritual interpretation 2, 3, 6–8, 11–13, 19–21, 24–6, 31, 38–9, 41–6, 50–51, 58, 60, 68, 70, 79, 82–3, 85, 94–5, 102–6, 108, 110, 113, 115, 117–22, 124–5, 127–8
St Paul's Cathedral 73, 80
Stock, Brian 2–3, 5, 24, 174
Sylvius, Petrus 39
Syms, Christopher 81–4

Tasso, Torquato 138
Terence 162
The Elementarie 164
Thirty-Nine Articles 6, 37–8, 44
transubstantiation 10, 17, 56, 62, 103, 105, 113
Trent, Council of 39, 67, 105
Turner, William 48
Tyndale, William 47
typology 22, 31, 49–51, 54, 57, 60, 83, 118, 128–9

Udall, John 69, 86
Udall, Nicholas 43
Una 140
Uniformity, Act of 5

vernacular 67, 70–71, 76, 78–9, 85–6, 89, 92, 95
Vernon, John 94
Virgil 135, 138
Vives Juan 78–9
vulgaria 72, 85, 94
Vulgate 46, 52, 67, 68, 71

Warres, James 61
Wastell, Simon 44, 58–60
Waswo, Richard 70, 71, 116
Webbe, Joseph, 80–81, 85, 91–2
Whitgift, Archbishop 39

Whittinton, Robert 72, 73, 74, 85
Wilson, Thomas 30, 31, 32, 78, 79, 168, 169

Wimsatt, William 10
Wise, Thomas 86
Wolsey, Cardinal 73, 74, 75, 76, 77